Communal Violence, Forced Migration and the State

Gujarat since 2002

Sanjeevini Badigar Lokhande

CAMBRIDGE
UNIVERSITY PRESS

CAMBRIDGE
UNIVERSITY PRESS

4843/24, 2nd Floor, Ansari Road, Daryaganj, Delhi - 110002, India

Cambridge University Press is part of the University of Cambridge.

It furthers the University's mission by disseminating knowledge in the pursuit of education, learning and research at the highest international levels of excellence.

www.cambridge.org
Information on this title: www.cambridge.org/9781107065444

First published 2015

Reprint 2016

Printed in India at Thomson Press (India) Limited.

A catalogue record for this publication is available from the British Library

Library of Congress Cataloging-in-Publication Data
Lokhande, Sanjeevini Badigar.
Communal violence, forced migration and the state : Gujarat since 2002 / Sanjeevini Badigar Lokhande.
pages cm
Includes bibliographical references and index.
Summary: "Examines the notion of citizenship for Muslims who were displaced after the Godhra violence in Gujarat in 2002"-- Provided by publisher.
ISBN 978-1-107-06544-4 (hardback)
1. Gujarat Riots, India, 2002. 2. Muslims--India--Gujarat. 3. Forced migration--India--Gujarat. 4. Citizenship--India--Gujarat. 5. Gujarat (India)--Ethnic relations. 6. Gujarat (India)--Politics and government. I. Title.
DS485.G88L65 2015
305.6'97095475--dc23
2015004530

ISBN 978-1-107-06544-4 Hardback

Contents

Acknowledgements

This book has been the result of almost nine years of research that began with a thesis at Jawaharlal Nehru University (JNU). It was also substantially written and shaped alongside my work in different capacities at the Tata Institute of Social Sciences (TISS) and London School of Economics project on 'Governance and the Governed' and the University of Mumbai. Before acknowledging my grateful thanks to people in various institutions, I must begin with people I met in Gujarat, where things first began to come together for the book.

Ayesha Khan, then a journalist with *Indian Express* in Ahmedabad who covered the violence in 2002 herself asked me if I had ever been in a riot. She went on to explain, 'that's why you don't understand. See in a riot if something is happening somewhere, you can run and go into some other lane and somehow escape, but in 2002 it was not like that.' My research initially occurred in the milieu of widespread national and international interest that the violence in 2002 generated at least for the first ten years before being popularly dismissed as the 'past' that panacea alleged to heal all wounds. Although it did not occur to me at the time of the interview, I had in fact in the past been in close proximity to the site of violence in two instances of riots during 1992–93 post Babri masjid riots and the riot after the Ramabai incident in Mumbai. With the exception of making me apprehensive about my safety for a few hours, my brief experience with riots had not otherwise affected my life in a major way. The displacement of Muslim families in the aftermath of the violence of 2002 therefore raised several questions including one that is central to this book, namely if displacement due to communal violence is in fact an aberration in the life of a citizen as it has been made out to be in the case of Gujarat or if it has larger implications.

My fieldwork in Gujarat from 2008 to 2009, on which this book is based, would not have been possible without the generosity and assistance of many people. I would particularly like to thank Achyut Yagnik for his in-depth understanding of Gujarat and his generosity in sharing it with others. I am grateful for conversations and suggestions and the people I met through him.

I am grateful to Prasad Chacko of Action Aid for introducing me to the city of Ahmedabad and for his invaluable help in my first few days there. I am particularly grateful to the victims of the violence in 2002, who allowed me, into their homes and who agreed to recount their painful stories with me, while others understandably refused to go down that path. In particular, I would like to thank Suraiyabano Aslam Khan Pathan, Noorjahan Kalumiyan Sheikh, the Meghrajis in Alliance Colony and Razzakbhai in Baroda among several others for their conversations and hospitality. I will always be grateful to Afroze appa and Altafbhai Sayyed for sharing their wealth of stories and insight as well as their hospitality. I am also grateful to Somnath Vatsa, who then worked with Action Aid, for not just his legal acumen but for discussions that proved invaluable in discerning major methodological issues and going after sources that would help me address them. Thanks are also very much in order to Fr Cederick Prakash for all the leads he gave and for the important sources he introduced me to. I am also grateful to Monica Wahi, Zaid Sheikh and Anna Diem for their friendship and warmth during my stay in Ahemadabad. I would particularly like to thank Sharifaben, Sister Celine and Sister Kavita for their support and hospitality during my fieldwork in Sabarkantha. I am also indebted to Yusuf Sheikh, Convener of Antarik Visthapit Hak Rakshak Samiti, Baroda and his wife for opening up their home to me and giving me access to the homes of many interviewees. Thanks are also very much in order for Johanna Lokhande for all the resources she shared with me in Baroda. I am particularly grateful to Sony Pellissery who was then at the Institute of Rural Management Anand (IRMA), Anand for discussions on methodology and policy studies that helped me with handling data. I am also grateful to Bharatiben Desai and the library staff of Gujarat Vidyapeeth and to their students for helping me with locating legislative assembly debates and their translation. I am also grateful to Dipankar Gupta whom I met unexpectedly during fieldwork in Ahmedabad, who generously introduced me to the person he was interviewing.

I am very grateful to faculty members at JNU where I was first encouraged to publish my research. Thanks are very much in order to Zoya Hasan who first as my thesis advisor and then as I wrote the book allowed me access to her time and her depth of knowledge that have made a world of difference in my writing. I am also grateful to Valerian Rodrigues for discussions and suggestions that my work has benefitted from but also for his friendship and support. I am especially grateful to Gurpeet Mahajan whose words I have hung on to since the early stages of my research and for the invitation to present my work at JNU as Visiting Fellow in 2014. I am also grateful to Gopal Guru for encouraging me to appreciate categories like internally displaced persons 'that shed light on particular realities', Anupama Roy for introducing me to readings, Rajarshi Dasgupta for suggestions on fieldwork and Amir Ali for introducing me to readings in political ethnography that proved to be very insightful.

It is a pleasure to thank senior colleagues at the University of Mumbai who have extended their support to my writing. In particular, I would like to thank Jose George and Surendra Jondhale for discussions and for watching out for me when I put in late hours at the university. I am also grateful to S. Parasuraman, Madhushree Sekher and Janaki Andharia for the freedom, support and facilities afforded at the green oasis of TISS campus in Mumbai that enabled me to add value to my research.

Parts of this book have been presented at seminars and I have undoubtedly benefitted from reviewers and audiences' questions and comments. I am particularly grateful to Barbara Harriss-White for her comments on a paper that I presented at the Oxford Sociology Conference on 'South Asia in Transition' at the Department of Sociology, University of Oxford and to Sumeet Mhaskar, Samina Luthfa and Irum Shehreen Ali for inviting me. I thank Janaki Andharia for her invitation and comments on a paper I presented at the 4th International Roundtable on Structuring Peace, State and Conflict Transformation: Prospects and Challenges in South Asia organized by Jamshedji Tata Centre for Disaster Management, Tata Institute of Social Sciences (TISS). I am very grateful to Sumeet Mhaskar for inviting me to University of Goettingen for the workshop on 'Revisiting Working Class Neighbourhoods in South Asia' in 2014. Grateful thanks to Soni Pellisery for the invitation to present my work at the National Law School of India University, Bangalore. I would also like to thank Kannamma Raman for the invitation to the national seminar on 'Challenges to Human Rights in the Twenty First Century', Sashwati Mishra for the invitation to the All India Criminology Conference on Organised and Transnational Crime: State and Non State Responses and Victims Perspectives by Indian Society of Criminology and Tata Institute of Social Sciences and Gurpreet Mahajan for the invitation to the Young Scholars' Conference organized by Jawaharlal Nehru University.

I am also grateful to Sujata Patel of the University of Hyderabad for incisive comments that went a long way in improving this work. I thank Joy Pachuau, Centre for Historical Studies for reviewing a chapter in the book. I am also very grateful to the anonymous reviewers at Cambridge University

Press whose comments and suggestions helped improve the manuscript. Thanks are very much in order also to Qudsiya Ahmed, commissioning editor at Cambridge University Press for her many skills at enabling an author to deliver the manuscript. I am also grateful to Madhushree Sekher for allowing me to draw on parts of my research presented at the international Authors Workshop of Tata Institute of Social Sciences and London School of Economics' project on Governance for the forthcoming volume *Governance and the Governed*. I am ever so grateful to Mrs Tiliya and Shruti Shah for helping me with translation of legislative assembly debates and to Jagdish Bhalke and Ajinkya Gaikwad for assisting me with research and Devika Kerkar for discussions on Sindhi Refugees that I benefited from.

Personally and academically, I owe a huge debt to Vasanthi Raman for conversations over several years and for opening her home to me in Delhi. Heartfelt thanks to C. B. Samuel and Selina Samuel for all their counsel during hard times and for being my parents in Delhi. Friends have been an integral part of this journey at various stages in the development of arguments in the book and it is my pleasure to thank John Thomas and Hoineihling Sithlou in particular for generous investments in time through various stages of the book. I also want to thank Shruti Joshi, Chandra Mallampalli, Satheesh, V. V. Linesh, Kamminthang Mantuong, Lipokmar Dzuvichu and Nathan Sigworth. For the lack of a better word, I have to say thank you to my parents Bhasker and Shalini Badigar for their selfless lives and my sister Salome for living this journey with me. I also have to thank my niece Sashyah for instructing me to include her name here and who has in fact contributed towards my well-being while writing this manuscript in more ways than she can imagine. Last, but most importantly, I thank my husband Ashish Lokhande for pulling me through times when I was convinced I would not make it and for enabling me to complete the submission. This manuscript would be nowhere near completion without his support.

Selected Glossary of Terms

Bandh	strike
Basti	habitation
Bigha	a unit of measurement of land equivalent to 2843.5 square yards and 47/80th of an acre. (Shah 2002: 222)
Chawl	tenement-like structures of one room houses lined up with a common corridor.
Colony	a collection of houses in sites usually marked by a boundary wall
Dandiya ras	traditional group dance with sticks
Dhamaal	riot
Galla	stall
Garba ras	traditional group dance
Hijrat	exodus
Ilakas	areas
Jamaat	occupational, caste or doctrinal group among Muslims
Josh	zeal
Kar sevak	a volunteer working for the Ramjanmabhoomi movement for the building of a Ram temple over what is believed to his birthplace over which a sixteenth century mosque now stands.
Kuccha	raw, in case of structures impermanent
Lari	hand cart
Lathi	long stick
Madrassa	a college for Islamic instruction
Maidan	field
Masjid	mosque

Mohalla	neighbourhood
Mood vatan	original place of residence/place that one belongs to
Pir/Peerzada	a saint who has both scriptural and mystical knowledge
Potlis	sac made by tying together the ends of a large piece of cloth
Ram dhun	chanting of prayers in particular to the deity Ram
Rath yatra	literally means journey by chariot that has religious connotations
Rashtra	nation
Samadhan	compromise
Sarpanch	the elected village chief who heads the village panchayat
Shila daan	brick donation
Shuttle	larger autorickshas that have a total of three rows of seats/ autorickshas that are shared by people going to different destinations along the same route are also called shuttle
Talati	village accountant
Toofan	storm, used to refer to a riot
Vatani	a resident/one who belongs to the place
Visthapit	displaced

Abbreviations

ABVP	Akhil Bharatiya Vidhyarthi Parishad (All India Students Federation)
AVHRS	Antarik Visthapith Hak Rakshak Samitee (Committee for the Rights of Internally Displaced Persons)
BBC	British Broadcasting Corporation
BJP	Bharatiya Janata Party
CM	Chief Minister
GOG	Government of Gujarat
GR	Government Resolution
IDPs	Internally Displaced Persons
INC	Indian Nation Congress referred to elsewhere as the Congress Party

IRMA	Institute of Rural Management Anand
MLA	Member of Legislative Assembly
MP	Member of Parliament
NCM	National Commission for Human Rights
NGO	Non Governmental Organisation
NHRC	National Human Rights Commission
PIL	Public Interest Litigation
PM	Prime Minister
RTO	Regional Transport Office
SEWA	Self Employed Women's Association
SHRC	State Human Rights Commission
UN	United Nations
UNHCR	United Nations High Commission on Refugees
US	United States

District Map of Gujarat

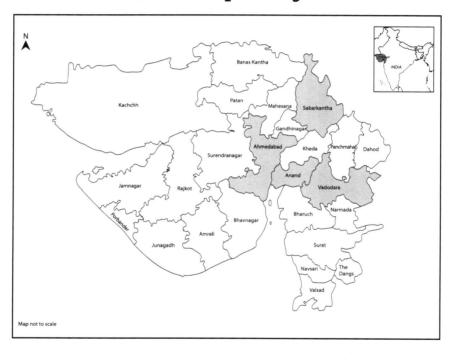

Introduction

In 2002, communal violence affected many parts of one of India's most prosperous states of Gujarat. The violence, sometimes described as India's most televized episode of communal violence, generated more commentary than any other previous instance, and yet by 2014, in the run up to the national elections, questions were raised about whether the violence was all that it was made out to be when the administration that was widely believed to be complicit in the violence went on to run one of the most economically successful state administrations in India. In addition to those who take on the mantle of 'naming names' such as journalists, political commentators, academics, writers and politicians, a large number of people on the many platforms of social media tried to articulate what was at issue in the cacophony of voices over facts and counter-facts.

A large number of reports by independent fact finding teams of journalists, academicians, politicians, non-governmental organizations (NGOs), investigative undercover journalists, as well as the National Human Rights Commission, condemned the failure of the state machinery that caused a large number of Muslims to flee their homes, and pointed to the state government's complicity in the violence. [1] In addition to this significant body of reportage, films such as the

---

1   Reports by Editors Guild Fact Finding Mission Report, Aakar Patel, Dileep Padgaonkar, B. G. Verghese, *Rights and Wrongs: Ordeal by Fire in the Killing Fields of Gujarat*, New Delhi, Editors Guild, May 2002; Amnesty International, *Justice the Victim: Gujarat State Fails to Protect Women from Violence*, http://www.amnesty.org/en/library/info/ASA20/001/2005 (accessed on 12 May 2010); Human Rights Watch, *'We have No Orders to Save You': State Participation and Complicity in Communal Violence in Gujarat*, 14 (3) (C), April 2002, http://www.hrw.org/legacy/reports/2002/india/ (accessed on 12 May 2010) ; Commonwealth Initiative for Human Rights, Citizen's Initiative, People's Union for Civil Liberties (PUCL), *Violence in Vadodara*, June 2002, http://www.onlinevolunteers.org/gujarat/reports/pucl/index.htm (accessed on 5 July 2010); People's Union for Democratic Rights (PUDR), *Maaro! Kaapo! Baalo!: State, Society and Communalism in Gujarat*, Delhi, May 2002, http://www.pucl.org/Topics/Religion-communalism/2002/maro_kapo_balo.pdf (accessed on 5 July 2010); and *Tehelka*, 4(43), 3 November 2007 among others.

award winning documentary *Final Solution* and artwork, not to mention almost relentless commentary on the violence for years to come, sought to capture what had happened and often sought to invoke the 'power of shame' to produce accountability and prevent such a situation from ever occurring again. However, in what befuddled left liberal commentators and academics, Narendra Modi who was in power at the time of the violence responded to this campaign with a campaign for pride named *Gaurav Yatra* and went on to win emphatic electoral support for three successive terms in the state. By 2008, increasingly, voices in mainstream media, some Muslim businessmen and even the head of a leading Islamic seminary began to urge Muslims[2] to participate in the economic progress facilitated by the same administration and to move on from the violence in 2002 when according to official estimates by the then home minister L. K. Advani, one and a half lakh people had fled their homes for 121 relief camps[3] across parts of north and central Gujarat.

'Things have returned to normal in Gujarat for everyone save some sections of the media, academicians and activists who keep recalling it', asserted the state's spokesperson for the ruling Bharatiya Janata Party (BJP) because, 'it (*accounts of the 2002 violence*) makes good copy'.[4] In the 2009 Gujarat assembly elections, Muslims publicly expressed support for the BJP-led administration in the state. In the run up to the 2014 elections a large number of media reports, some academics and websites described the violence as just another riot that lasted for the whole of three days that did not justify the vilification of Narendra Modi[5] who went on from first being demonized and then idolized to become the prime minister of India all in little over 12 years. This book seeks to understand and explain these years through the unlikely lens of displacement that centrally engages with the question of whether communal violence and the displacement it engenders is

2   Maulana Vastanvi's comments as Vice Chancellor of Darul Uloom Deoband created an uproar that forced him to step down. Viewed on 28 March 2011, http://articles. timesofindia. indiatimes.com/2011-01-27/india/28367708_1_maulana-vastanvi-seminary-resignation-issue.

3   Bharat Desai, 'Fear Still Stalks Gujarat', *Times of India*, 27 March 2002, http://articles. timesofindia.indiatimes.com; Dionne Bunsha, 'The Crisis of the Camps', *Frontline* 19 (8) (13–26 April 2002), http://www.frontline.in.

4   Yamal Vyas (BJP Spokesperson for Gujarat) in discussion with author, 10 February 2009.

5   Madhu Purnima Kishwar, *Modinama: Work in Progress*, Madhu Purnima Kishwar, Manushi Trust, http://www.manushi.in/docs/Modinama-ebook.pdf; economists Jagdish Bhagwati and Arvind Panagariya in a letter to *The Economist*, 12 April 2014.

an aberration in the life of a citizen as it is popularly made out to be, or if it has larger implications.

The 2014 national elections saw BJP capture power at the national level for the first time with an emphatic majority in the Lok Sabha with 282 seats out of a vote share of an estimated 31 per cent.[6] Founded in 1980, BJP is the political wing of the family of right wing formations called the Sangh Parivar working for the revival of a lost Hindu golden age before the advent of foreign aggressors, that includes a number of organizations the most prominent of which are the Rashtriya Swayamsevak Sangh (RSS) or the Association of National Volunteers a paramilitary organization that also serves as an advisory body, the Vishwa Hindu Parishad (VHP) or the World Council of Hindus that imitates Christian organizations as an ecclesiastical structure that seeks to unify Hindus and resist Muslim and Christian aggressors (Jaffrelot, 2001, pp. 388–411) and Bajrang Dal (BD) or the army of Hanuman, which is a loose structured federation of militant youth. The Sangh Parivar also has many others groups that specifically cater to sections of society such as students, women, trade unions and farmers. Groups in the Sangh Parivar are cadre-based and while in the past there have been differences between ideologues in the RSS and the political wing of the BJP under more moderate leaders such as Atal Bihari Vajpayee (Narayanan, 2014), the various organizations are united in the ideology of *Hindutva* of exclusive cultural nationalism. The 2014 elections were an epoch making national election as no political power had gained substantial power, let alone an emphatic majority in the national government of India in the name of Hinduism, combined more recently with good governance, since independence from British rule and Partition of the Subcontinent.

The Partition to create the modern states of India and Pakistan had caused one of the largest displacements of people in the twentieth century comparable with the displacements produced by the Second World War in Europe. During the Partition an estimated 12 million people were displaced in divided Punjab alone and an estimated 20 million in the Subcontinent as a whole. In addition to this there were forced migrations that occurred in waves especially from Bengal that went on for more than half a century (Zamindar, 2007, 6; Chatterjee 2007, pp. 995–1032). Despite the horrors of Partition at a time when the scaffolding of newly formed state structures were yet to fall in place and safety was a central

---

6   'BJP's 31 per cent Lowest Vote Share of Any Party to Win Majority,' *Times of India*, 19 May 2014.

concern, that people including Muslims in India looked to the state to provide safety is perhaps an indication of the potency of the emancipatory ideal of the nation-state created by the Indian national movement. In both the newly formed postcolonial states of India and Pakistan displaced persons were an integral part of the first two Five Year Plans where refugee rehabilitation plan was part of the universal and rational programme for development of the nation as a whole. In case of Muslims that formed a minority in Delhi for instance this programme initially involved their rehabilitation into mixed areas and then to 'Muslim areas' when they no longer felt safe in mixed areas due to the perception that due to the Partition Muslims had lost the right to live there. Notwithstanding the limited capacity of states, their failure and allegations of betrayals, taking care of displaced persons was an important aspect of establishing the legitimacy of newly formed states (Zamindar 2007, pp. 9, 26, 28).

In the climax of the 1973 Hindi movie *Garam Hava*, set in Uttar Pradesh in the aftermath of the Partition of India where people continued to be faced with the dilemma of whether to migrate to Pakistan or remain in India, Salim Mirza, an elderly Muslim shoemaker in Agra has to deal with the dilemma of whether to move to Pakistan or stay back in India. The film has been hailed for its poignant picturisation of the questions that partition raised for millions of ordinary citizens, among those being that of displacement and the hope of finding citizenship. Initially Salim Mirza chooses to stay back with his wife and two grown children even when members of his own extended family leave their ancestral home one by one to live in Pakistan, a land of plenty, by the reports of the women who come back to visit with exaggerated accounts. Despite his firm belief in the ideals of the freedom struggle, the travails of his everyday existence make him realise the change in the power equations in the new republic where his community is reduced to a minority. The family is hard pressed on all sides because of the vitiated atmosphere that makes it difficult for him to even earn a living. The last straw in that time of instability is when his daughter commits suicide after a second relationship is unfruitful because the man does not return from Pakistan to marry her. On what is to be his journey to finally migrate to Pakistan, having packed all his belongings and closed his ancestral home, along the way he sees his son who has decided to join his friends of other communities, agitating for their right to employment as citizens. Something turns in Salim's mind seeing this and he turns back, perhaps an indication of a decision to live life and struggle as a citizen of India rather than seek citizenship with co religionists in another country.

Cut to the present reality and most observers would find the existence of democratic and constitutional structures and peaceful co-existence among communities in most parts of India. However, every once in a while, violence among religious communities called communal violence has occurred in some parts and that has led some scholars to even describe communal violence as endemic to India.[7] At times when this communal violence has played out on the streets, depending on the time taken for authorities to restore law and order, the rampaging of mobs has caused damage to life and property causing people to flee their homes either temporarily, permanently or to even relocate eventually to find safety in the numbers of one's own community while groups have come together in the name of 'citizens' initiatives to highlight the plight of victims and to organize relief.[8] And yet while most of the scholarship and ongoing debate on communal violence so far has attempted to understand the causal aspects of such violence, there have been fewer attempts to understand the effects of violence[9] and fewer still on those who flee their homes when state institutions are rendered ineffectual to guarantee their safety.

Gujarat, one of India's most prosperous states has had a history of considerable success in the pursuit of economic growth and has projected itself as a model for good governance under the leadership of Narendra Modi who was chief minister of the state for three consecutive terms. Gujarat however has also had, despite many syncretic elements in its culture (Singh, 2002; Yagnik and Sheth, 2005), a history of communal violence. India's westernmost state, which shares a land and water boundary with India's neighbour Pakistan described as an enemy in

---

7   Paul Brass, 2003, *The Production of Hindu-Muslim Riots in Contemporary India*, New Delhi: Oxford University Press, 6. Riots have also occurred in Pakistan and their frequency has increased since 1992.

8   Veena Das uses 'citizen's groups to describe such collectives in her 2007 book, *Life and Words*, University of California Press, 182. It is noteworthy however, that in polarized situations such as those of major communal violence in 1969 and 1985 riots in Ahmedabad, the 1984 anti Sikh riots, the 1992 riots in Mumbai as well as in 2002, civil society groups have mobilized efforts for relief and rehabilitation of displaced people as 'citizens groups'.

9   See Veena Das, (ed.), 1992. *Mirrors of Violence: Communities, Riots and Survivors in South Asia*, New Delhi: Oxford India Paperbacks; Rowena Robinson, 2005, *Tremors of Violence: Muslim Survivors of Ethnic Strife in Western India*, New Delhi: Sage Publications; Darshini Mahadevia, 2007, 'A City with Many Borders: Beyond Ghettoization in Ahmedabad,' in Annapurna Shaw ed., *Indian Cities in Transition*, New Delhi: Orient Longman, 341–89; and Veena Das *Ibid*.

government departments, legislation and policy,[10] has like some other border states, what is known colloquially as, the Disturbed Areas Act. However, besides the fact that Gujarat has never experienced insurgency or secessionist movements and the dynamics of society and polity in the state are very different from those of other states considered as frontier areas of the Indian territory that have Disturbed Areas Act, the legislation commonly referred to by a similar name in Gujarat[11] was intended to empower the Collector and to prevent further polarization of living spaces during the 1980s when instances of communal violence frequently occurred and people turned increasingly to their co-religionists to create enclaves of safe zones that have been described elsewhere (Jaffrelot, 2012) as ghettoes.[12] Communal violence was therefore not without precedent in Gujarat and yet the violence in 2002 created an upsurge of interest and drew national and international attention to the state that has been has been vital politically for the growth of the BJP. While riots have known to be localized phenomena (Brass 2003, p. 149), many hold that the violence in 2002 was different.

> Earlier we would hear that a riot has taken place in one place but we were still eating and doing our thing at our own houses. Even if there was a riot in one place you could run out of one *galli* (street) and escape to another but 2002 was different.[13]

On 27 February 2002 a large number of volunteers for Hindu right wing groups called *karsevaks* were returning to Gujarat from Ayodhya by the Sabarmati Express. Some of them were caught in an altercation in the early hours of the morning when the train stopped at the railway station in Godhra, a town with a

---

10 The Custodian of Enemy Property is a government of India department. The Enemy Property Act of 1968, Enemy Property (Amendment and Validation) Bill 2010 are legislations enacted after the 1965 India-Pakistan War.

11 'The Gujarat Prohibition of Transfer of Immovable Property and Provisions for Protection of Tenants from Eviction from Premises in Disturbed Areas Act, 1986'.

12 The Act that was first promulgated in 1986 in the context of Ahmedabad has been extended to other areas and retained by successive governments including during Narendra Modi's tenure as chief minister. However, the act has been ineffective in stemming increasing polarization in parts of Ahmedabad where they had already occurred to the extent that living spaces are divided by borders. Moreover in the run up to the 2014 elections the VHP advised its members to pressurize the government to extend it to other parts of Gujarat to prevent Muslims from cohabiting with Hindus (Vijaysinh Parmar, 'Evict Muslims from Hindu Areas: Pravin Togadia', *Times of India*, 21 April 2014).

13 Ayesha Khan (then a journalist for Indian Express, Ahmedabad), in discussion with the author, 13 December 2008.

large Muslim population. They were returning from a *mahayagna* (a grand ritual) organized by Vishwa Hindu Parishad (The World Council of Hindus) in Ayodhya in the northern state of Uttar Pradesh that was part of sustained mobilization for the construction of a Ram temple at what is believed to be the birthplace of Ram over which a sixteenth century mosque called Babri Masjid has stood since more than four centuries.[14] After the altercation at the Godhra railway station, the train stopped a few metres away from the station again and subsequently a mob from the nearby *basti* (habitation) of Muslims surrounded the compartment attacking it with stones and in the melee that ensued the compartment caught fire as a result of which 57 people including women and children were burned alive. The then chief minister, Narendra Modi visited the station at 2 o'clock the same day and the bodies, some of which were burned beyond identification, were brought to a hospital in Ahmedabad. By the evening of the same day the chief minister announced that he suspected the role of ISI (Inter Services Intelligence of Pakistan) in the killings and announced that there would be a state wide *bandh* (strike) the next day to mourn the deaths. Already right wing groups of VHP and BD had given a call for state *bandh* the next day and for a *bharat bandh* (nationwide strike) on 1 March. The newspaper *Sandesh*, a leading Gujarati daily carried a front page report that stated that before the burning of the train 10–15 Hindu girls were taken from the train compartment and burned and that their bodies were badly mutilated.[15] As shops and establishments remained closed the next day i.e., on 28 February organized mobs of hundreds led by the VHP and BD began to take to the streets armed with sticks, swords, petrol, cooking gas cylinders and even guns and hand-made bombs in violence that affected 15 to 16 districts[16] and was most intense in the districts Ahmedabad, Anand, Mehsana, Sabarkantha, Panchmahal,

---

14 The Ramjanmabhoomi movement led by the BJP has sought to mobilize national support since the late 1980s for the construction of a temple in Ayodhya. Right wing activists mobilized around the disputed site by such campaigns as *shiladan* (donation of bricks) and collection of construction material near the disputed site. This was despite the matter being subjudice and the Supreme Court injunction issued on the matter over the disputed site in the wake of the demolition of the Babri mosque in 1992 by right wing activists that had led to riots in different parts of India. On 26 February 2002 there were repeated disruptions by members of parliament (MPs) in Parliament demanding that the *karsevaks* gathering in Ayodhya be arrested and the construction material collected there be seized.

15 *Sandesh*, 28 February 2002, quoted in Citizens' Initiative, 2002, *How has the Gujarat Massacre Affected Minority Women: Survivors Speak*, http://cac.ektaonline.org/resources/reports, (accessed on 10 March 2011) Fact Finding by a Women's Panel.

16 *Frontline*, 19(12): 8–21, June 2002.

Vadodara, Bharuch and Dahod. Families were burned alive in their homes, a large number of women raped, people were stabbed and stoned, their houses damaged, and shops and businesses owned by Muslims were looted and set on fire. The violence caused at one time more than one and a half lakh Muslims to flee their homes and others to permanently relocate to places of Muslim concentration while an estimated 82 relief colonies came up in ten districts of Gujarat for Muslims, who did not return to their earlier homes.

Communal violence is an important theme in Indian politics since colonial times. Colonial administrators had used the term 'communal' to refer to sectarian conflicts that was subsequently used by them as well as scholars, policy-makers and in common parlance to refer to conflict between religious communities especially between the majority Hindus and Muslims that constitute the largest minority[17] of nearly 150 million citizens. Communal violence along with violence by extreme left wing groups referred to as naxal violence and terrorism that accounts for most of the violent deaths in India, constitute the major forms of non-state violence that challenge the entity of the state that in Max Weber's famous formulation has the legitimate use of force. Although enumeration of incidents of communal violence has serious methodological and logistical problems in India given that home ministry of the government of India, whose responsibility includes the reporting of law and order, has stopped the regular publishing records of riots since 1985 (Brass 2003, pp. 60–67) according to one estimate, from 1961 to 2002, except for two years, there was one or more riots every year in India (Engineer 2004, pp. 230–35). In another estimate of communal incidents between Hindus and Muslims from 1950–95 in 28 Indian cities, 7173 lives were lost as a result of communal incidents (Varshney and Wilkinson 1996, p. 19). According to estimates compiled from analysis of newspaper reports from the period 1960–93 to enumerate the number of communal incidents in which there was at least one death for India as a whole and by state, communal incidents between Hindus and Muslims rose during the 1960s reaching a peak in 1969, declined between 1971 and 1977, and then began a sharp increase during the years from 1978–93 (Varshney and Wilkinson 1996, p. 19). According to Paul Brass, 'Rioting and killing in the years between 1990 and 1993 reached peaks not seen since 1947.' In these years communal violence took place in two waves of riots across large parts of

---

17   India is among the three largest Muslim countries in the world. Amartya Sen. 2006. *Identity and Violence: The Illusion of Destiny*, New Delhi: Allen Lane and Penguin Books, 60.

northern and western India that have been associated with mass mobilizations by the VHP and BJP for building the Ram temple in Ayodhya. In the significant scholarship on communal violence the role of the state, civil society and communities involved has been analysed to determine causality and processes of communal violence. Rich empirical and theoretical accounts have sought to explain communal violence through social science,[18] anthropological[19] and psychological[20] lenses employing essential, instrumental and constructivist arguments[21] that examine the role of communities involved, the concepts of state or civil society or a combination of these.[22] In one of the more recent works it has been argued that communal violence is not just sectarian violence but a more complex phenomena where tensions within the Hindu social order due to the state's redistributive policies led to the increase in communal violence and the rise of 'Hindu nationalism' in Ahmedabad, Gujarat and subsequently at an all India level as well (Shani, 2007). Ornit Shani argues that prolonged instances of communal violence brought to sharp relief a fragmented state to which the unitary cultural nationalism of the BJP presented an alternative. What also needs to be taken into account however, is the fact that in Gujarat, periods of prolonged communal violence were also contemporaneous with important policy decisions in the state in the 1980s that proved to be decisive during the opening up of the economy leading to structural transformation and economic

---

18 Such as Paul Brass, 2003, *The Production of Hindu-Muslim Riots in Contemporary India*, New Delhi: Oxford University Press, 6. Jan Breman, 2002, 'Communal Upheaval as Resurgence of Social Darwinism', Economic and Political Weekly, 20 April; Jan Breman, 2004, The Making and Unmaking of an Industrial Working Class: Sliding down the Labour Hierarchy in Ahmedabad, New Delhi: Oxford University Press; Ethnic Conflict and Civic life: Hindus and Muslims in India, New Haven and London: Yale University Press, 2002.

19 Veena Das, 2007, *Life and Words*, University of California Press; Rowena Robinson, 2005, *Tremors of Violence: Muslim Survivors of Ethnic Strife in Western India*, New Delhi: Sage Publications.

20 Ashish Nandy, Shikha Trivedy, Shail Mayaram, and Achyut Yagnik (eds.), 1995, *Creating a Nationality: The Ramjanmabhoomi Movement and Fear of the Self*, New Delhi: Oxford University Press; Sudhir Kakar, 1990, 'Some Unconscious Aspects of Ethnic Violence in India', in Veena Das (ed.), *Mirrors of Violence: Communities, Riots and Survivors in South Asia*, 134–45, New Delhi: Oxford University Press.

21 From Ashutosh Varshney's classification in *Ethnic Conflict and Civic life: Hindus and Muslims in India*, New Haven and London: Yale University Press, 2002.

22 Ornit Shani, 2007, *Communalism, Caste and Hindu Nationalism*, New Delhi: Cambridge University Press, 267–93.

growth through diversified and rapid industrialization spurred by an aggressive industrial policy (Hirway, 2000). This has sought to be explained by the thesis that while economically rather than having a broad-based, egalitarian agenda the state has chosen to ally with drivers of privatized economic growth namely the national and international big business elite, for popular measure, it pursues a majoritarian Hindu nationalist agenda that ensures its legitimacy socially and culturally (Nikita Sud, 2012). In the same explanation, from the understanding of the state as emerging from a protean make up of ideas, institutional practices and politics, it has been argued that government's support for the cultural nationalist agenda has been constrained by alternative norms and pressures thereafter. In another volume that sought to portray the amorphous character of the everyday state however it was argued that despite the efforts of the entity of the state in India to maintain 'the myth of neutrality through spectacles' such as inquiry commissions, *mohalla* committees etc. it continues to have evident majoritarian biases (Hansen, 2000, pp. 31–67) notwithstanding the stated constitutional ideal of secularism. To say that the state is not a unitary entity but a multi-hued lattice and a protean, amorphous entity need not occlude the possibility of the dominance and paramountcy of certain trends in it.[23]

Violence does inevitably beg the role of the state constructed as the neutral arbiter of public interest and the guarantor and protector of life. In recent times there has been renewed interest in unpacking the meaning of concepts such as the state particularly for those who study governance[24] and among anthropologists to understand what constitutes the state.[25] The entity of the state constituted by ideas, rituals, institutions and organizations is conceptualized rather than a monolith, as a protean, disaggregated and banal entity. There is the thesis that

---

23 Sanjeevini Badigar, 2013, 'Gujarat and its Protean State', Economic and Political Weekly 48(39): 35–37.

24 Among others, Joel Migdal, 2001, *State in Society: Studying how States and Societies Transform and Constitute one Another*, Cambridge: Cambridge University Press; Francis Fukuyama, 2004, *State Building: Governance and the World Order in the Twenty First Century*, Ithaca, N.Y.: Cornell University Press; Mark Bevir and R. A. W. Rhodes, 2010, *The State as Cultural Practice*, Oxford: Oxford University Press.

25 See Akhil Gupta, 1995, 'Blurred Boundaries: The Discourse of Corruption, The Culture of Politics and The Imagined State', *American Ethnologist* 22: 375–402; Jonathan Spencer, 1997, 'Postcolonialism and the Political Imagination', *Journal of the Royal Anthropological Institute* 3: 1–19; C. J. Fuller and John Harriss, 2012, 'For an Anthropology of the Modern Indian State', in C. J. Fuller and Veronique Benei (ed.), *The Everyday State and Society in Modern India*, 1–30, New Delhi: Social Science Press.

the empirical reality of state in society is much more complex than has been previously acknowledged where state and society are disaggregate and mutually transforming (Migdal, 1994, p. 3). In the scholarship on new 'governance', the analytical lens has also shifted from grand theories of representative democracy to processes of government in action with a focus on efficiency and capacity (Bevir 2010, 2011). In India the existence of a shared modern nationalist culture and of the state as an organizing concept through which society imagines its cohesion, order and sovereignty (Hansen, 2000, p. 34) has been noted, as has also the overriding importance of vernacular idioms and folk understandings in popular politics that are far removed from theories of liberal democracy (Michelutti 2007, p. 654). The idea of the state as a neutral arbiter in conflict , widely perceived as being essential in the governance of a democratic state and crucial to the aura of the state as an entity above society that gives it legitimacy (Hansen 2000. p. 36) is an idea that is questioned in this account of what followed the violence in 2002.

In the significant and copious literature on communal violence, the fact that some people are forced to flee their homes at such times is at best acknowledged for instrumental reasons such as to clear slum land of encroachments or as a peripheral consequence. In recent times however, displacement has received greater analytical visibility. Drawing out Deleuze and Guattari's contention that in history analysis is from a sedentary point of view in the name of a unitary state, Liisa Malkki argues that there is a sedentary bias in social science that privileges the study of settlement as normal and pathologizes movement and displacement (Malkki, 1992, pp. 24–44). Refugees for Hannah Arendt however, represent the *avant-garde* of their people in exposing the limits of existing polity[26] (Arendt 1943, 1973, p. 277). Agamben also argues that, the refugee is the sole category in the otherwise ubiquitous and entrenched framework of the nation-state that affords the possibility of the imagination, to begin with, of new forms and limits of political community (Agamben, 1995, p. 119). Arendt argued that displacement was 'symptomatic of a malaise inherent in the very structure of a nation-state' where despite the existence of constitutional structures and rule of the law in the Europe of her times the state had been transformed from an instrument of the law into an instrument of the nation when people concluded, 'quite democratically, namely by majority decision, that for humanity as a whole it would be better to liquidate certain parts thereof.' Importantly, she also asserted that history could

26 Hanna Arendt, 'We Refugees', originally printed in *The Menorah Journal*, 1943, reprinted in Marc Robinson, *Altogether Elsewhere: Writers in Exile*, London: Faber and Faber.

very well repeat itself if constitutional structures become irrelevant in the face of the 'will of the people' (Arendt, 1962, pp. 275, 299).

Displaced populations first became a focus in human rights discourses that emerged in the post-war era that underlined the need to protect subjects from their own states. Human rights discourses and normative developments have led to greater analytical visibility although not as historical moments in a progression of time or to constitute a genealogy of rights. People have always moved due to fear of persecution, conflict, natural disasters etc. although it is widely believed, never on the scale that was first witnessed during World War I. The etymology of words such as *hijrat* (exodus), alien, exiled, displaced, stateless, refugee etc. indicate cultural, social and political understandings for people fleeing to seek refuge existed before, though not as a legal status.[27] It is however the displacement of hundreds of thousands of people after the First World War that is considered to be the first time in the West that displacement appeared as a mass phenomenon on an unprecedented scale (Arendt 1962, pp. 267–303; Agamben 1995, pp. 114–19). Arendt draws attention to the fact that the emergence of displacement as a mass phenomenon coincided with the spread of the modern nation-state throughout Europe. In the complex of ideas and events called modernity there was also the manifestation of the idea of the modern polity of nation-state as a single, unified collectivity confined within territorial borders, ruled by an authority whose origin was not from the divine above but from the people below, bundled into a single entity that was to guarantee rights of the members of the nation-state i.e.. the 'citizens.' While the *Déclaration des droits de l'Homme et du Citoyen* or the Declaration of the Rights of Man and of the Citizen from the French Revolution in 1789 is often credited for creating a horizontal membership of the 'citizen' as opposed to the traditional hierarchical one of the subject as it defined the rights of all the estates of the realm as universal, what is often less acknowledged is that the subsequent spread and universalization of this potent idea coincided with more people being displaced that ever before. The figure of the refugee according to Arendt, therefore presented the radical crisis of the very concept of the nation-state where although its project was to guarantee the rights of man *par excellance* (Arendt 1962, pp. 267–303), the inscription of the native (that is bare life) in the legal order of the nation-state, as Agamben goes on to argue, left no

---

27 Paul Tabori cited in Sophia A. McClennen, 2004, *The Dialectics of Exile: Nation, Time, Language and Space in Hispanic Literatures*, US: Purdue University, 15.

space for 'something like the pure man in himself' within the political order of the nation-state (Agamben 1995, p. 116).

After World War II, given the staggering numbers of masses in motion for which no national government was willing to guarantee protection to initially the Allied forces and subsequently a host of international bodies sought to attend to the situation before the United Nations High Commissioner for Refugees (UNHCR) was established in 1951. Owing to the crisis of stateless people in Europe the discourse on displacement for years came to be seen through international lens i.e., across national boundaries (Malkki, 1995, p. 502). With the formation of the UNHCR refugees came to be seen as an international, social and humanitarian problem. One reasoning is that this was due to a 'powerful sense of post-war shame and responsibility for the predicaments of the people who were fleeing the holocaust and yet were so often refused entry when they were in most desperate need of asylum' that shaped principal elements of international refugee law and related legal instruments (Malkki, 1995, pp. 495–523). Some norms such as those against genocide, crimes against humanity and principle of racial non-discrimination have acquired the import of *jus cogens* and although there is contestation over what principles should constitute this category, there is near universal agreement for the existence of *jus cogens* norms that are fundamental and overriding principles of international law over which no derogation is ever permitted.[28] The wave of decolonization and the cartographic redrawing of boundaries of erstwhile colonially ruled countries in subsequent years leading up to the 1960s created a new definition for 'unprecedented' in mass displacements. In 1967 the Protocol Relating to the Status of Refugees, made the Geneva Convention the universal instrument of refugee law. In subsequent years in different parts of the world regional refugee law instruments such as the Organisation of African Unity Convention Governing the Specific Aspects of Refugee Problem in Africa (1969) and the Cartagena Declaration of 1984 for Latin America expanded the situations under which refugee status is recognized as foreign aggression, occupation (for Africa), foreign domination, events seriously disturbing public order and, in the case of Cartagena declaration to massive violations of human rights and domestic conflict (Deng, 1998, p. 9). However such regional instruments as well as the Geneva Convention Relating to the Status of Refugees were all restricted to those people who crossed an international border.

---

28 Jus Cogens, Legal Information Institute, Cornell University Law School, http://www.law. cornell.edu/wex/jus_cogens.

The refugee regime led to the articulation of the rights of the displaced in international terms and therefore above the nation-states. At the heart of the category of refugee however was the question of protection of the rights of those who 'owing to a well-founded fear of being persecuted for reasons of race, religion, nationality, membership of a particular social group, or political opinion' had to flee their home country and therefore that of discrimination due to membership to different social groups within the nation-state. While the backdrop of the World Wars and the development of the refugee regime led to the question of those displaced due to membership of different social groups being viewed primarily from an international lens as those outside the boundaries of the nation-state, the debates on citizenship rights quite centrally engage with the question of discrimination due to membership of different social groups and majority and minority cultures within the state and within the polity with much insularity between the two. Further, the spread of the modern nation state as the entrenched operative framework not only meant that every piece of land across the globe was laid claim to by some nation state (Malkki 1992, 24-44) but also that the ultimate owner of all land within boundaries of the nation state was declared by law to be the 'state.' Thus under the doctrine of eminent domain the state, as the ultimate owner of land, has the power to take any land including private property under the reason of public purpose such as providing civic amenities, creating infrastructure and other modern amenities for 'development' of national and local economies. The fact that this dispossesses some of their land and impoverishes them was widely seen as an inevitable and necessary price for the greater common good of development. Studies by anthropologists and sociologists particularly since the 1980s however have demonstrated the social, cultural and economic costs of displacement due to development (Dreze, Samson and Singh1997; Cernea and Mc Dowell 2000; Baviskar 2005; Fernandes and Thukral 1989; Scudder 2005).

In the United Nations (UN) in the last decades of the twentieth century it was realized that in international normativity there was a blind spot when it came to those who lived in refugee like situations and had not crossed an international border. Reasons of *realpolitik* cannot be entirely discounted for this enlightenment about internally displaced persons (IDPs) in the post-Cold War world where countries developed cases of 'compassion fatigue' and 'host country predicament' (Vincent and Sorensen, 2001, p. 4) so that fewer people who found themselves in refugee-like situations could escape national boundaries if they wanted to. B. S. Chimni has also pointed to the growing tension in international refugee law 'between its language of protection and the ground reality of rejection' (Chimni, 2000). In 1998, the UN introduced the category of Internally Displaced Persons (IDPs) and definde them as,

> persons or groups of persons who have been forced or obliged to flee or to leave their homes or places of habitual residence, in particular as a result of or in order to avoid the effects of armed conflict, situations of generalized violence, violations of human rights or natural or human-made disasters, and who have not crossed an internationally recognized state border (United Nations 1998, p. 2).

The principles identify the rights and guarantees of internally displaced persons. While not legally binding, the principles draw extensively on legally binding provisions of international humanitarian and human rights law and, by analogy, on the basic principles of refugee law (Kalins, 2000, p. 2) and have led to significant advances in the rights of IDPs. In 2009, some governments in Africa legally bound themselves to these principles through a regional instrument, the Kampala Convention, adopted by a special summit of the African Union in Kampala, Uganda on 23 October 2009 that came into force in a little over three years when by 2014, 22 governments had ratified it. This means that these countries are required to incorporate these provisions into domestic law and are legally bound to protect the rights and well-being of those displaced by conflict, violence, natural disasters and other human rights abuses. Most importantly however, recognition of the innovation of the category of IDPs is important because the Guiding Principles that place 'primary duty and responsibility' on 'national authorities' to 'provide protection and humanitarian assistance to internally displaced persons within their jurisdiction'[29] brings to the fore the underlying and longstanding issue of physical exclusion and discrimination against groups-based on ascriptive conditions within the nation-states. The category of IDPs strings together hitherto separate and separate 'domains' of study of citizenship, refugee studies, displacement due to development and disaster management.

The category of IDPs emphasizes the element of choice, which is why it does not apply to persons who move voluntarily from one place to another solely in order to improve their economic circumstances. Robert Muggah reiterates that internal displacement occurs when coercion is employed, where choices are restricted and where they are facing more risks than opportunities by staying,

---

29 Principles 3, 25, United Nations.

which is purported to distinguish it from 'voluntary' or 'economic' migration (Muggah, 2003). Peter Penz argues that the element of coercion is not always straightforward and therefore it is misleading to view coercion and choice as mutually exclusive. Choice is not eliminated, merely restricted (Penz, 2003, p. 84; Das 1996, pp. 1509–14). Though violence and coercion are considered benchmarks in determination of IDPs, Ranabir Samaddar has pointed out that categories like this do not take into consideration structural violence as one of the 'push factors' of displacement. The notion of forced is so narrowly defined, that the structural violence permeating these societies escapes one's attention, (Samaddar, 2004, p. 23). The distinction between coercion and choice becomes unclear in situations of extreme poverty where people have no choice but to move to another place to seek their livelihood. This problematic is evident in the case of rural to urban migrants in India. For example a poor farmer faced with drought and starvation hardly has a choice but to move.[30] A more direct example of structural violence is in 2005 when Dalit homes were burnt in Gohana due to upper caste resentment at their development. In case of displacement due to communal violence as well displacement can be dispersed and take place incrementally over a period of time and coercion is not as evident.

Since the innovation of the category of IDPs what has come to be known as forced migration studies has become a growing domain of scholarship particularly since the late 1990s.[31] The current scholarship on IDPs provides empirical

---

30 Thanks to Gopal Guru for drawing attention to this limitation of the category of IDPs.

31 Francis Deng, the UN appointed International Commissioner for the rights of Internally Displaced Persons, gleaned international law, refugee law and humanitarian law to produce *Internally Displaced Persons: Compilations and Analysis of Legal Norms*, and formulated the UN Guiding Principles on IDPs. The Internal Displacement Monitoring Centre along with the Norwegian Refugee Council has regularly produced a constructive compendium of sorts of internally displaced persons around the world through Global IDP Surveys. Through their work on displaced populations Francis Deng, Roberta Cohen, David Akorn have provided descriptive accounts of situations of displacement around the world, highlighting the plight of the displaced in the light of the UN Guiding Principles. In *Caught between borders: response strategies of Internally Displaced Persons* by Sorensen, Birgette Refslund and Mark Vincent, and *Living in Limbo: Conflict Induced Displacement in Europe and Central Asia* by Steven B. Holtzman, and Taies Nezam, compare accounts of IDPs in South Asia and across Europe and Central Asia to identify patterns in the experience of displaced populations and highlight major issues of concern for IDPs such as livelihood, material well-being, employment and relationship with the state. The importance of the book is that it compares the poverty, employment and other indicators of the displaced with that of local populations in the same country rather than comparing the situation of displaced with international human rights instruments, thereby giving a more accurate

accounts and detailed descriptive accounts of local situations in the light of normative developments at the international level. However, due to the historical context in which the category emerged and the role of the UN in normative developments with regard to displaced persons, the discourse on displacement has emphasized neutrality and humanitarian aspects in order to intervene in a world of sovereign nation-states. This context is carried forward in most of the scholarship on internally displaced persons so far that is couched in the language of human rights and studies displacement primarily from an international lens that emphasizes the humanitarian aspects of the plight of displaced persons. Liisa Malkki, however, points out that the overtly humanitarian emphasis of studies on the displaced often has the effect of depoliticizing the issue of displacement (Malkki, 1995, pp. 495–523). Moreover this also has in effect retained the inside-outside dichotomy of entrenched statist perspectives by which the radical, probing potential of the lens of displacement has inadvertently been blunted.

Satish Deshpande, however, argues that communal violence involves spatial strategies to shape space. Arguing that the concept of nation involves ideological and material contests, he holds that neighbourhoods are an important part of the spatial strategy of *Hindutva* where the cultural nationalist imagination of the nation is sought to be realized. Neighbourhoods, he points out, are seen as an important site to conquer among the ideologues of *Hindutva* (Deshpande 2000, pp. 167–211). Given that displacement turns the analytical spotlight on exclusionary aspects of the nation state and taking a cue from Agamben who uses

---

picture of the plight of the displaced. However, being a macro level study *Living in Limbo* does not provide narrative accounts to describe the instances, which give rise to the statistics or explain processes of displacement. Given that in most countries, several groups are seen as similarly impoverished and that there is competition among deprived groups for resources from the state, S. B. Holtzman and Taies Nezam make a strong case to argue that displaced have a specific pattern of 'vulnerability' that deserves the state's attention. With a focus on the condition of being displaced rather than overly emphasizing the distinction of formally created categories such as refugees and IDPs, especially given the history of conflict along borders in South Asia, Paula Banerjee, Sabyasachi Basu Ray Chaudhuri and Samir Kumar Das have, in *Internal displacement in South Asia*, given a rich, descriptive account of displaced persons in the region. *Forced migration in the South Asian region: Displacement, Human Rights and Conflict Resolution* edited by Omprakash Mishra brings out the major issues that have dominated debates in the emerging area of forced migration studies such as those of responsible sovereignty postulated by Roberta Cohen and the arguments by Peter Penz regarding the subjective element of coercion, which is a defining element of the category of internally displaced persons. *Dimensions of Displaced Persons in Northeast India* edited by C. J. Thomas chronicles the several cases of internal displacement in the region.

the lens of displacement to emphasize a topographical rather than cartographical understanding of space, in this book the study of neighbourhoods, namely a focus on topographical dimensions is used to bring to light processes of displacement that have important explanatory value.

The city of Ahmedabad that has witnessed a large number of riots has featured prominently in scholarship related to Gujarat after the violence that rocked the state in 2002 (Robinson, 2005; Jasani, 2008; Gupta, 2011). A long time resident of Vadodara who worked in Ahmedabad as a journalist at the time of the violence in 2002 pointed out that Ahmedabad is not Gujarat and what happened in Ahmedabad could not be extended to the whole of the state. 'It (communal violence) is there in Baroda as well but if you only look at Ahmedabad you will come away with a very skewed picture of Gujarat.'[32] An endeavour was therefore made during the author's fieldwork conducted in 2008–09 to draw in sources from rural as well as urban areas in the districts of Ahmedabad, Baroda, Anand and Sabarkantha. In addition to the two cities of Ahmedabad and Baroda and two smaller cities of Anand and Himmatnagar two additional semi-urban areas, Modassa and Idar, which have a large Muslim populations and which became shelters for the displaced from rural areas of Sabarkantha and the surrounding districts were also taken up as Sabarkantha has the largest number of displaced persons. Further villages such as Ode, and Kidiad that suffered high death tolls; Mogri, a village in Anand district where Muslims have not returned; and Deshotar, a village where a majority of Muslims have returned were also taken up for research.

A collector in the Ahmedabad Municipal Corporation pointed out very matter of factly that 'You can't prove anything by showing so many people moved from here to there.'[33] Beside the fact that any study on population movements would pose significant methodological challenges especially in our globalized times where with increasing mobility, people's movements within and beyond borders seem to constitute huge masses of unaccounted population the collector's assertion made much methodological sense in that people move for a host of reasons and to establish causality would require evidence that is not discernable in existing forms of aggregate data in the public domain whether in census or land and property

---

32 Ayesha Khan (then a journalist for Indian Express, Ahmedabad), in discussion with the author, 13 December 2008.

33 The Collector (The District Collector Office, Ahmedabad), in discussion with the author, 8 December 2008.

market data, which do not publish social aspects such as caste and religion. In this book therefore the analysis is mainly informed by field work and interviews with displaced persons, community workers, NGO practitioners, academics, media professionals, officials and party functionaries.

Given the inside/outside dichotomy that characterizes refugee studies that has been critiqued and the need to undertake rigorous archival work to bring out the evolution of institutional practices of governing populations flows, (Samaddar 2004, pp. 21-35) this book uses a complex of ethnographic data, government resolutions, policies, correspondence of the government of Gujarat with the National Human Rights Commission (NHRC) and National Commission for Minorities (NCM), court cases, reports of state appointed commissions of inquiry, independent and media reportage and Gujarat legislative assembly debates since the formation of the modern state of Gujarat in 1960 to 2003 to study the handling of population movements due to communal violence. It employs the probing lens of displacement to examine Gujarat since 2002 to argue that displacement is not only symptomatic of the state being taken over by a majoritarian vision of the nation by which minorities may be threatened, but that in our globalized times it entails a shift in the very idea of the state in terms of what can rightly be expected of it and the source of its legitimacy.

The first chapter lays out the context of the book, namely the state of Gujarat by examining the demographic spread of the state, various population movements and the processes associated with them such as industrialization, deindustrialization and liberalization that have played a significant role in shaping the polity of Gujarat to find that neither communal violence nor displacement are without precedent in Gujarat. The next chapter, therefore, examines what happened in 2002 that led to national and international outrage. It reconstructs circumstances and processes in the journey of victims of communal violence from being *vatanis* which loosely translated means citizens or inhabitants to having to flee their homes through their stay in temporary dwellings such as relief camps, rented accommodations or houses of relatives and friends to relief colonies or houses in places of Muslim concentration and being identified by NGOs as *visthapith* or displaced people. Chapter 3 examines the response of the complex of state institutions and functionaries to the situation in 2002 in comparison with previous instances of communal violence to argue that what was distinctive about the violence of 2002 was the response of the state. The many instances of communal violence in Gujarat afford opportunities to examine the governance of communal violence from a comparative perspective across time across different levels of authority of the entity of the Indian state. In the violence in 2002, given the lacuna left by the state, Muslim organizations stepped in for relief and rehabilitation and set up relief colonies. The next chapter examines the phenomena of relief colonies and the various contestations and negotiations arrived at so that by 2009 an increasing number of Muslims in Gujarat publicly expressed support for Narendra Modi. The last chapter examines the impact of these events in the larger political universe through contributions of the civil society and the battle in the theatre of the court for their larger implications on the Indian polity.

1

Demography and Population Movements in Gujarat

Gujarat, the westernmost state of India with its landmass reaching out into the Indian Ocean, forked by the gulfs of Kutch and Khambhat to form a large coastline, has had a history of maritime trade going back to four millennia as well as of migrations from within and outside the subcontinent. The state has been known historically for its culture shaped by mercantilism, industrialization and entrepreneurship and most recently for its unabashed march towards economic liberalization, as the self professed and popular model of economic growth and good governance. It has historically had a high number of immigrants and migrants that came as traders, nomads, missionaries, travellers, merchants, refugees and with the development of industries particularly since late 1800s, as work related migrants. It is a highly urbanized state with 31.10 per cent of its population living in urban areas. This high level of urbanization is nowhere more visible than in the district of Ahmedabad where 80.2 per cent of the population lives in urban areas while 19.8 per cent lives in rural areas.[1]

This highly urbanized state has come to be characterized in recent times for its economic growth but also for the violence in 2002. Violence however is not without precedent in Gujarat. Communal violence in the state has led to the highest per capita of deaths due to such violence in the country and the highest number of casualties in a single cluster of riots (Parekh, 2002). In trying to find meaning and explain the events of 2002 broadly two images of Gujarat have emerged, one of the state with a culture of syncretism that has been interrupted since the 1980s by right wing mobilization and another as a state prone to violence with repeated instances of caste and communal conflict. To look at Gujarat, this chapter, therefore, employs the contending lenses of citizenship as well as displacement in that while one marks or at least formally signifies membership or inclusion – the other marks physical exclusion. There is a rich body of scholarship

---

1   Government of India, 2001, Census of India, District Census Handbook, Ahmedabad, 27.

on the state including those by anthropologists or sociologists that has been added to by academic attention to Gujarat after the violence of 2002 and while this chapter does not share the expertise of those disciplines it examines and draws on existing scholarship by them on the state to lay out the context for subsequent chapters. Given the sedentary bias of social sciences that has come to be questioned,[2] this chapter examines the demographic profile of Gujarat with respect to the entrenched framework of the state as well as other collectivities of membership such as caste and religion through which people relate to land and the faultlines that they become for forced migration as the context of subsequent chapters.

Geography and demography

Linkages between land and human habitations have been made not just in common sense assumptions but disciplines of geography and anthropology as well.[3] While a number of factors have shaped Gujarat's demographic spread and settlement pattern, for the Anthropological Survey of India, 'Gujarat's ecology explains its ethnographic features'. The Anthropological Survey of India's, *People of India*, attributes the demographic spread and culture of Gujarat to its location on the western coast of the Indian subcontinent, to the North of the Indian Ocean along which it has a large coastline that has since as far back as four millennia linked both inland and overseas trade routes and facilitated maritime trade through sea ports such as Mandvi, Kandla, Dwarka, Bhavnagar, Porbandar, Veraval, Gandevi, Surat and Bharuch in South Gujarat with two major gulfs Cambay and Kutch that have led to immigration of various people groups across time. As many as 206 communities i.e., 71.28 per cent in today's Gujarat claim to have migrated to the state at some time in the past. 60.90 per cent of Gujarat's enumerated communities, which is higher than the national average of 40.93 per cent, can recall their migration in oral tradition (Singh, 2002, p. xxiv, 6). The state that has historically attracted migrants continues to do so even today and as it grows in population density and is ranked sixth among other states that were the most preferred

---

2   For a discussion on literature in anthropology on linkages between culture and place see Liisa Malkki, 1992, 'National Geographic: The Rooting of Peoples and the Territorialization of National Identity among Scholars and Refugees,' in 'Space, Identity, and the Politics of Difference,' *Cultural Anthropology* 7 (1): 24–44, http://www.jstor.org/stable/656519.

3   Ibid.

destinations within India (Government of India, 2001b). Different communities in Gujarat have since 1900 travelled and settled outside India as labourers, traders and businessmen to countries as far apart as Uganda, Zanzibar, Mozambique, Natal in South Africa, West Asia, United Kingdom, United States and Fiji among others. Since the 1960s, the attraction of migrating overseas especially among the middle classes has caught on to the extent that there are entire villages known as (Non Resident Indian) NRI villages where most of the young have emigrated to other countries. The Gujarati diaspora particularly the landowning caste group of *Patidars* now known as *Patels* continues to invest and give back to villages, cities and towns in Gujarat through investment in infrastructure such as schools and hospitals in their original village. Unlike some of the southern states however majority of such donations are transmitted directly or through relatives rather than formal channels due to their distrust of government bureaucracy (Rutten and Patel, 2007). The ideological role of *Hindutva* and religious sentiments also influence many overseas *Patels* to donate directly to temples and religious organizations (Dekkers and Rutten, 2011, pp. 16–18).

The western border of Gujarat is also part of the international border between Pakistan and India. However the massive displacement of millions at the time of Partition that left a trail of destruction of life and property did not affect Gujarat in the scale and intensity that it did Punjab and Bengal as displaced Hindus including Gujaratis and Maharashtrians from Pakistan settled in cities of Bombay presidency[4] while 2.2 per cent of those Muslims who migrated to Pakistan were from the Bombay Presidency, which the present state of Gujarat was then a part of.[5] The Sindhi Hindus however who were historically influential in trade and bureaucracy and had up until then enjoyed patronage and protection of rulers before their exodus from Sindh in Pakistan as an aftermath of the Partition suffered huge social, emotional and material losses. (Bhavnani, 2014, pp. xxiv–xxv; Zamindar, 2007, 62–64). Until the fencing of the border was completed there continued to be movement across the border for familial and other ties among communities. A large wave of migration occurred in 1965 during the war between India and Pakistan when 8000 Hindus from Pakistan crossed the Thar

---

4   Sarah Ansari, 2005, *Life After Partition: Migration, Community and Strife in Sindh*, Karachi: Oxford University Press, quoted in Vazira Fazila and Yacoobali Zamindar, 2008, *The Long Partition and the Making of Modern South Asia: Refugees, Boundaries, Histories*, New Delhi: Penguin Viking.

5   Quoted in Rajmohan Gandhi, 1968, *Patel: A Life*, Ahmedabad: Navajivan Publications, in Achyut Yagnik, *Op.cit*.

Parkar district in Sindh on to India. While Gujarat remained unaffected by this in-migration as the state of Rajasthan was the host state at that point in time, the death of Balwantrai Mehta, the then chief minister of Gujarat, as a result of his plane being shot down by Pakistan, had led to increasing feelings of animosity against Pakistan (Shah, 1970, p. 188). In 1971 when Pakistan and India went to war again and India occupied a large part of Thar Parkar desert, of the 90,000 Hindus who decided not to return when the territory was restored to Pakistan after the Shimla Agreement, Gujarat received a large number of Meghwal (Dalit) families from the region who were given land to resettle in Kutch (Jayal, 2013, pp. 90–91).

According to official estimates Hindus form the majority in the state at 89.9 per cent while Muslims are the largest minority at 9.0641 per cent among other minority communities such as Christians, Sikhs, Buddhists and Jains (Government of India, 2011). The social stratification for the majority population in Gujarat along caste lines is distinctive in that while according to the *varna* hierarchy of the Hindu social order where status is accorded in descending order to *Brahman, Kshatriya, Rajput, Shudra* and the untouchables or *ati shudras*,[6] in Gujarat the *Vanias* who belong to a *varna* lower than that of the *Rajputs* who belong to the *Kshatriya varna* are ranked higher than the *Rajputs* in local ritual hierarchy due to the importance accorded to trade and commerce in the region and their sanskritization (Shah, 2002, p. 64). Also, the middle order caste grouping of *Kshatriya* comprises 28.8 per cent of the total population compared to the national average of 15.50 per cent and the lowest percentage of the caste category traditionally known as *Shudras* at 12.8 per cent as against the national average of 29.1 per cent while upper caste *Brahmins* and *Vaishyas* are 7.27 per cent and 9.34 per cent respectively, which are comparable for corresponding figures nationally. Despite the numerical preponderance of *Kshatriyas*, which is more the result of political shifts and the federating of castes in the last few decades (Shah, 1975), it is the caste group of *Patidars* that have since the nineteenth century[7] risen first with ownership of land and subsequently in other professions and politics of the state to achieve social mobility in central Gujarat (Pocock, 1972) and become among the most influential communities in the state. Social stratification among

---

6   The caste groupings mentioned here are those used by the Anthropological Survey of India, *Op.cit.,* 25. These are the four main *varnas* groups of Hindu social hierarchy in the order of Brahmins, the highest, followed by Kshatriya, Vaishyas and Shudras. These groups comprise many castes and each caste is divided into various sub groups.

7   A. M. Shah traces the political ascendancy of *Patidars* to the eighteenth century (A. M. Shah, 2002, 35).

87 enumerated Muslim communities in Gujarat, the largest number of Muslim communities for any state in India, shows the existence of a hierarchy among them with *Syeds* as the highest followed by *Shaikh, Moghul* and *Pathan*. There are also other agrarian castes such as *Malek* and *Molesalam Girasia*, trader and artisan communities such as *Memon, Khatri, Khoja, Bohras* and service communities (Singh, 2002, p. 13; Engineer, 1989). Muslims that historically converted to Islam from Hinduism include *Bohras, Khojas* and *Memons* that claim to have converted from upper castes Hindu communities; agrarian communities such as *Patel* Muslims and *Rajputs* such as *Rangrej, Samma, Sepai, Sumra, Langha, Miyana, Kher* etc as well as those from artisans communities such as *Pinjara, Nagori* and *Lohar.* The *Arab* and *Baloch* communities occupy the middle order. A section of Muslim communities converted from lower castes and artisans follow their ancestral occupations. (Singh, 2002, p. xxv)

The Anthropological Survey of India (ASI) seems to be making a case for the existence of a culture of syncretism in Gujarat by pointing out various elements of commonality of socio-religious practices and intercommunity linkages especially among communities such as *Wagher, Banjara, Patel, Salat, Samma, Sanghar, Pinjara, Lohar* and *Multani* that are found among both Hindus and Muslims and continue to share language and cultural traits such as naming patterns and many elements of life cycle ceremonies. Their data on Gujarat suggests that, 'within an eco cultural sub region or a cultural linguistic region there is a larger sharing of traits among all communities across religious divide' which includes consumption of foods based on crops/grains locally grown, dress, elements of material culture, kinship structure, many a ritual of life cycle ceremonies, and dance forms such as *garba ras* and *dandiya ras* that are found in celebration across communities. Achyut Yagnik and Suchitra Sheth in the *Shaping of Modern Gujarat* also point out that communities and sects such as *Pirana* and *Pranami*, which amalgamated the teachings of the established religions, the evolution of Gujarati language and literature, emergence of Indo-Islamic and later Indo-European architecture (also Patel, 2007), the development of classical Hindustani music and introduction of new musical instruments from western Asia and Europe indicate a cultural synthesis that occurred historically.

However, with the frequency of riots in places like Ahmedabad and Vadodara, especially in the 1980s, 1990s and in 2002, communal violence for residents of these cities had almost become a given as an elderly lady said in jest about communal violence in Ahmedabad, '*maro ne kato, khao ne piyo*' (kill and cut, eat and drink) implying that life goes on along with these incidents of violence.[8] The violence in 2002 led to a significant body of independent and media reportage that documented gross human rights violations so that the state was categorized as a 'Hindutva lab' (Dayal, 2002) and the 'installation of the Hindu rashtra' (Sarkar, 2002). Scholars however have suggested more recent origins to this violence (Parekh, 2002; Yagnik and Sheth, 2005; Thapar, 2004; Nussbaum, 2007) given that between 1969 and the next major riot in 1985 there was relative calm and more recently the characterization of the state as a Hindu *rashtra* has been contested as one-sided categorization[9] (Sud, 2011). On the other hand however, the description of the state as a cultural frontier (Breman, 2002, p. 1485) and the emphasis on its violent history with respect to instances of caste and communal violence (Ghanshyam Shah, 1970, 1987, 1994; Engineer, 1985) stand in contrast to descriptions of an idealized and lost cosmopolitanism in Gujarat (Jasani, 2010). Insights into this puzzle formed by contradicting images of Gujarat can be explored in major socio economic processes that shaped the construct of the modern state and membership in Gujarati society.[10]

Authority and membership

How do people relate to land? Family, kinship, religion, tribe, feudal ties and various other collectivities signify ways in which people relate to authority in a geographic space or location prior to the overshadowing, seemingly ubiquitous embrace of what is called modernity and the form of modern polity – the state with its principle of membership i.e., citizenship. The idea of Gujarat in its modern form as an administrative subdivision of India was realized in 1960 after the demand for a separate state heightened under the Mahagujarat Movement for the formation of a separate state of Gujarat out of the Gujarati speaking areas of the bilingual state of Bombay. This included the former administrative territories of Bombay presidency that formed the mainland that are referred to as north, central and south Gujarat; the commissionerate of Kutch of the small peninsula of Kutch,

---

8   Ayesha Asuben Siddiqbhai (elderly homemaker, Ahmedabad), interview by author, October 2008.

9   Achyut Yagnik (writer, commentator and activist, Ahmedabad) in discussion with author, 10 October 2008.

10 Joel Migdal argues that states may mould but they are also continually moulded by the societies in which they are embedded. (Migdal J. Kohli and Shue 2001, 2).

over 200 princely states from the peninsula of Saurashtra or Kathiawad and the large princely state of Baroda, smaller states like Rajpipla etc. All these regions that were united as one administrative unit of Gujarat were to be governed by the Indian Constitution. However, the normative construct of the modern state as the comprehensive political authority within a given territory has, as has been more recently acknowledged, a more complex empirical reality. The encounter with the colonial state and modernity affected social and political reality in the Indian subcontinent not quite in the same way as it did in Europe in that what emerged in the West in waves of nation building were sought to be simultaneously transferred to state authority even as traditional organizing principles such as caste and religion, although reconstituted, persisted. It has been postulated that relationships between ruler and ruled and political belonging to territorial states were tenuous under traditional conditions in pre-colonial Indian power centres where, due to an 'absent' centre the caste system governed boundaries and controlled transactions between social groups more than any of the political authorities of regional kingdoms or empires. Belonging to a political community in pre-colonial times was thin in contrast to modern practices as belonging was more diffused across layers of caste, region etc. and membership to caste was of greater significance than membership to a political community as people who inhabited a particular space could be part of different kingdoms in a short space of time (Kaviraj, 1994, pp. 116,122). Loyalty to a single religion could not also be assumed as a guarantee of subjects' support to their rulers (Thapar, 2004, p. 170). A widely accepted argument is that under the colonial gaze, hitherto fuzzy identities of membership to communities had congealed through modern practices of systematic gathering of information on communities for their enumeration that would go on as a corollary to contribute to the creation of abstract identities such as Hindu and Muslim (Kaviraj, 1994, p. 116) and open up possibilities for violence. The erstwhile polities and their subjects, united as one administrative unit of the democratic republic of the modern Indian nation-state, were to be governed by the Indian constitution that articulated a horizontal membership of citizenship over the many hierarchies of Indian society. However, when the Indian constitution sought to guarantee rights to historically marginalized communities through a system of reservation of seats in national and state legislatures, government jobs, educational institutions and in electoral constituencies it had the unintended effect of linking rights of individual citizens to collectivities such as caste and tribe (Tambiah, 1996) thereby perpetuating their importance. As states made reservation policies that fixed percentages of quotas in government employment and education for marginalized groups listed as Scheduled Castes, Scheduled Tribes in the constitution and in the contested and expanding category of Other Backward Castes (OBCs),[11] it put boundaries on the scope of social mobility and access to public resources making caste a basic category in the construction of citizenship (Shani, 2007, p. 63). Thus in the world's largest democracy that is India, given the perpetuating importance of these other categories of membership within citizenship and the competing forms of order, 'integrating frameworks of authority' (Kohli, 2001, p. 106) are difficult to find.

Various socioeconomic processes shaped the polity and capabilities of the state in Gujarat. Gujarat's mercantile history in the state put it on the map with international trade since the sixteenth century and provided fertile ground for the establishment and growth of modern industries. With the opening of the first textile mill in Ahmedabad in 1861 and the subsequent laying of the railway line between Ahmedabad and Bombay, processes of modern industrialization started to take root and spread so that by 1911 there were 53 mills in Ahmedabad and textile mills in many parts of Gujarat, which fuelled the migration of people from rural to urban areas who were recruited as labour in the mills. By 1950 half of Ahmedabad that came to be known as the 'Manchester of India' earned its employment from textile enterprises (Breman, 2002). Existing cities such as Ahmedabad, Baroda, Surat and Rajkot saw the influx of people and newer cities and towns developed as industries diversified and spread. People belonging to upper castes, such as *Nagar Brahmins* and *Vaishnav Vaniyas* as well as some agrarian communities including *Kanbi*, *Khatri* and Muslim communities who diversified into trade and money lending were among the first to benefit from and dominate modern processes as well (Yagnik and Sheth, 2005, pp. 103,111). Gujarat also began to attract migrants from neighbouring states of India as the state invested in large public sector industries under the Nehruvian model of development and also followed a policy of promoting small and medium scale industries. Ahmedabad is the largest industrial metropolis of the state that to date attracts people in large

---

11 The Indian constitution fixed reserve quotas in the Lok Sabha (lower house of the Indian parliament, state legislative assemblies, government jobs and educational institutions as 14 per cent for Scheduled Castes (SCs) and 7 per cent for Scheduled Tribes (STs). The constitution also provided for creation of reservation for 'any backward class of citizens' (Article 16 (4)) but did not establish clear criteria for establishing backwardness and instead decreed the determining of criteria on the basis of social and educational backwardness by commissions appointed by the President (Article 340 (1)).

numbers from the neighbouring states of Rajasthan, Maharashtra and UP (Singh, 2002, pp. 8–9). Migration from rural areas to smaller developing towns also significantly increased with the development and diversification of industries. A drought from 1984–88 led to further migration from urban to rural areas so that by 1980 Gujarat was among the most industrialized states of the country, and by 1991, one in three Gujaratis lived in a city (Yagnik and Sheth, 2005, pp. 228–29).

The expansion of working population also brought about the gradual organization of collective action of labour since early 1900s most notably through the dominant trade union the Majoor Mahajan Sangh (MMS) known in English as the Textile Labour Association (TLA), the first labour union in India due to the efforts of Anasuya Sarabhai coupled with the leadership of Mahatma Gandhi. MMS had a unique character that under the influence of Gandhi combined traditional patron client relations determined by family ties and values of avoidance of conflict and compromise with non-violent agitation to form what was at one time the largest and most organized labour force in the country (Breman, 2004, p. 42). The MMS in its heydays had membership of over 150000 members that with considerable success fought for rights for workers to engineer a composite membership that emphasized collective interests over caste and religious interests through a strategy of class harmony rather than class conflict (Breman, 2002, p. 1486). However, kinship networks and belonging to caste and religious community played an important role in recruitment and functioning of MMS so much so that entire departments were almost exclusively under the control of a particular caste or community. While Ghanshyam Shah draws attention to the fact that departmental unions corresponded to caste and communal groups as did living spaces of workers to argue that the labour movement was not successful in forging a strong overarching working class identity over caste and communal identifications (Shah, 1970, p. 197), Jan Breman holds that it did in some instances, such as the 1969 riots serve as a space for intercommunal harmony and mutual protection against communal violence (Breman, 2002, p. 1486), which is a phenomenon witnessed more in urban than rural areas.

Particularly in its rural areas Gujarat along with Maharashtra in western India has had the distinction of having the most successful and largest number of cooperatives in India with the union of dairy cooperatives' brand of Anand Milk Union Limited (Amul) and Self Employed Women's Association (SEWA)'s cooperative banks acquiring renown around the world for their achievements. Village economy in central Gujarat has been markedly different from that of other parts of the subcontinent in that while other regions were only slightly monetized, the heartland of Gujarat was monetized since pre-colonial times (Hardiman, 1998, p. 1563) and farmers had engaged in commercial farming for more than a century. The cooperative movement started in 1904 when the British colonial government introduced the Indian Co-operative Societies Act that proved to be particularly successful in parts of Gujarat. The Charotar tract in central Gujarat had a history of efficient milk production that in 1920s the British provincial government harnessed through a contract given to a private company named Polson Diary. It was to supply milk from Kheda district to the government milk scheme in Bombay city. Following discontent over the terms and conditions of the company, milk producers decided to organize themselves on cooperative lines and supply milk directly to Bombay and were encouraged by nationalist leaders such as Sardar Vallabhbhai Patel and Morarji Desai. Under the leadership of Tribhovandas Patel in 1940, village level cooperative societies were formed that were organized at the district level organization under the Kaira District Co-operative Milk Producers Union that expanded to form Amul. Under the leadership of Verghese Kurien, who first interned with the organization but was asked to stay on, Amul became a national brand and what came to be known as the Anand pattern of cooperatives was recommended by the then prime minister Lal Bahadur Shastri to be replicated across the nation. Under Operation Flood, a national dairy development programme in 1970 that sought to replicate the Anand pattern nationally, supported by donations from the European Economic Community (EEC) and World Food Programme, went on to become the world's largest programme of dairy development with three million members that exports milk to other countries in Asia and by 2014 accounted for 15 per cent of global production (Sood, 2014).

While it was widely believed even by planners in the Planning Commission that cooperatives in Anand transformed a milk deficient area into a milk sufficient one, it was in fact already an area that had a surplus of milk production that successfully organized cooperatives by local initiative rather than state intervention (Attwood and Baviskar, 1988, p. 17). The cooperative model went on to become a central aspect of India's planned economy in an effort to redistribute risks and rewards to weaker members of community as a major tool to achieve social and economic goals such as increasing production and mobilizing underutilized resources to reinforce social justice, equality of opportunity and social solidarity through its democratic set up. However while cooperatives were sought to be initiated and encouraged through state subsidies and state intervention, a large number of them did not succeed. While those that succeeded such as the dairy, oil seed and cotton cooperatives went on to become important bases of power it is important to note however that these cooperatives were informal cooperative groups of selective alliances to overcome serious technological obstructions in production and not a system of communal solidarity (Attwood, 1988, pp. 69–87). While the cohesion of landowning *Patidar* castes identity was vital to the success of dairy, cotton and oilseeds cooperatives they ended up being the chief beneficiaries themselves and dominated many of these cooperatives (Patel, 1988, p. 375; 1995, p. 255). A large number of small farmers from Kshatriya and other castes also benefitted greatly from the cooperatives but not poor landless labourers. Thus leadership in the cooperative movement in terms of majority in management committees, chairmanship etc. predominantly comes from the dominant caste of the region. Therefore while *Avanavils, Chaudharies* and *Rajputs* dominate cooperatives in Valsad and Surat, Mehsana and Saurashtra respectively, *Patidars* dominate in other areas such as Surat, Bharuch, Vadodara, Ahmedabad, Kheda (Phansalkar, 1997, p. A-144). Cooperatives, therefore, did not remove or weaken biases of caste and economic scale. They, however, became important bases of power as some leaders of cooperatives acquired skills in mobilization of men and resources to compete for leadership positions in the cooperatives. Many went on to become members of central and state legislatures.

Prior to the formation of the modern state of Gujarat in both Bombay presidency as well as princely states it was the traditional upper castes of *Brahmins* and *Vaniyas* who formed the bulk of government employees. The *Patidars* forming 14 per cent of the population consolidated their growing economic and social base even politically by securing a quarter of the assembly seats in five assembly elections from 1957 onwards. The *Patidars* constituted a large proportion of the Congress Party's rural base in Gujarat since the time of the Indian National movement when it was a bastion of the party and where the Kheda and Bardoli *satyagrahas*[12] were fought and Gandhi's constructive programme was first tried although Gandhi's efforts were also met with significant resistance in Gujarat (Yagnik and Sheth, 2005, p. 191). While Patidars were conservative in their approach in the rural context, they were more militant than the Gandhian and middle class

---

12 Satyagraha literally translated as firmness in adhering to the truth is an important tenet of Gandhian thought and political action. Translation from Anthony J. Parel, 2013, *Hind Swaraj and other Writings,* New Delhi: Cambridge University Press, xci.

Congress leadership (Hardiman, 1981). Faced with the growing dominance of the *Patidars*, the Rajputs who were not numerically strong but sought to find a place of reckoning in the emerging polity formed the Kshatriya Mahasabha in 1948 by creating a caste combination called *Kshatriya* that combined their numbers with another traditionally arms bearing community, the *Kolis*. This combination, however, did not then make a significant show electorally and upper and middle castes dominated all political parties in Gujarat.

Land, citizenship and displacement

Sociologists have pointed out that land continues to deliver economic, social and political power to those communities who own it in rural India (Srinivas 1955; Mendelsohn, 1993, p. 807) as is evident among land owning communities in Gujarat. In Gujarat the *Patidars*, which means shareholder that spread from only landholding groups to the broad *Kanbi* group during the nineteenth century (Hardiman, 1981) control almost two thirds of land in regions of central and northern Gujarat while the numerically largest *Kolis* are landowners and politically dominant only in Saurashtra. The *Anavils* that are numerically smaller than the *Patidars* are the predominant landholding community in south Gujarat. Other landholding communities include *Brahmins*, *Rajputs*, and certain Muslim communities. *Barias* and *Vaghris* are small landholding communities while *Dalits* are usually landless.

The modern state of Gujarat inherited policies from the Bombay presidency that itself had retained some policies of the colonial British administration toward land. This included the distinction between private and government property and that all uncultivated land was property of the government, part of which was sought to be brought under cultivation by giving it to tenants and levying a rent, while part of the property was allowed to be used by the public for free. Such policies such as the distinction between government and private land as well as certain practices of taxation existed even before the British. However, the British while apparently allowing traditional practices to continue, tried to rationalize policies towards land, (Shah, 2002, pp. 134, 148, 204) reconstituted the basis of power of dominant castes, encouraged commercial agriculture among them and strengthened them by granting property rights to them (Hardiman, 1998, p. 1542). In the modern Indian nation state where Article 19 defined the right to property, which was subsequently amended under Article 33, state relations to property were supposed to broadly have the following dimensions of taxation powers, police powers to protect property and prevent people from using property in a way prejudiced to others and that of eminent domain. Also in a continuation of colonial policies towards land under the doctrine of eminent domain the state, as the ultimate owner of land, has the power to take any land including private property under the reason of public purpose such as providing civic amenities, creating infrastructure and other modern amenities for 'development' of national and local economies against payment of compensation.

Given however, that actual ownership of land in rural areas continued to remain concentrated in the hands of a few landlords under the impetus of the national movement's emphasis on social justice along with other social movements for land reform, Gujarat was among other states in the newly formed democratic republic of India where land reform measures were undertaken. Land reform sought to abolish intermediaries that existed between the state and cultivators; give 'land to the tiller'; regulate the size of landholdings and redistribute surplus among landless, marginal farmers. Under the land reform measures undertaken after independence The Bombay Tenancy Agricultural Land Act 1948 was implemented in Gujarat that then came under the erstwhile state of Bombay. According to an important provision called 'Farmer's day' inserted in the Act in 1956 with a view to give tillers rights over the land, if any person legally tilled the land of any other person on 1 April 1957, he was entitled to purchase the said land. According to official estimates, the beneficiaries of these reforms included 1,77,171 people from Scheduled Castes, 2,58,132 from Scheduled Tribes and 8,42,822 from the 'other' category (GOI, 2001, p. 12). Land reforms had also been enacted in Saurashtra through the Saurashtra Land Reforms Act, 1952, giving occupancy rights to 55,000 tenant cultivators over 12 lakh acres of land, out of 29 lakh acres held by *girasdars*, spread over 1,726 villages. The balance was left for their personal cultivation (Teltumbde, 2011, p. 10). Although administrative machinery and legislations were passed to implement land reforms they barely impacted the inequality in ownership of land as each of the provisions were subverted in practice (Sud, 2012, pp. 76–80). For instance, the ban on owning land eight kilometres away from an agriculturist's residence was lifted as well as the right to cultivate government surplus land through *eksali* (one year) schemes where landless and *Dalits* and OBCs cultivated land for decades and were forced to hand it back to their upper caste landlords by the government. Subsequently, the government of Gujarat enacted the Estates Acquisition Act through which it acquired cultivable and uncultivable land wasteland and *gochar* land, that in many instances was sought to be acquired by landless *Dalits*, which continues to remain with them without regularization by the government (Teltumbde, 2011, p. 10). Land reform measures were implemented with more success in the princely state of Saurashtra where *Kanbi-Patidar* who were former tenants of Rajput intermediaries become land owners rather than in parts of central and north Gujarat where *Patidars* controlled substantial tracts of land but where the state machinery comprising largely upper and middle caste *Brahmin*, *Vania* and *Kanbi* communities failed to do the same (Desai, 1971). The chief beneficiaries of land reforms thus turned out to be middle caste group of *Kanbi-Patidars*.[13]

In some rural areas the issue of landless Dalits seeking to till government owned surplus land led to conflict. A group of Ahmedabad mill workers associated with Dalit Panther Movement had encouraged landless Dalits to acquire *gochar* land (grazing land) from the government that developed into routine clashes between Dalits and Patidars that escalated in 1981 over the murder and burning of a Dalit youth. This was followed by the socioeconomic boycott of Dalits by the rest of the village. The government surplus land that the government rented out to landless and marginal groups for a period of a year, as well government owned surplus cultivable and uncultivable *gochar* land up to an estimated two lakh of which was encroached upon by landless Dalits under the leadership of mill workers in Ahmedabad and the instances of violent eviction of Dalits from these lands have remained a moot point for violence against Dalits such as in 1999 when an 800 strong mob of upper castes tried to violently evict Dalits from 125 acres of land in Pankhan, Saurashtra. This is also true of Dalits trying to vacate land for which they acquire title deeds from the possession of upper castes (Teltumbde, 2011, pp. 10–11).

Such displacement that occured on the margins largely went unnoticed as successive governments of Gujarat followed a policy of emphasis on rapid industrialization and modernization of agricultural production such as the 'Green Revolution' in 1960 under which the production of cash crops was encouraged through initiatives like large irrigation projects, subsidized electricity and credit resources for farmers, the chief beneficiaries. Since the 1960s the economy in Gujarat grew faster than the national economy. In addition

---

13 *Kanbi* is a large agricultural caste, and *Patidar* is the designation originally claimed by those sections, which were holders of land rights i.e., those who held a *patti*. The name was applied to families of superior economic and social standing.

to the culture of entrepreneurship in Gujarat, successive governments enacted favourable policies by which the state showed consistent increase in rate of growth from 3.32 per cent in the sixties to 4.95 per cent in the 70s to 5.67 per cent in the 80s and 90s (Hirway, 2000, p. 3106). Bodies such as the Gujarat State Finance Corporation (GSFC) established in 1951, Gujarat Industrial Development Corporation (GIDC) established in 1962 and Gujarat Industrial Investment Corporation (GIIC) established in 1968 also went on to do better than their counterparts in other states. Under the principle of eminent domain, the state as the ultimate owner of land and natural resources acquired land for public purposes for 'development'. The fact that this dispossesses some of their land and impoverishes marginal farmers was seen as an inevitable and necessary price for the greater common good of development in policy-making all over India.[14] Movements that challenged this model of development due to the involuntary migration of people from their places of original residence did not find many takers in Gujarat both in the state apparatus and in society at large. The most publicized and longstanding case in this regard is the Sardar Sarovar Project (SSP), the first and largest of major dams was built as part of the Narmada Valley Project, India's largest river project which involves the construction of 30 major, 135 medium and 3,000 minor irrigation schemes along the river Narmada and 41 of its tributaries. According to an estimate the SSP was supposed to irrigate 19 lakh hectares of land and submerge 19 villages in Gujarat, 33 in Maharashtra, 182 in Madhya Pradesh as well as submerge 13,744 hectares of forest area (Srinivasan, et al., 1989, p. 339). The Narmada Water Dispute Tribunal (NWDT) was constituted in 1969 to deliberate over the distribution of Narmada waters between the Gujarat, Madhya Pradesh, Maharashtra and Rajasthan. NWDT delivered the award in 1978 for sharing of water among the riparian states, which were to receive the natural resources and fix compensation for those to be displaced by the dam. However, while the NWDT's award fixed the nature and quantum of compensation to be given to displaced persons, which was a definite advance in large dam related displacement and relocation in India, it had adopted a very legalistic notion of land harking back to colonial times and had not at all appreciated the fact that most of those displaced who were to suffer for the cause of displacement were

---

14 India's first prime minister famously said to those displaced by the Hirakud Dam, 'If you are to suffer, you should suffer in the interests of the country'. Invariably, a majority of those estimated 65 million displaced people between 1950 and 2005 (Fernandes, 2009, 180–207) chosen to suffer for the county came from already marginalized groups (Lobo and Kumar, 2009, 9).

primarily *adivasis* or tribals whose existence was very closely intertwined with the land (Iyengar, 2002, 122–23). A large number of the displaced also had little knowledge of their displacement or provisions for relief and rehabilitation.

Since 1980s NGOs such as Gujarat Chhatra Sangharsh Vahini or Action Research in Community Health and Development (ARCH-Vahini), which started visiting the *adivasis,* got involved in helping the affected people obtain adequate resettlement. However, successive governments ignored problems related to relief and rehabilitation of the project that was touted as the answer to the problems of areas facing acute water scarcity up until the 1980s when first middle class activists from Gujarat and Mumbai and subsequently national and international activists got involved in the struggle for the rights of the displaced. Since a large number of the 'oustees' are *adivasis* the issue of displacement by the SSP raised the larger issue of preservation of *adivasi* culture versus their assimilation in the mainstream (Baviskar, 1995). The Narmada Bachao Andolan (NBA) i.e., the Save the Narmada Movement led by Medha Patkar since 1985 and other civil society organizations have opposed the principle of *eminent domain,* which requires few who are invariably already marginalized to give up their land and home for the benefit and development of the majority arguing that such development is in fact destruction. Estimates for number of people to be displaced by SSP ranged from 6603 families according to the NWDT, to independent estimates of that range from a conservative 7,600 families to 400,000 (Kothari, 1996, p. 1479). NBA's calculation of number of displaced includes those in the submergence areas, catchment areas and other measures related to the dam such as compulsory afforestation. The World Bank also following NBAs reasoning for assessing Project Affected People held that the figure of those displaced rose to six times the then existing estimate of 40,000 families. Since the NBA's involvement in 1987 the campaign for the rights of the displaced became a no-dam campaign that received much support by scholars and activists outside Gujarat but was vehemently opposed inside Gujarat.

The state machinery instead sought to mobilize support for the dam through publications and advertisements. Workers of the then ruling party, the Congress Party staged violent protests and disruptions against Medha Patkar. On the basis of its Independent Review Mission (IRM) report headed by Bradford Morse in 1991–92 to review resettlement and rehabilitation related to those affected by the project, the World Bank withdrew from the project in 1993. The report was welcomed by the anti-dam movement but strongly criticized and publicly burnt in Gujarat. On the question of rehabilitation for *adivasis* who depended on forest produce, the government accused them of being thieves, law breakers and encroachers in its affidavits to the Supreme Court (Morse, 1992, p. 126) that eventually ruled in favour of increasing the height of the dam. While activists such as Medha Patkar and Baba Amte who follow Gandhian principles of non-violence and *satyagraha* made headway through dialogue with other state governments of Maharashtra and Madhya Pradesh that was in fact the state most affected by the dam, the government of Gujarat resisted all dialogue and acted stringently against protesters and leaders even invoking the Official Secrets Act and calling the movement anti-national (Hardiman, 2004, p. 233). Such a display of the state's authority however has not always been as apparent in other arenas.

Displacements: Political, caste and communal

The state apparatus in Gujarat for long was led by the social groups of the upper and middle castes namely the *Brahmin-Vania-Patidar* combine. In 1969 Congress split into Congress (I) for Indira led by Indira Gandhi and Congress (O) for organizational leadership led by Morarji Desai. While Congress (I) led by Indira Gandhi at the national level and consequently in Gujarat sought to mobilize poor and deprived groups, which would provide the new electoral support base, many upper caste Congressmen defected to join Congress (O) in Gujarat. This period also witnessed a number of protests due to shortage of foodgrains and increasing prices and what was perceived as callous and corrupt attitude of the government. Students and professors of the Gujarat University in Ahmedabad started a movement against corruption called the Navnirman Movement in 1974, which the predecessor of the BJP, the erstwhile Jana Sangh and the Congress (O) successfully identified themselves with (Shah, 1974, p. 1433). The formation of the Congress (O) had created a void in the support base of the Congress (I), which it tried to fill by the creation of a new combination of electoral support in the 1970s. The new combination known by the acronym KHAM was a combination of *Kshatriyas, Harijans, Adivasis* and Muslims. The formula helped Congress win an emphatic victory in the 1980 elections. For the first time not a single member from the *Patidar* community had a cabinet rank while a majority of ministers in the new cabinet were from either *Kshatriya, Harijan, Adivasi* or Muslim communities and the chief minister Madhavsinh Solanki himself came from a lower caste *Kshatriya* community. These developments, however, had the effect of antagonizing the upper castes as well as the middle castes who felt a threat to their economic and political dominance. The Madhavsinh Solanki government, however, had not brought about a paradigmatic change in the policy priorities of the state and adhered to a policy of rapid industrialization with the intention of making Gujarat a 'mini-Japan'.

In 1972, the Congress-led government had appointed the Gujarat Backward Classes Commission under the chairmanship of AN Baxi to identify communities that were socially and educationally backward in Gujarat and to determine redistributive action for them in the lines of what had been done for Scheduled Castes and Scheduled Tribes in the constitution. The Baxi Commission identified backward communities on the basis of caste and submitted its report in 1976 recommending 10 per cent reservation for 82 identified castes. In 1980, six months after the KHAM strategy brought Madhavsinh Solanki-led Congress government came to power, protests against the reservation for scheduled castes by upper castes medical college students started in Ahmedabad. Although reservations were accepted in many states in India, Gujarat was one of the few states that experienced long drawn anti-reservation agitations once in 1981 and again in 1985. Unlike other states like Maharashtra, Tamil Nadu, Bihar and Uttar Pradesh, Gujarat did not have a backward caste or non-Brahmin movement until 1940s and even the national movement had been led by upper and middle castes namely *Brahmins*, *Patidars* and *Vaniyas* (Shah, 1987, p. AN-158).

The protests against reservation in 1981 turned violent and attacks that were mainly aimed at Dalits started in the industrial and working class areas of Ahmedabad and spread to middle class localities (Yagnik and Bhatt, 1984) and to other towns and cities. Public property was burned in arson, Dalit *bastis* (habitations) were set on fire in many parts of Ahmedabad. In other towns and rural areas there were also instances of violence against Dalit youth leading to forced migration of Dalits to neighbouring towns. (Shah, 1987, p. 167). The violence that went on for three months and had further spread to 18 out of 19 districts in Gujarat and to the many *Patidar* dominated villages of north and central Gujarat claiming a reported a death toll of 40 before subsiding after the High Court rejected the petitioners' plea opposing reservations (Kohli, 1990, p. 252). After groups that had not been listed by the Baxi Commission Report demanded to be included on account of their backwardness, the Solanki government appointed another commission under the chairmanship of retired high court judge C. V. Rane to look into the possibility of inclusion of such groups. The Rane Commission submitted its report in 1983 and identified Socially and Educationally Backward Classes/Castes (SEBC) included income along with occupation in place of the earlier caste-based identification. It also recommended an increase of 18 per cent to the existing reservation of 10 per cent for the identified SEBCs. The Commission's Report was initially ignored and when the Solanki government decided to implement it after 14 months, it replaced class with caste as the criterion of backwardness. The government appointed another committee under the chairmanship of Harubhai M. Mehta to look into the claims of additional 239 castes for inclusion into the original list of 82 communities (Shani, 2007, p. 58). The Solanki government's decision to increase reservations in government jobs and educational institutions led to protests leading to the outbreak of rioting again in 1985.

The agitation that once again was begun by upper castes' opposition to the reservation led to closing of schools and colleges, arson looting and outbreaks of violence over a period of seven months. In the course of the violence, which began as caste conflict, the killing of a Muslim boy gave a communal turn to the events and tensions began to spiral. The law and order situation only seemed to worsen after the police went on rampage after the killing of a police officer (COI, 1990, p. 215). Muslims complained that they faced losses to life and property due to connivance of the police with rioters. After a lull when violence broke out again, eight members of a Hindu family were burnt alive in a locality in Kalupur area of Ahmedabad followed by Hindu retaliation. The Solanki government's reservation policy was not implemented and the agitation subsided after the government reached a settlement with its employees. According to one estimate 220 people had died in the riots by 1986 (Shani, 2007, p. 88).

Both the anti-reservation riots of 1981 and 1985 saw increasing leadership and participation of the middle class. Among the first entrants to the emerging middle class in the region since colonial times included government employees that belonged to upper castes of *Brahmins* and *Vanias*. Parsis, *Patidars, Rajputs,* Muslims, artisan castes and untouchable castes were also subsequently added to their number. The anti-reservation agitation was a contest between upper and middle caste members of the middle class and the new lower caste entrants to the middle class (Shah 1987, p. AN-155). By 1981 processes of deindustrialization started in Ahmedabad and there was rapid informalization of labour economy. The share of the educated unemployed in the total unemployed increased from 57 per cent in 1980 to 75 per cent in 1994. It has been estimated that the percentage share of technically qualified labour power in the aggregate amount of main workers in Gujarat was less than one in 1981 while the percentage of educated labour power above matriculation was 15 per cent in the same year (Hirway, 2000, p. 3112). In a milieu of increasingly crowded and intense competition for a share in the limited pie of educational and employment opportunities that afforded social mobility, an aspirational and expanding middle class felt a strong sense of deprivation with its new entrants. The middle class composed predominantly of members of upper and middle castes that dominated educational institutions and the media, as well as the bureaucracy and police therefore had ideological penetration as well as access to state machinery. These agitations, thus, saw different professional associations such as the Ahmedabad Bar Association and the Ahmedabad Medical Association that supported the struggle and went on a sympathy strike (Spodek, 1989, p. 769) while business organizations such as cloth dealers, dealers in foodgrains, books etc. joined in to criticize the government (Shah, 1987, p. AN-155).

In 1990 when BJP leader L. K. Advani sought to undertake a *yatra* (campaign through publicized journeys) from Somnath in Gujarat to Ayodhya in Uttar Pradesh to mobilize nationwide support for the Sangh Parivar campaign to build a temple at what is believed to be the birthplace of a revered Hindu god Ram where a sixteenth century mosque now stands, the *yatras* left a string of communal clashes in their wake. When Advani was arrested in Bihar, there were communal riots in most towns and cities in Gujarat. During the BJP's campaign for the building of a Ram temple in Ayodhya in 1992 when *karsevaks* (religious volunteers) climbed on the Babri mosque and demolished it, riots between Hindus and Muslims broke out in different parts of India. In Gujarat too rioting was reported from several places including the otherwise peaceful city of Surat that had not witnessed a major riot for 65 years but recorded the highest death toll of 190 in the 1992 violence.[15] Violence and increasing insecurity of Muslims since the 1990s corresponded with increasing religious fundamentalism on the other side of the international border in Pakistan by the increased insecurity of Hindus and especially Dalit Hindus with rising religious fundamentalism, religious persecution, forced conversions and violence against women. Since early 1990s as a result of the increased vulnerability of Hindus, particularly in Punjab, Pakistan as many as 17000 people, who came to India as visitors with valid travel documents, stayed on and applied for citizenship (Jayal, 2013, p. 90). The next major instance of violence occured ten years later in 2002 when the burning of the compartment of a train after an attack by a mob in a Muslim locality killed 57

---

15 *Ibid.*

people including women and children and a large number of *karsevaks* who were returning from Ayodhya. This incident was followed by violence that spread to a large number of districts in Gujarat as a result of which according to conservative estimates more than 1000 people,[16] most of whom were Muslims, lost their lives and more than one and a half lakh Muslim families were displaced. The violence and subsequent displacement of Muslims led to national and international outcry.

Communal violence has occurred in other parts of India as well but in Gujarat Ahmedabad, in particular, has the dubious distinction of riots that have continued for long periods and periods of generalized violence that have extended for months particularly during the 1980s and 1990s. While the state authority manifested decisively and with an iron fist with regard to the Save the Narmada Movement that gathered national and international support in the 1980s and 1990s, elsewhere there was the aspect of an ineffectual and fragmented state, with regard to Ahmedabad where the nexus between state functionaries and law enforcers with bootleggers involved the parallel economy of transporting and supplying liquor where it was illegal in prohibition Gujarat and with the land mafia in Vadodara. This fragmentation was manifested more starkly during prolonged instances of violence such as the 1985 riots that went on for seven months. According to Jan Breman, when processes of deindustrialization started in Ahmedabad by 1981, with the decline of the trade union, the sparse space for dialogue and moral authority built on collective action, and social consciousness that transcended communal identification, had also declined (Breman, 2002, p. 1486). With violence disrupting everyday life during the 1985 riots, people in affected areas turned to their own communities for the delivery of essential services such as security and food. Local strongmen who delivered in times of need such as Latif Khan for Muslims, developed such goodwill among those he helped in times of trouble that he won elections to the Ahmedabad Municipal Corporation in 1987 contesting as an independent. The 1985 riots also saw militant right wing organizations of the Sangh Parivar such as the VHP that had attacked Dalits in the 1981 riot provide much needed help to them in times of curfew when food provisions were scarce. Ornit Shani has argued that the fragmentation in the Hindu social order caused by politics of redistribution of the state found an alternative in the politics of recognition provided by the right wing ideology of 'Hindu nationalism'-based on the idea of a unitary Hindu identity (Shani, 2007, pp. 121, 155).

---

16 http://news.bbc.co.uk/2/hi/south_asia/4745926.stm, (accessed on 24 February 2006).

It is important to note however that, despite the aspect of an ineffectual state during periods of violence, this was also a period of rapid industrialization, diversification of the industrial base and structural transformation in the economy of Gujarat that went on to witness a high rate of growth of the state's Net State Domestic Product (NSDP) and the highest rate of per capita income among 16 states in the post-liberalization period from 1990–91 onwards although agriculture lagged behind. This was facilitated by important policy developments in a state where liberalization was met with little popular resistance (Kohli, 2012) and in a culture that accords great importance to trade and commerce. The state's industrial policy rolled out a red carpet for industries and made crucial policy decisions that aggressively pursued new industrial investments, accelerated industrial development and placed the state at the forefront of industrial development in the 1990s. These included the establishment of industrial estates that were provided amenities in several parts of the state by GIDC, the provision of infrastructural needs such as electricity, water and connectivity through rail and road, the setting up of four important corporations of GIIC, GIDC, GSFC, and Indextb (Industrial Extension Bureau) to provide finance, power and significant investments in infrastructure. The state's leadership in policy-making in the post-liberalization period is evident in that Gujarat's Industrial Policy 1991–95 was already in operation when the central government declared the New Industrial Policy 1991 (Hirway, 2000, p3109). The latter half of the 1990s also marked a shift in Gujarat from Congress to the BJP when the BJP came to power in 1995.

The rise of BJP

As far back as the 1974 Navnirman Movement, the BJP through its predecessor, Jan Sangh, the political wing of Sangh Parivar had successfully aligned itself with the upper castes and the middle class through causes such as anti-corruption and anti-reservation. In the 1981 agitation against reservations by upper caste students as well, Akhil Bharatiya Vidyarthi Parishad (ABVP), Sangh Parivar's student wing was the first organization to protest reservation of seats in medical colleges. It also initiated the agitation aimed at the beneficiaries of the reservation system namely the *adivasis* and Dalits and also took the agitation to the middle class localities of Ahmedabad. The Jan Sangh's alignment with the anti reservation agitation, which the Congress (O) also supported and its subsequent support for

Jayprakash Narayan's call for 'total revolution' gave it credibility with the middle classes. According to the Commission of Inquiry (also known as the Dave Report) instituted to investigate into the 1985 riots, the *Patels* of Khaira and north Gujarat and the students belonging to ABVP 'combined together to intensify the anti-reservation agitation'.[17] The Congress's combination of redistributive measures with electoral politics that had united the upper castes in opposition had found a ready ally in the BJP. In 1986 during the annual *rathyatra* procession from the Jagganath temple in the old walled city of Ahmedabad when violence broke out yet again amidst continuing tensions from riots in the previous year, the BJP and VHP openly invited Dalits to join the 'holy war' against the Muslims. From 1987 to 1992 through a series of *yatras* by BJP leaders in open air vehicles accompanied by public speeches and meetings *en route*, the BJP sought to mobilize a Hindu unity through its ideology of Hindutva. The issue of building a temple in the contested site in Ayodhya was mobilized into a national political issue by the BJP in the 1980s. Through its *yatras* and *ramshila pujans* (the worship of bricks) that were collected from different parts of the country and taken to Ayodhya the BJP sought to mobilize support across all castes and classes of Hindus. In 1990, the BJP came to power in Gujarat for a few months through a coalition arrangement along with the Janata Dal. During L. K. Advani's rathyatra in 1990 violence erupted on a large scale in many areas during which an estimated 220 persons were killed. Narendra Modi, who was then BJP's General Secretary in Gujarat, organized a series of meetings and a *bandh* at the time.[18]

Through the 1980s and 1990s the BJP came to dominate social and economic bases of power such as professional organizations, educational institutions and cooperative institutions at the local level in both rural and urban areas. For instance during the election of the Chairperson of the Kaira District Cooperative Milk Producers Union where the established practice of election is that the union's board members are themselves elected by village society members, after the BJP came to power in 1995, the government directly nominated three members to the board. Although the Kaira District Cooperative Milk Producers Union's brand Amul went to court and won the case, it was only the beginning of a larger shift where eventually all district unions barring two came to have BJP affiliated chairpersons. Moreover the tradition of elections for chairpersons of milk federations gradually eroded as more and more federations came to be headed

---

17 Justice V. S. Dave, *Op.cit.*
18 Achyut Yagnik and Suchitra Sheth, *Op.cit.*, 260.

by government nominated chairpersons while faced with the twin challenges of political interference in cooperatives and competition from private players (Sood, 2014, p. 28).

Although there wasn't a large scale instance of violence between 1992-93 and 2002, in a ten day spate of violence against Christians from December 1998 to January 1999, Christian churches and institutions were attacked in the tribal dominated districts of Gujarat while there were reports of the state police's refusal to register complaints.[19] In 2001, Narendra Modi replaced Keshubhai Patel as chief minister of Gujarat. In the same year an earthquake in Kutch claimed 13,000 lives and left large scale destruction in its wake. Although relief and rehabilitation work in Kutch was severely criticized initially given the scale of damage and destruction and the administration's inability to cope with it, Narendra Modi who headed the Gujarat State Disaster Management Relief Funds himself led reconstruction efforts that were projected as a nationalist effort to rebuild Kutch. The chief minister's leadership during the subsequent year when violence rocked the state in 2002 however led to national and international censure and outrage. In the face of independent reportage alleging his administration's complicity in the violence, Narendra Modi however, resolutely remained on his post even leading a *gaurav yatra* (procession of pride) to campaign for elections that were due. He went on to win the 2002 elections with an emphatic majority and continued to be repeatedly voted to power in Gujarat in 2007 and again in 2012 serving as chief minister for 14 years before being elected as prime minister of India in 2014. Under his chief ministership Gujarat pursued a business friendly (Kohli, 2012) approach, continuing the policy of previous governments of emphasizing development with a notable check on corruption to reap rich dividends in economic growth.

Neighbourhood profiles

Gujarat is economically one of the fastest growing states in India whose prosperity is sometimes reflected in the residential spaces in the state. *Patidar* families in the Charotar belt in central Gujarat that were the main beneficiaries of the Green Revolution moved out of their traditional places in the centre of the village to build plush residential plots at the edge of the village or moved to nearby district towns (Rutten, 2002, p. 265). The 1981 census noted that

---

19 Human Rights Watch, *Politics by Other Means: Attacks Against Christians in India*, 1 September 1999, http://www.unhcr.org/refworld/docid/3ae6a84b4.html, (accessed 23 June 2011).

out of the 18,114 inhabited villages enumerated in the state most were multi-community villages.[20] These villages have not only members of the same religion (12.6 per cent) but also of other religions (59.8 per cent).[21] Muslims can be found living in villages and cities among members of their own community as well as side by side among members of other communities. In remote villages of Panchmahal, one or two Muslim families of traditional trading communities such as Bohras, Memons as well as those that have taken to trade in recent times such as Mansooris, who lived in isolated tribal dominated villages and ran local businesses such as grocery shops and petty businesses such as flour mills, were not uncommon. In cities and urban centres such as Rajkot, Surat, Nadiad, Anand, Himmatnagar, Bhavanagar etc. mixed living settlements were not uncommon.[22] However, there has been an increasing polarization of living spaces in Gujarat. In the run up to the 2014 national elections, the VHP along with Bajrang Dal outfits belonging to the Sangh Parivar led by VHP president Praveen Togadia staged a street protest outside a house purchased by a Muslim resident in Meghani circle of Bhavnagar to protest a Muslims' buying of property in a Hindu area. He urged his audience to prevent such deals from taking place by marking an area as Hindu through the organization of the public chanting of prayers such as *Ram dhuns* or forcibly taking possession of the house so that even if legal action were to be taken it would take years to be resolved in India's justice system that has a huge backlog of cases.[23]

Nowhere is the segregation of living spaces more evident than in Ahmedabad, the largest of the three metropolitan cities of Gujarat state and the seventh largest metropolis in India. The apparently cosmopolitan areas of bungalows and middle class residential apartments, Gandhian institutions such as Gujarat Vidyapeeth (a Gandhian University) and the Sabarmati Ashram, premier educational institutions, malls and restaurants and even brands of international eatery chains that are vegetarian without exception fall on the Western side of the river Sabarmati

---

20 Cited in Takashi Shinoda, 2002, *The Other Gujarat*, Mumbai: Popular Prakashan, xi.

21 Government of India, Census of India, 1981, series 5 col. 1981 cited in K. S. Singh, *Op.cit*, 15.

22 Rabiya Ismailbhai Vohra, (homemaker, Mogri Siswa Relief Colony, Anand) interview by author, 20 February 2009, Professor Ghalimhbai Walibhai Memon (retired principal, Himmatnagar) interview by author, 30 March 2009 and Fakhruddin Ibrahim (businessman, Godhra) interview by author, 7 March 2009.

23 Vijaysinh Parmar, 'Evict Muslims from Hindu areas: Praveen Togadia', *Times of India*, 21 April 2014, http://timesofindia.indiatimes.com.

while the old city with its ancient gates and living spaces and working class areas around the mills where Dalits, Muslims and OBCs with their non-vegetarian food habits live, in addition to the industrial periphery that developed in the 1980s, fall on the eastern side of the river Sabarmati. Upper caste Hindus and Jains traditionally follow vegetarianism that signifies piety as well purity from what are perceived as polluting non-vegetarian habits. However, these practices by extension have been extrapolated to all of Gujarat, not just culturally where non vegetarianism is looked down upon but even officially when Narendra Modi, then the chief minister attributed reports of malnutrition in the state to vegetarianism and figure consiousness of Gujaratis.[24]

Ahmedabad is known for its fabled *pols* where communities have historically lived in close proximity but distinct from one another in ancient and now often dilapidated living spaces. *Pols* are enclosed living spaces of houses connected by very narrow and interconnected streets guarded by a gate for protection. The narrow alleys, gates and passages of low ceiling were intended to make it difficult for mobs of attacking thieves or armies to enter. For centuries a *pol* served as a residential area for members of the same caste or castes with similar social status and within a caste, families across class distinctions live in the same *pol*. Therefore communities across the caste hierarchy lived very close to each other but separate from one another. With the establishment of textile mills *chawls* that were one or two storeyed structures of one room houses lined up with a common corridor came up on private land to house workers of the textile mills that also became a part of the city's topography. In these working class areas Dalit and Muslim workers lived side by in mixed living areas. However, in mills jobs came to be associated with specific communities so for instance spinners were mostly Dalits while weavers were mostly Muslim and workers preferred to live with their kin in particular localities in proximity to mills so that even working class localities were based on communities (Shah, 1970, p. 197). As the textile mills flourished, the owners of the mills moved out of the old city and settled in bungalows and apartments of two to three rooms in housing societies on the western side of the river Sabarmati while Muslims strengthened by remittances from the gulf initially moved in and refurbished these ancient houses.[25] Housing societies continued to maintain caste cultures (Shah, 1987, AN-163) through practices and informal rules of eating and living

---

24 Indira Hirway, 'Not Vegetarianism or dieting Mr. Modi', *The Hindu*, 27 September 2012.

25 Sujata Patel quoted in Ayesha Khan, 2012, 'How to Profit from a Disturbed Area', *FountainInk*, 3 October, http://fountainink.in/?p=2784.

and through names such as Thakorwas, Muslim society etc that clearly indicate caste and community thereby reproducing caste dynamics in these apparently cosmopolitan parts if western Ahmedabad, which is also the more serviced area of the city with access to water, sewage system, garbage collection, gas pipeline and public transport. *Vanias* including Hindus, Jains live in upmarket Navrangpura, Paldi and Usmanpura areas,[26] while the Dalits of low income groups live in low income areas and on the city's periphery.[27]

Such division is not peculiar to the city of Ahmedabad,

> Divisions in cities have always existed. It is not the fact that they are divided that is the particular characteristic of the partitioned city today; rather, it is the source and manner of their division. Some divisions arise of economic functionality, some are cultural, and some reflect and reinforce relationships of power; some are combinations of all three (Marcuse, 2003).

In Ahmedabad, according to Darshini Mahadevia, the city structure, which earlier reflected divisions on the basis of class, now increasingly appears to be divided by religion where a series of communal riots in 1980s, 1990s and in 2002 led communities to shift to areas that they consider safe and hence, has increased the localized congregation of people belonging to one religion or caste into a particular region of the city (Mahadevia, 2003, p. 362).

Juhapura in particular is a case in point here. Juhapura was a village in the periphery of Ahmedabad that in 1970 became a site for a reconstruction programme of the Ahmedabad Municipal Corporation (AMC) along with NGOs in Sankalit Nagar for flood victims who had been displaced from the banks of the Sabarmati River.[28] Despite its distance from the main city, the building of Sankalit Nagar also opened up the possibility of housing for the expanding middle class of the city looking for affordable housing alternatives.[29] Sankalit Nagar had both Hindu and Muslim occupants as did other residential complexes that came up in

---

26 Darshini Mahadevia, 2003, *Development Dichotomy in Gujarat*, New Delhi Research Foundation for Science, Technology and Ecology.

27 Darshini Mahadevia, 2007, 'A City with Many Borders: Beyond Ghettoisation in Ahmedabad', in Annapurna Shaw (ed), *Indian Cities in Transition*, Orient Longman, 363.

28 Achyut Yagnik (writer, commentator and activist, Ahmedabad), interview by author, 21 October 2008.

29 Zakia Jowher (Indian Social Institute, New Delhi) in discussion with author, New Delhi, 4 April 2009. Zakia was living in Paldi, Ahmedabad during the violence in 2002 and subsequently moved to New Delhi.

the following years. With each riot however more and more communities moved into localities with their caste fellows and co-religionists. In 1990 following Advani's arrest during *rath yatra*, BJP and VHP called for a general strike and systematic attacks were made on government property and upper class Muslim homes while in the industrial neighborhoods of Ahmedabad, Dalits and Muslim clashed. In 1985 only one high wall had come up between a *Patidar* and a Muslim neighbourhood. By the end of 1990, the residents of almost all Dalit *chawls* near Muslim *chawls* in the industrial areas had erected high walls around them, interrupted by iron gates (Nandy, 1998, pp. 114–15). In the 1992–93 communal violence that erupted in several parts of India due to the demolition of Babri Masjid, Muslim property including homes were burned again and once again residents of areas such as Bapunagar in Ahmedabad were rendered homeless. By the 1990s there were very few localities with mixed populations from the two communities in Ahmedabad. For instance while Dalits migrated out of Dani Limda and Shah Alam areas, Muslims from the walled city with fewer choices in other parts of Ahmedabad, moved into areas like Dani Limda and Shah Alam and increasingly, to upcoming Juhapura, an area that had few paved roads or proper sewage systems. Juhapura had an estimated population of 1.5 lakh to which 50,000 were added at the time of the violence in 2002. Juhapura also has 30 per cent Hindu population. However, with the influx of Muslims since the late 1980s, Hindus moved out of the older residential areas into areas like Gupta Nagar and Praveen Nagar.[30] Juhapura gradually became a Muslim dominated area so that even buildings with Hindu names such as Amba Towers have only Muslim residents. Muslims who would have liked to live in cosmopolitan settings and in the more serviced western parts of the city have no choice but to live in Juhapura or any one of the pockets of Muslim concentration in the city.[31] Public and private sector banks are known to have designated Muslim concentration areas as 'negative or red zones' where they do not give loans for housing or

---

30   Dr Hanif Lakdawala (Director, Sanchetna Community Health and Research Centre, Ahmedabad), in discussion with author, 24 October 2008.

31   Javed Ameer (Action Aid, Ahmedabad) in discussion with author, 5 January 2009. Javed and his wife, a lecturer at a prominent college in Ahmedabad and struggled in vain to get a loan for a house back in the 1990s in places that are considered to be cosmopolitan parts of Ahmedabad such as Vastrapur, Satellite etc. Even banks were not willing to give them loans for houses in these parts because of their Muslim names and suggested that they take up a house in areas of Muslim concentration.

other purposes.[32] Living spaces of communities in other parts of the city are also not difficult to discern in Ahmedabad where localities are referred to by the communities living there such as a Hindu *ilaka*, area/ territory or Muslim *ilaka* and where these spaces are separated by corners, streets, roads and name plates that serve as 'borders'.

Ahmedabad cannot be extrapolated for the rest of Gujarat. However, there are obtrusive signs of the polarization of the population elsewhere as well. Baroda, in particular, has seen a fair number of riots due to religious processions especially in its old city areas such as Wadi, Panigate and Fatehpur areas where co-religionists and community members live in pockets. However, compared to Ahmedabad, Baroda had a number of areas with mixed living areas in many localities.[33] After the violence in 2002 however, city space in Baroda also shows clear signs of polarization with even government residential colonies that are otherwise known to be mixed living areas of employees belonging to those of a particular community. The Gujarat Tractor Company's Residential Quarters and the Patrakar (journalists) Colony in Tandalja have less than five Hindu families as Tandalja is a Muslim dominated area.[34] During the series of *yatras* held by the BJP since the late 1980s and particularly L. K. Advani's *rathyatra* from Somnath to Ayodhya, the VHP put up signboards in each city and town *en route* declaring them to be cities of a Hindu *rashtra*. Signboards declaring a place to be Hindu *rashtra* are not uncommon to date in Gujarat.[35]

These processes of segregation were also visible in relief and rehabilitation work after the massive earthquake that hit the Kutch region in Gujarat on 26 January 2001 where an estimated 13,000 people were killed and 900 villages were reduced to rubble.[36] The massive earthquake destroyed ancient structures,

---

32 Justice Rajindar Sachar, *Op. cit.*, 22 and Javed Ameer (Action Aid, Ahmedabad) in discussion with author, 5 January 2009.

33 Ayesha Khan (then a journalist with Indian Express, Ahmedabad) interview by author, Ahmedabad, 13 December 2008. Ayesha grew up in Baroda in the upmarket Ellora Park but had to move out of her home of 17 years in the midst of the violence.

34 Tripti Shah (activist and lecturer, Vadodara) in discussion with author, Tandalja, Vadodara, 19 February 2009.

35 For instance the road from the relief colony of displaced Muslims at the outskirts of Himmatnagar to the main city in Himmatnagar was marked with a signboard which says 'Here begins the Hindu Rashtra'.

36 Edward Simpson and Malathi de Alwis, 2008, 'Remembering Natural Disaster: Politics and the Culture of Memorials in Gujarat and Sri Lanka', *Anthropology Today*, 24 (4): 7.

temples, mosques, administrative buildings and entire neighbourhoods and left tens of thousands dispossessed and displaced. Relief had poured out nationally and internationally at the time. It has been argued that relief work after the earthquake was used as an opportunity to rebuild Kutch in exclusionary nationalist imaginations (Simpson and Corbridge 2006). Upper caste homes were relocated away from the destruction and away from Dalit and Muslim homes. The Vishwa Hindu Parishad (the World Council of Hindus) sponsored the rebuilding of a village but it was to be used only to relocate caste Hindus.

The most unusual *toofan*

For people who live in communally sensitive areas in Gujarat, communal violence is localized violence that occurs every now and then but does not always disrupt their 'normal' lives. In Godhra, considered to be a communally sensitive town where riots occur frequently, a businessman explained, '*Abhi har ghante do ghante mein hota hai* (every hour or two hours it (*riots*) happens)…there would probably be one or two deaths, *aur bas kuch nahi* there was nothing more to it.'[37] At Wadi in the old city in Baroda for instance where narrow streets are lined with tightly packed houses on both sides in a densely populated and overcrowded living space that has a large Maharashtrian presence, riots have known to erupt among other reasons, over fights during religious procession like the Ganesh festival processions. However, such incidents did not lead to apprehensions about security, as a Maharashtrian lady explained that one has to just know how to get out of a troubled spot.[38] Abdul Majid Abdul Salaam who was a resident of Dariyapur, an area classified as communally disturbed, before moving to Naroda Patiya says about Dariyapur, that 'these little things keep on happening its nothing much. A little keeps happening. People who understand don't do it; people who don't understand do it.[39]'

Large scale instances of communal violence however have had more apparent effects. In the 1969 communal violence in Ahmedabad there were instances of displacement in the sites of violence such as in Saraspur, Gomtipur and

---

37 Nooruddinbhai Mandalowala (businessman, Godhra), interview by author, Vadodara, 24 February 2009.

38 Jyotsna (housewife, Wadi, Vadodara), 25 February 2009. Jyotsna was sure that her husband who grew up in Wadi and runs a garage there knew the alleys inside out and can help anyone get out should any trouble or riot arise.

39 Abdul Majid Abdul Salaam, (Embroiderer, Ahmedabad) interview by author, 26 January 2009.

Chamanpura.[40] The Commission of Inquiry headed by Justice Reddy that examined the 1969 riot recorded that, 'Throughout the night of 19 September 1969,' 'incidents of arson, murders, and attacks on Muslims and places of worship escalated. By the morning Muslims families particularly in the suburban, eastern areas, had begun leaving their homes to safe areas, and 'the stream in the morning almost became a flood within 24 hours' (Reddy Commission Report, 1970, p. 157).[41] Fleeing Muslims gathered in the railway station and in camps established by Muslim organizations and there were reports of trains carrying Muslims being stopped and attacked. There were indications of planning and organization behind the violence such as people moving with voters lists, provision of inflammable material and even the provision of transportation facilities for violent mobs, which led to attacks on Muslim's lives and properties and included violence against children, rape of women and the mutilation of their bodies and sex organs and burning alive of poor labourers (Shah, 1970, p. 195). For Noorjahan Kalumiyan Sheikh who was 17 and newly married when the 1969 riots broke out, the atmosphere in 1969 was as dangerous as in 2002. Since the time she moved in to live with her in laws after marriage in 1969 till the 2002 violence, she lived in Asarwa Kadiyeki Chali in Chamanpura, a working class neighbourhood in Ahmedabad where Dalits and Muslims lived side by side, where she paid a miniscule amount of rent under the old tenancy laws. According to her account, during the 1969 riots 20–25 Muslims were burned alive and the women were raped in the house next to hers where Pathans lived. Noorjahan's family returned after about two years but hers was the only Muslim family to go back to their house in Asarwa Kadiyeki Chali. According to her they could continue to live there because they lived just like Hindus. '*Humara vyayhaar apne Hindu jaise hi tha rehne pehannemein*', (our behaviour and sense of dressing were like Hindus.)[42]

After the riots in 1969 there was a socioeconomic boycott of Muslims and some Hindus as well as Muslims moved out of parts of Ahmedabad such as Saraspur (Shani, 2007, p. 124) and other areas in the more ancient parts of city that had witnessed large scale rioting where their particular communities has been attacked,

---

40 Professor Abid Samshi (reitred college Professor, Ahmedabad) in discussion with author, 28 October 2008, Noorjahan Kalumiyan Sheikh, (elderly widowed homemaker, Ahmedabad) interview by author, 27 October 2008.

41 See Justice J. Reddy, 1970, *Report of the Commission of Inquiry: Ahmedabad Communal Disturbances (1969)*, Ahmedabad: Government of Gujarat. (Henceforth, Reddy Commission report).

42 *Ibid.*

to places of greater concentration of their own communities (Shah, 1970, p. 187; Shani, 2007, p. 120). After the violence Muslims refused to be rehabilitated in the places of original residence in the walled city areas that were surrounded by Hindus, the predominant sentiment and rationale being that they could only get security in their community. The AMC had then allotted temporary accommodation to some of the displaced, most of which were Muslims in plots adjacent to Gujarat Housing Board flats in the working class area of the then upcoming New Bapunagar. In 1985 this same area of Bapunagar as well as Gomtipur on the eastern industrial belt of Ahmedabad, beyond the railways suffered severe communal violence and mass-scale destruction, which left thousands of people displaced. Approximately 2500 houses were damaged and 12,000 Muslims had been displaced including instances where people's houses had been burned more than a few times (Shah, 1970, pp. 113, 123, 187). A relief camp was opened at Aman Chowk to provide shelter for hundreds of Muslims who had fled there in the midst of the violence.

The government of Gujarat had at that time given some of the displaced houses at Indira Garib Nagar in Bapunagar. However, in 1985 when the riots broke out against reservation and finally took a communal turn, Bapunagar became the site of pitched battles and some Muslims there were rendered homeless again and had to take shelter in camps. As was witnessed in 2002, even at that time marriages were conducted in the camp itself during that time of vulnerability. Shehnajbano Aslam Ali Sheikh and her sister got married in Aman Chowk camp where they were taking shelter. She recalls that even then, mobs had used gas cylinders to blow up walls of houses and that a girl in her neighbourhood had been raped. 'The *mohalla* (neighbourhood) people faced them *samna kiya* but they were with tear gas, policewale were supporting them then what can we do.' After staying for about a year in the camp even after it had closed down, they eventually did return to their house in Bapunagar, which had been burned. 'We used to get scared but then everyone got together, the Muslims. Then everyone started staying. For how long will we stay on rent they said. Then everyone went to their own houses.' In the latter half of the 1980s with declining mills and increasing incidents of communal violence some Muslims moved to the industrial periphery of Ahmedabad where over the years areas of Muslim concentration such as Vatwa have developed. At that time, a lot of people moved in to this industrial area on the periphery by squatting and occupying land. Authorities turned a blind eye to this development due to the cheap labour it provided to the industries nearby.[43]

---

43   Fr. Cederick Prakash (Director, Prashant, NGO, Ahmedabad),16 March 2010 and Afroze

In the 1990s, during Advani's *rath yatra*, middle class Muslim houses were targeted by the VHP.[44] A Muslim lecturer in one of the prominent colleges in the city of Ahmedabad recollected how she and her brother had to leave their house and stay with friends and relatives for a few days while their parents apprehensively stayed back after they found a note stuck on the door which said, *Musalmano amaro vistar chodine do* (Muslims leave our area). In two days even her parents moved out of their house in a prominent locality where the elite of Ahmedabad lived on the western side of the river Sabarmati. Their decision proved timely as their house was eventually burned and their possessions looted. The attack on their home in 1990 deeply etched their distinctness along with fear for this family of lecturers and civil society leaders that had until then chosen not to live in overcrowded areas of concentration of their own community but among their associates in the more serviced part of a city, which on the outside seems to have a cosmopolitan setting. After the attack they were among other Muslims in Ahmedabad who had to relocate to another place.[45]

Some localities had witnessed communal violence in villages, towns or cities through acts of arson, rioting etc. at some point in the past but these had not always caused displacement. Rabiya Ismailbhai Vohra a Muslim from Nadiad even witnessed a Hindu lose his life by a stray bullet of the police in her own courtyard during the 1992 post-Babri masjid riots. That however was not reason enough to move then because there was no threat to her life. 'Earlier they used to only burn Muslim shops', they would not do anything more says Imtiaz Pathan's mother who has seen rioting on more than one occasion around Gulbarg Society that was the site of a major carnage in 2002 where 69 people lost their lives and where she sustained major burns and injuries herself and also lost her husband along with 10 members of her family. Even in the old city there are instances of those whose houses were in the 'site' of communal violence in the 80s and 90s and who would choose to return to their homes, even if it meant living in anticipation of violence.[46]

and Altaf Sayyed (brother and sister duo are Nyayapathiks, workers for NGO Nyayagrah, Sayyedwadi, Ahmedabad), 4 December 2008.

44 Dr Hanif Lakdawala (Director, Sanchetna Community Health and Research Centre, Ahmedabad), in discussion with author, 24 October 2008; Professor Abid Samshi (retired college Professor, Ahmedabad) 28 October 2008; Zakia Jowher (Indian Social Institute, New Delhi) 4 April 2009; Lecturer at College (identity withheld on request) in discussion with author, 7 January 2009.

45 *Ibid.*

46 Zakia Jowher (Indian Social Institute, New Delhi) in discussion with author, 4 April 2009. The woman referred to is her grandmother.

Sarfarazbhai Munshi, a rickshaw driver who lived in Chamanpura Ahmedabad, has witnessed at least two other riots in the past echoes what seems to be a common refrain, '*Aisa toofaan humne kabhi nahi dekha*. (we have never seen such a riot)[47]' Despite having lived in a communally sensitive area like Dariyapur for several years before moving to Naroda Patiya, Abdul Majid Abdul Salaam will not brook any comparison between what happened in 2002, and the small riots that break out every now and then in parts of the old city and working class neighbourhood localities,

> See don't bring the name of Dariyapur in this at all, *bekar baat hai* don't bring Dariyapur in here at all. This thing that happened, in Patiya where I stayed there for seven to eight years ... such a riot has happened, and Allah knows, talking much about it is not a good thing, all wrong things happened.

Despite the existence of modern forms of economy and polity in Gujarat, caste and communal identifications have persisted and perpetuated in importance while the party that has successfully managed to wield power in the state since 1995 through the articulation of a unitary Hindu identity is the BJP. While commentaries and works of scholarship on Gujarat since 2002 have described gruesome instances of violence and subsequently high levels of economic growth under Narendra Modi's leadership as unprecedented, both economic growth as well as gruesome communal violence, including violence against women and children have occurred in the past as well. However, the violence of 2002 is somehow perceived as different from them. Why was the violence in 2002 different and why did it cause displacement to the extent that it did? While the events of 2002 led to an upsurge of independent and media reportage and academic interest in the violence, the meteoric rise of Narendra Modi and BJP in Gujarat and at the national level in 2014 has led to the questioning of the outrage around the violence of 2002 described as another communal riot.[48] The displacement of Muslims is also dismissed as migration between communities that has always happened.[49] The next chapter, therefore, examines what happened during the violence in 2002 and in particular processes in the population movement to examine the migration-displacement question.

---

47 Sarfarazbhai Munshi (rikshaw driver,Ahmedabad) interview by author, 30 November 2008.

48 Economists Jagdish Bhagwati and Arvind Panagariya in a letter to *The Economist,* 12 April 2014.

49 Yamal Vyas (Spokesperson for BJP in Gujarat, Ahmedabad)10 February 2009.

2

Vatani to Visthapit
Violence and Displacement in 2002

On 28 February 2002, as black smoke emanated from shops, kiosks and houses, for Zakia Jowher who climbed to her terrace in her house in Paldi for a bird's eye view, it looked like the city of Ahmedabad was burning. The smoke was evidence of things burning but she was unable to gauge where it came from and her own experience in the past made her feel like it was all around and not far from her own house.[1] The communal violence that began in Gujarat on February 2002 went on till June 2002 while sporadic incidents of violence continued in the tense atmosphere in the state right up to the end of the year and into the first few months of the next year. While it is considered to be elementary knowledge that collective violence 'rarely – indeed almost never – engulfs an entire city or town' , (Brass, 2003, p. 149) given that beyond media generated perceptions of simultaneity, it is the 'sites of violence' that are important in understanding communal violence, what was in fact pervasive and seemed to engulf the entire northern and central region of Gujarat at that time and what was even felt by Muslims outside the state (Kirmani, 2008, p. 57), was fear and insecurity.

The insecurity caused by the violence, led a large number of Muslims to flee their homes for places of concentration of their co-religionists in urban and rural areas in the state. The Antarik Visthapith Hak Rakshak Samiti or Committee for the rights of IDPs that was formed in 2007 described those living in relief colonies or who had relocated as *visthapith* (displaced persons) using the UN formulated Guiding Principles on Internally Displaced Persons. The Guiding Principles that articulate the rights of IDPs before displacement, during displacement and after displacement provide a useful template to track displacement. However, processes of displacement encountered in Gujarat presented complexities that do not easily fit trajectories of flight, displacement and post displacement scenarios what with the place that is often identified as the trigger of the violence, Godhra, becoming

---

1 Zakia Jowher (Indian Social Institute), in discussion with the author, April 2009. Her house in a middle class locality in Ahmedabad was attacked in 1990 as well.

a site for relief camps, Muslims in some instances either returning to live at the site where they witnessed gruesome violence such as Naroda Patiya violence, or those classified as *visthapith* moving but a few kilometres from their original homes. The government of Gujarat for its part maintained that those who live in 'resettlement colonies' do so of their own volition.[2]

This chapter, therefore, seeks to address the apparent poser of whether the population movement during and after the violence was migration or displacement by chronicling what happened. In interviews with survivors of the violence and displaced, especially those from rural areas, the word *vatani*, which comes from the Urdu word *vatan* or country and means one who belongs to a particular place, often came up. Many of those categorized as *visthapith* or displaced, especially those from rural areas described themselves as being *vatanis* for many generations of the places from which they were displaced. This chapter reconstructs circumstances and processes in the journey from places of original residence to being identified by NGOs as *visthapith* or displaced people. It begins by examining the sites of mass carnages and instances of generalized violence within Ahmedabad and in other parts of Gujarat that converted localities where Muslims lived into marked spaces or pitched battlegrounds and in others forced people out of their homes, before drawing out the situations and contingencies that further caused Muslims to move out of their homes. While time is the thread of this account produced years after the violence and, therefore, gives a bird's eye view, it is individual narratives that shed light on processes, causes and questions of what constitutes forced migration due to communal violence.

A normal anomaly: Routine displacement

With a chuckle at her own ingenuity, 60 year old Noorjahan Kalumiyan Sheikh says she left her home on the eastern side of the Sabarmati river among working class areas of Ahmedabad in Asarwa Kadiye ki Chali along with her family after hearing about what had happened in Godhra in the wee hours of 28 February itself. Having witnessed communal violence in 1969 where a mob burned Muslims in

---

2   Government of Gujarat, 'Status Report of the Displaced Families in Gujarat with Reference to NCM Delegation visit on 15/10/2006,' file RTI-102008-Information-18-A1, Social Justice and Empowerment Division, Sachivalaya, Gandhinagar, August 2008. While Muslim organizations, NGOs and the media referred to these colonies as relief colonies, the Government of Gujarat in its report to the NCM refers to these as 'resettlement colonies'.

a house in her locality, she knew that if there was trouble in Godhra there would be trouble in her locality as well.

> We knew that if it happened in Godhra it will definitely happen here. In 1969 we had seen it in front of our eyes. *Ahko dekhi haal kara ne? isliye chet jawe* (we had seen them do it in front of our eyes hadn't we? thats why we were alert.) We first removed our son and daughter in law and we came to the station and from there we all got scattered. Like she went to her mother's house, I went to mine. Then the *dhamaal* (riot) happened. We couldn't take anything, everything got cleaned out. Ours was the only house there so moving becomes important doesn't it?[3]

Few other Muslims were as quick to anticipate the violence that was to come even in the 'city with many borders' (Mahadevia, 2007, p. 341) that is Ahmedabad that had witnessed a polarization of the population along religious lines even prior to 2002 evident in the demographic spread of Muslims in pockets in the walled city, slums in the industrial suburbs in the eastern periphery, *chawls* in working class areas divided by Hindu and Muslim *ilakas* (areas), among middle class and upper middle class societies in the upmarket Paldi area and a few colonies in Navrangpura on the western side of the river Sabarmati and in large settlements such as Juhapura, that the word ghetto seems inadequate to describe.

Some however in the walled city and in the working class neighbourhoods, had witnessed violence earlier, and like Noorjahan also anticipated trouble when they heard of fire in the train at Godhra. Earlier when riots broke out, many Muslims from such neighbourhoods would head straight to the railway station and to their respective villages or those of their relatives from there. They would return after about 10–15 days when tensions in the city cooled down.[4] According to Khatunbibi Sayyed who had also witnessed the 1969 riots when she fled with her family, many Muslims in Bapunagar and Chamanpura had left the locality on the same day of the burning of the train coach in Godhra i.e., 27 February 2002 itself. She left her home in the morning of 28 February as soon as her neighbours warned her of arson that had broken out with the burning of a bakery in her locality. She left with whatever money she had and a few important papers, apparently familiar with the possible course of events.

---

3   Noorjahan Kalumiyan Sheikh (homemaker, Ahmedabad) interview by author, 27 October 2008.

4   *Ibid.*

In 1969, Khatunbibi had to leave her home when her husband, reacting to the violence around the locality got anxious, and they moved out with their children and a small *potli* (sack) with their belongings to seek refuge in a *chawl* in Kalupur, a locality that has a large concentration of Muslims. There was rioting on the streets *maaram kati maaram kati*, (killing and bloodshed all around) and her Hindu neighbours hid her in their house since she reasons, *pehle wale Hindu acche the* (the earlier ones were good Hindus).

Her 45 year old son, Sirajbhai reminds her about another time they had to flee their homes for safety in 1985–86, after the anti-reservation riots turned communal. Then they had to flee in the middle of the night to Jamalpur, another locality where there are a large number of Muslims who had set up a camp for those displaced then. In 1985 their house was broken into and looted. Like several others they could not take any of their possessions with them save some money and important papers like the ration card. Again in 1992, in the riots after the Babri masjid demolition she had to flee again and take refuge in a camp in Bapunagar. In 2002, Khatunbibi knew she had to go to a camp again for safety but was prevented from going there because of the restriction of movement and police *bandobast* (arrangement), so she went instead to a *chawl* inhabited by Muslims called Patel ni chali. She had no prior acquaintance of the people in the chawl but there were others like her who had come there looking for refuge and the residents allowed them to stay and eventually set up a camp where she stayed on for up to four months.[5]

Places like Bapunagar and Gomtipur that are known to be communally sensitive also saw a lot of violence on 28 February 2002. The years of riots that these localities had witnessed led to communities clustering together within the same locality, so that the Hindu side is distinct from the Muslim side and the point where one side ends and the other begins is commonly referred to as 'border'. It was after the 1985 riots that Bapunagar came to be partitioned into Hindu and Muslim areas through a distress selling of houses from both communities into their respective *ilakas* areas separated by the border (Shani, 2007, p. 127). During the 2002 violence, in the case of such localities, the 'border' became the frontier to be defended. Khatunbibi's son, Sirajbhai was living on the 'border' in Old Bapunagar at the time of the violence in 2002. He sent his children to the interior of Bapunagar, where he knew it would be safe and stayed back with his wife to face the mob '*samna karne*' at the border where his house was. After three days

---

5   Khatoonbibi Sayyed (homemaker, Ahmedabad) interview by author, 27 October 2008.

he decided to pull back and go to the interior of Bapunagar himself where other Muslims of the locality had started collecting food and clothes among themselves for people who had fled their homes.[6]

Ahmedabad, 28 February 2002

Most Muslims however, seemed to be caught unawares by the violence that started on the 28 February. The worst case, in terms of casualties was that of Naroda Patiya.[7] Naroda is an industrial suburb on the eastern periphery of Ahmedabad where there are a large number of small scale industries that have attracted a large number of migrants. To house these migrants, slums have come up on the agricultural land around the area, where as is typical of many slums, only after many years basic facilities like water have become available. Naroda Patiya was a 'mixed *basti*', in that Muslims as well as Hindus lived in the area, although Muslims usually lived in the same row or in clusters such as Noorani Mohalla. Several people who had lived in Naroda Patiya for years have affirmed that despite the frequency of communal incidents in Ahmedabad, that area was not prone to violence.[8]

The residents of Naroda Patiya were therefore caught completely unaware as a mob began to gather in front of the entrance of the locality since 9 o' clock in the morning of 28 February. Mayaben Kodnani, member of the Gujarat legislative assembly (MLA) was present at the time at Naroda Patiya and left

---

6   Sirajbhai Nathubhai Sayyed (mechanic, Juhapura, Ahmedabad) in discussion with author, 27 October 2008.

7   For detailed testimonials of survivors of violence see among others, Concerned Citizens Tribunal Report, 2002, *Crimes Against Humanity: An Inquiry into the Carnage in Gujarat* (Vols 1–3), Citizens for Justice and Peace, Mumbai; Human Rights Watch, *We have No Orders to Save You: State Participation and Complicity in Communal Violence in Gujarat*, Vol. 14 No. 3(C), April 2002, http://www.hrw.org/legacy/reports/2002/india/ (accessed 12 May 2010); Citizen's Initiative, PUCL, *Violence in Vadodara*, June 2002, http://www. onlinevolunteers.org/gujarat/reports/pucl/index.htm (accessed 5 July 2010); PUDR, 2002, *Maaro! Kaapo! Baalo!: State, Society and Communalism in Gujarat*, New Delhi: Secretary, Peoples Union for Democratic Rights.

8   Among others Aishabibi Abid Ali Pathan (homemaker, former resident of Naroda Patiya, lost her husband in the violence, Ahmedabad) interview by author, 19 December 2008 and Noorjahan Abdul Kadir Shiekh (homemaker, former resident of Naroda Patiya, lost her husband in the violence, Ahmedabad) interview by author, 19 December 2008. Both these women had lost their husbands in the violence on 28 February 2002.

after encouraging the mob and speaking to the police who were already present at the spot. Mohamammad Khalid was among the few residents gathered near the entrance to watch the gathering mob when bullets fired from the police near the entrance injured him in his spine and killed several others.[9] Soon the mob led by the likes of Bajrag Dal activist Babu Bajrangi (Babubhai Patel) advanced into the *basti* and chased its Muslims residents around in their own locality for hours. The bullet that entered Khalid's body and was removed only days later left him without the use of his legs as a paraplegic for life. In the case of his brother-in-law however, the wound proved fatal and his sister Aishabibi was left holding his corpse through the entire day and most of the night that the ordeal lasted. She had fled to the adjacent State Reserve Police (SRP) quarters for help with his body and finding none had taken refuge in a vacant room from which she heard sounds of violence for hours until she lost consciousness herself.[10] Many families were separated and gruesome killings, rapes and the burning alive of men, women and children continued for the most part of the day. Only those Muslims who managed to go to the nearby SRP quarters before 11–12 am or those who hid themselves somehow managed to escape that day. At 11:30 pm in the night, when the police came to escort the survivors, people initially refused to come out for fear of being attacked again. Some of the survivors still believe it was the organizers of Shah Alam camp who came to take them and not the police.[11] The violence in Naroda Patiya and Naroda Gam had claimed 95 victims[12] although the estimated death toll remained much less for years as officials waited for seven years before declaring the missing as dead.[13] The police van took the survivors to Muslim majority areas such as Shahibaug and Shah Alam.

Gulbarg Society was another colony located in a 'mixed' area in that in the *chawls* that surrounded the area, Muslims lived alongside Dalits. Older people in the locality recall having to flee their homes in 1969 riots as well, in order to

---

9   Mohammad Khalid Sayyed (mechanic, former resident of Naroda Patiya, Ahmedabad) interview by author, 24 October 2008.

10 Aishabibi Abid Ali Pathan (homemaker, former resident of Naroda Patiya, Ahmedabad) interview by author, 19 December 2008.

11 Noorjahan Abdul Kadir Shiekh (homemaker, former resident of Naroda Patiya, Ahmedabad) interview by author, 19 December 2008.

12 'Gujarat Riot toll goes up from 952 to 1180', *Times of India*, 16 February 2009. Death toll of 95 is the figure confirmed by the Supreme Court appointed Special Investigation Team (SIT).

13 'Gujarat Riot Missing Declared Dead', *Times of India*, 19 March 2010, http://articles. timesofindia.indiatimes.com.

seek safety in Shahibaug, a Muslim dominated area.[14] In earlier riots like the anti-reservation riots in 1985, when tensions were running high, some families also left their houses temporarily for a school in Bapunagar for two to three days and returned when the situation got better without much loss to property.[15] Gulbarg Society was a colony surrounded by *chawls* on one side and railway tracks at the back.

Ehsan Jafri, its prominent resident who came from a humble background,[16] but had achieved much success eventually becoming Member of Parliament (MP) for the Congress Party when Amar Singh Chaudhary was chief minister of Gujarat. Gulbarg housing society was already built like a fort with two feet wide and 20 feet high boundary walls in addition to a barbed fence surrounding it, an indication of the feeling of insecurity that already existed. Whenever a riot broke out, some people from the neighbouring slum would take shelter in Gulbarg since there was a State Reserve Police post outside his house[17] and in the past Jafri had used his influence to ensure police action when a mob had surrounded and attacked the colony in the 1986 riots (Engineer and Tanushri, 1986, p. 1346). On 28 February 2002, Ehsan Jafri spoke to the Ahmedabad Commissioner of Police, PC Pandey who came to Gulbarg Society in the morning and assured him of protection and left.[18] Soon a mob of thousands including residents and members of the Vishwa Hindu Parishad (World Council of Hindus) of the locality gathered in front of the society.[19] Some Muslims from

---

14 Sarfaraz Abdul Qadar Munshi (autorickshaw driver, former resident of chawl in Chamanpura, Ahmedabad), interview by author, 30 November 2008; and interview with Aisha Asuben Siddiqui (resident of Siddiqabad Colony, Juhapura, Ahmedabad), 29 October 2008.

15 Noorjahan Lalsahab Sheikh (homemaker, former resident of chawl in Chamanpura, survivor of Gulbarg Society violence, Ahmedabad), interview by author, 29 October 2008.

16 Professor Ansari (retired Professor, Ahmedabad) interview by author, 11 December, 2008.

17 Imtiaz Shahid Pathan (employee of Electrical company, former resident of Gulbarg Society, survivor of violence, Ahmedabad), 12 July 2008. Also, Ashish Khetan, 2007, 'Safehouse of Horrors,' *Tehelka*, November 3: 43.

18 Imtiaz Shahid Pathan (employee of Electrical company, former resident of Gulbarg Society, survivor of violence, Ahmedabad), interview by the author, 12 July 2008 and Sarfarazbhai Abdul Qadar Munshi, (rickshaw driver, Ahmedabad) interview by author, 30 November 2008. See also *Concerned Citizens Tribunal Report*.

19 Suraiyabano Pathan (homemaker, former resident of Gulbarg Society, survivor of violence,) interview by author, 12 July 2008 and Imtiaz Shahid Pathan (survivor Gulbarg violence) interview by author, 12 July 2008.

the *chawls* nearby had fled to Gulbarg society for refuge, others fled to the railway station nearby even as the mob increased in number and started breaking down shops belonging to Muslims. Only some of those who fled to Gulbarg for safety lived to regret their decision.[20] The restive mob started pelting stones, which the young men from inside the colony threw back in defence. The few armed policemen in front of the society were ineffectual and according to survivor's accounts unresponsive to the situation. The mob kept up the offensive for hours demanding the surrender of Ehsan Jafri who went out to the mob at 2:30 pm and was hacked to death and his body burned. A gas cylinder was used to bring down one portion of the wall and the mob stormed in to inflict their wrath on those inside. At 5:30 pm the police came to escort the remaining few who had climbed up to the second floor of Jafri's house even as the rest of the structures and buildings burned. The survivors of Gulbarg society, as in the case of Naroda Patiya recall their reluctance to come out when the police came to escort them in the evening. The mob surrounded the police vehicle as well and it took two more hours till the harrowed survivors reached Shahibaug, an area of Muslim concentration. 69 people were killed, and many women raped and burned in the rampage of the mob on that single day in Gulbarg society.[21]

Violence in other parts of Ahmedabad

Besides the instances of mass murders in Naroda Patiya and Gulbarg Society, violence caused several deaths in other parts of Ahmedabad on the 28 February 2002 particularly in Saraspur, Shahwadi on the southern periphery of Ahmedabad and in Meghaninagar, Sundaramnagar and Behrampura as well.[22] Another Muslim ghetto on the periphery that saw large scale violence was Vatwa. Vatwa is a settlement among industrial suburbs on the eastern periphery in the south of Ahmedabad. On 28 February, itself a large number of housing colonies of Muslims were gutted in fire forcing the residents to flee.

---

20 Noorjahan Lalsahab Sheikh (homemaker, former resident of chawl in Chamanpura, survivor of Gulbarg Society violence, Ahmedabad) interview by author, 29 October 2008.

21 Imtiaz Shahid Pathan (employee of Electrical company, former resident of Gulbarg Society, survivor of violence, Ahmedabad) interview by author, 12 July 2008. Also Ashish Khetan, 2007, 'Safehouse of Horrors,' *Tehelka*, November 3: 43.

22 Manas Dasgupta, '140 Killed as Gujarat Bandh Turns Violent', *The Hindu*, 1 March 2002. Also, *Times of India*, 1 March 2002 and 2 March 2002. See also *Concerned Citizens Tribunal Report*.

But it wasn't only the periphery or the eastern side of Sabarmati that was attacked on that day. Paldi, an upmarket locality on the more serviced side of the city in western Ahmedabad, which is known for the presence of rich *Vanias*, Jains and a few colonies that house upper middle class Muslims, also witnessed attacking mobs. While mobs surrounded and threw *kakdas* (burning rags) and hand made bombs into some of these housing societies inhabited by Muslims, one colony that particularly attracted the wrath of the mob was Delite Apartments with eyewitnesses claiming to have seen the revenue minister who was subsequently murdered, Haren Pandya, accompanying the mobs.[23] In other colonies that were a few meters interior from the road, residents had to keep a constant vigil every night for their security for three months till the violence continued as no amount of personal contacts with state functionaries proved useful to assure them of their safety.[24] As soon as they had a chance to in the evening, almost all the residents of the colonies including doctors, advocates, a retired judge of the high court and social workers surrounding Delite fled their home for houses of relatives in areas of Muslim concentration and community halls in Juhapura, which became a haven for several Muslim families all over Ahmedabad.

Among the islands of peace in the city where no violence was reported were Ram-Rahim Nagar and Janata Nagar in Ramol, despite the fact that among the residents was a survivor of the fire in the train carnage at Godhra. The residents of the colonies had an almost equal proportion of Hindus and Muslims, which is why VHP apparently dithered from action in Ram-Rahim Nagar that had a record of maintaining peace through previous episodes of communal violence. In previous instances of violence during the 1980s and 1990s, the residents reportedly maintained cooperation and peaceful coexistence among themselves. Like other places with Muslim residents however, the residents had to keep a

---

23 Resident of Paldi (name withheld on request), interview by author, 29 January 2009. Haren Pandya had also appeared before the Concerned Citizen's Tribunal claiming that the Chief Minister had said that they should allow people to vent their anger and not come in the way of the Hindu backlash. Pandya was shot dead in March 2002 after his morning walk barely 2 kms from his home allegedly by those wanting to avenge the 2002 violence. All accused were subsequently acquitted by the High Court. It has been argued that Pandya's murder was in fact a political murder because of his testimony to the Citizen's Tribunal. See R.K. Mishra, 2007, 'A Murder Foretold: The Riots Tribunal admits Haren Pandya had deposed before it' Outlook , Nov. 19, http://www.outlookindia.com.

24 Zakia Jowher (Indian Social Institute), in discussion with the author, April 2009. Also, Dr. Lakdawala (Director, Sanchetna Community Health and Research Centre, Ahmedabad), in discussion with author, 24 October 2008.

night vigil themselves for the months that the violence lasted.[25] There and in other parts of Ahmedabad there was a distinct lack of police presence or their being far outnumbered by the mobs armed with weapons such as swords, *dharia* (scythes), chemicals, *lathis* (sticks), inflammable substances such as petrol as well as voting lists, that through the name, revealed the community that the person belonged to and the place of residence. Looting of properties that were attacked took place in what had become a free for all situation while mobs that had a festive and carnivalesque aspect to them (Sarkar, 2002) prevented fire brigades from reaching affected areas to douse fires.[26]

Violence in other parts of Gujarat

While close to 200 deaths had taken place in a single day of violence in Ahmedabad, other cities like Vadodara, Surat and Viramgam also witnessed stabbings, arson and stone pelting.[27] In Vadodara, fourteen people were killed when a mob set fire to Best Bakery, owned by a family in Hanuman Tekdi. Curfew was imposed in the old city areas of Vadodara that are known for their communal sensitivity such as Karelibaug, Wadi, Navapura, Raopura, Panigate and City police stations after mobs initiated burning and looting of property and incidents of stabbing.[28] Curfew was imposed in 26 towns and cities in the state including parts of Ahmedabad, Vadodara, Surat, Rajkot, Anand, Nadiad and Kaira.[29] Even the capital city of Gandhinagar witnessed violence with groups of people attacking the old secretariat building and the building of the Wakf Board was burned down.[30]

By the afternoon of 28 February violence had picked up in rural areas in several parts of Gujarat as the provocative reporting of the vernacular press got circulated

25 Sanjay Pandey, 'Ram Rahim Nagar an Oasis of Peace', *The Times of India*, 3 March 2002, http://articles.timesofindia.indiatimes.com.

26 'Votaries of Harmony Become Victims', *Times of India*, 1 March 2002, http://articles. timesofindia.indiatimes.com; 'Firemen to go on temporary strike', *Times of India*, 11 May 2002, http://articles.timesofindia.indiatimes.com.

27 Manas Dasgupta, '140 Killed as Gujarat Bandh Turns Violent', *The Hindu*, 1 March 2002, http://www.hindu.com.

28 '3 killed as Violence Continues in Vadodara', *Times of India*, 24 March 2002. http://articles. timesof india.indiatimes.com.

29 Manas Dasgupta, '140 Killed as Gujarat Bandh Turns Violent', *The Hindu*, 1 March 2002.

30 'Curfew in Gandhinagar for the First Time,' *Times of India*, 2 March 2002, http://articles. times of india.indiatimes.com.

and meetings and rallies were held to discuss what had happened. Already on the same day in several villages of districts of Ahmedabad, Vadodara, Panchmahal, Kheda, Mehsana and Sabarkantha there were incidents of mobs burning Muslim fields, shops, establishments and houses. Muslims hid in fields or wherever else they found refuge and some of them from villages like Kuha, Onganej and Chiloda found their way to camps in Ahmedabad.

In Panchmahal district as tribals participated in the violence for the first time, Muslims who were from trading communities like the *Bohras* who had been shopkeepers in remote tribal villages for generations were caught completely unawares when they were attacked and fled to the jungles and hillocks.[31] Interestingly in Godhra, where it all began and where there is the highest proportion of Muslim presence at 40 per cent as compared to 4.6 per cent in the whole district of Panchmahal (Lobo and Das 2006, p. 13), Muslims did not have to flee their homes because of attacks.[32] However, in Visnagar town, in Mehsana district eleven family members of two Khan brothers were hacked and burnt in one of the predominantly Hindu localities, Deepda Darwaza, leaving just three survivors. In the districts of Anand, Dahod, Kheda and Sabarkantha as well attacks on Muslims properties forced them to flee for their lives. After the first day of rioting itself 140 people were estimated to be dead from media reportage. As violence, considered by many to be unprecedented, continued the army was called in and deployed by 1 March after two days.[33]

The violence intensified in the rural areas on the next day when Muslims fleeing from their village in Dellol were attacked and killed as were 26 Muslims in Panderwada who were attacked and some burned to death. Ode village in Anand district is known as an NRI (Non Resident Indian) village due to the large number of *Patels* who have migrated to developed countries and who have contributed towards the village infrastructure. Yusufbhai Vohra whose house was located next to his

31 Nooruddinbhai and Fakruddin Najmuddin Mandalowala (businessmen based in Godhra with shops in interior villages in Panchmahal) interview by author, 24 February 2009. Also Memon family (resident Kifayatnagar Relief Colony, Himmatnagar, Sabarkantha) in discussion with author, 30 March 2009.

32 *Ibid.*

33 Rajat Pandit, 'Centre delayed deployment of paramilitary forces', *Times of India*, 2 March 2002, http://articles.timesofindia.indiatimes.com. The incident of the burning of the coach of Sabarmati Express took place on 27 February. After 24 hours chief minister Narendra Modi asked the Home Ministry for the army to be sent in at 6 pm on 28 February. After another 24 hours, on 1 March the army was finally deployed.

brother's among houses of *Kanbi Patels* in the villages had returned from his Friday prayers while the rest of his family was watching TV when the villagers gathered in a mob in front of their house. Out of Yusufbhai's extended family only a few , who were not on the ground floor, managed to escape to the vacant house of an NRI neighbour, while the rest were trapped in the house when a mob surrounded it and set it on fire.[34] Further up ahead another house was set on fire as well resulting in the death of 24 Muslims that day who were burned alive. The members of the Vohra family who managed to escape at night walked to Sureli, a village with a significant Muslim population six kilometres away. Even the other *mohallas* in Ode came under attack and were burned to the ground. In the early hours of the morning when the mob went away, some Muslims tried to flee to Sureli. 'At night some stayed back here, some left for Sureli. Where one found a way they left there, to save one's life.'[35] Villages like Sureli that were villages of predominantly Muslim population became places of refuge for fleeing Muslims in rural areas.

However, residence in an area of Muslim concentration was not always a guarantee of safety as experienced by villagers in Nava Station, a village populated by Muslims and surrounded by Hindu-dominated villages near Deodar at Banaskantha district in north Gujarat. A group of around 200 people attacked it and killed at least four persons before police dispersed the mob by which time at least six persons were killed. According to NGO functionaries in Idar, villages with Muslim population such as Haripur and Kesarpura in Sabarkantha, that had become places of refuge for Muslims from neighbouring villages, 'were not attacked, because they had a Muslim majority, but even these places were on alert because if 20–25 villages got together and attacked then again they would be in trouble.'[36] The size of the population of a pocket of Muslim concentration, therefore, seems to have played an important role in their ability to ward of an attack and protect themselves at that time of violence. The Bharat Bandh declared by VHP on this day had turned violent in a few places outside Gujarat as well such as in parts of UP, Rajasthan, Andhra Pradesh and Haryana.[37]

---

34 Yusufbhai Vohra (survivor of Ode carnage) interview with author, 19 February 2009.

35 Rafiq Mohammed Sayyed (survivor of mob violence, Ode, Anand) interview with author, 6 March 2009.

36 Usmanbhai and Harenbhai, (Nyaya Pathiks (Peace and Justice Community Workers with Nyayagraha) at Deshotar village, Sabarkantha) in discussion with author, 19 March 2009.

37 'Mixed Response to Bandh', *Times of India*, 2 March 2002, http://timesofindia.indiatimes. com.; 'Curfew Bound Rajasthan Towns Peaceful', *Times of India*, 2 March 2002, http://

While the army was finally deployed after two days, it could not guarantee the security of villagers at Sardarpura in Mehsana district where mobs attacked and surrounded Muslims who had taken shelter in a house and electrocuted it leaving upto 33 dead.[38] At Kidiad village in Sabarkantha as well Muslim villagers waited in the house of their ex *sarpanch* Salimbhai Sindhi for up to two days where they had hoped the violence would not affect them. When the police came to their village on 2 March, they warned them of danger and advised them that as they were minorities, it would be better for them to take their women and children to a safe place. However when the villagers packed themselves on to two tempos (a process which took several hours) and left the village, they were stopped on the highway by a mob in Panchmahal district and 74 among them including women and children were killed by the mob and only a few managed to flee and save their lives.[39]

Even as the chief minister claimed that the situation was returning to normal, official figures of death and destruction reported – a total of 289 deaths from over a dozen troubled spots, including Ahmedabad, Mehsana, Sabarkantha, Dahod, Vadodara, Bhavnagar, Rajkot and Surat.[40] Violent incidents continued even on March 3, such as the one involving the death of two British Muslim nationals who were murdered by a mob on the highway close to Prantij. While central Gujarat and the rest of the state remained calm with sporadic incidents of violence, in Ahmedabad violence continued for the fifth day as mobs were back on the streets, indulging in large scale arson and killings even as a large number of migrant workers started to flee the city.[41] After six days of violence despite

---

timesofindia.indiatimes.com.; 'Minor Incidents during UP Bandh', *Times of India*, 2 March 2002, http://timesofindia.indiatimes.com., 'Bandh Evokes Good Response in Eastern Districts', *Times of India*, 2 March 2002, http://timesofindia.indiatimes.com.; 'Kaithal Mosque Burnt, Punjab Bandh Partial', *Times of India*, 2 March 2002, http://articles.timesofindia.indiatimes.com.

38 Resident of Satnagar Navi Vasahat, (Relief Colony Sabarkantha), in discussion with author, 29 March 2009. Survivors said 31–33 people had died while *The Hindu* reported 30 deaths, Leena Misra, 'More Riot Cases May Come from the Cold', 9 August 2003, http://articles.timesofindia.indiatimes.com.

39 Salimbhai Sindhi, (erstwhile *sarpanch* of Kidiad village and resident of Al Falaha Colony, Modassa), interview by author, 22 March 2009. Also Ayyubhai Sindhi and Ayeshabibi Sindhi (erstwhile residents of Kidiad, Al Falaha Colony, Modassa), interview by author, 22 March 2009.

40 'Modi Says Tension Down – Statistics Tell Another Story', *Hindustan Times*, 3 March 2002.

41 'Exodus Begins as Violence Starts to Taper Down,' *Times of India*, 4 March 2002, http://articles.timesofindia.indiatimes.com.

stray incidents of stabbing and burning of people a scaling down of violence was finally reported and curfew was lifted in majority of the 30 towns and cities where it had been imposed. Despite the scaling down of violence there seemed to be little respite for Muslims due to instances of violence such as when 150 Muslims were found hiding in the fields after mobs attacked and killed twelve people in Ajanwa village on 2 March. A family that fled that village was told to wait in a house for the police to come and pick them up when the group was attacked by a mob and six members of the family were killed in an incident on 5 March.[42] For a few days after that amidst continuing tensions there were no reports of violence until 11 March when Muslims in Panvad village in Vadodara district were attacked.[43]

Flight

Since 28 February when the violence began, an increasing number of Muslims had begun to flee their homes and seek refuge in Muslim dominated areas in cities like Juhapura in Ahmedabad, Tandalja in Vadodara, Ismail Nagar or Hadgood in Anand. In the case of rural areas people fled to villages and towns with significant Muslim populations such as Modassa, Idar and Himmatnagar. For many women, the traditional place of safety where one can have the least reserve or formality, their mother's home *pier* (maiden home) was the place they took refuge in along with their families.[44] In Himmatnagar, in the house of a retired college principal 40 members of his extended family and friends from Khedbrahma, a communally sensitive town in Sabarkantha, lived from the beginning of the violence till the time tensions abated a few months later.[45] Some lived on rent or in relatives' houses but came to the camp to eat food. Kinship ties were instrumental in providing shelter at those times of need.

Hundreds of youth continued to roam the streets, brandishing swords, daggers, axes and iron rods and creating panic among Muslims of all classes in all areas of Baroda as well. A retired employee of Gujarat Tractor Company described how

---

42 'Muslims Held to Ransom over FIR', *Times of India*, 6 May 2002.

43 'Two Die in Riots in Vadodara', *Times of India*, 11 March 2002, http://articles.timesofindia.
    indiatimes.com.

44 A large number of women who were interviewed went to their mother's house, *pier* in
    Gujarati.

45 Ghulambhai Walibhai Memon (retired Principal and resident of Noor Colony,
    Sabarkantha), interview by author, 30 March 2009.

he and his family felt watched as they continued to stay in their home in a colony made by the government housing board, and therefore of mixed residency. They continued to be on guard themselves and decided to leave their house at the crack of dawn when they thought the mob would be away on a break. They locked their house and left with their daughter on a scooter to their relatives' home on the outskirts of Baroda in Nimeta village. Their relatives were in no better position than them because they were also the only Muslim family in the village and the continuing reports of violence began to make them feel unsafe again. Again in two days relatives from Baroda sent a police escort for them and they came to Machipeeth in the old city in batches, after sending women and children first, the family reached another relative's place where they stayed for a month before finding a rented house in Tandalja, an area of Muslim concentration whose population has shot up even more after the 2002 violence.

Mansoori Abbas Dawoodbhai was a successful shopkeeper who traded in grains in new Shinol village in Sabarkantha district. When he was threatened by some members of his own village on 28 February he sent his wife and children to his uncle's house in nearby Old Shinol village. Some of his friends among the villagers also accompanied him there. He hid and watched as a mob burned his shop and house. He was fortunate that his son's house that was attached to his did not burn because it shared a wall with the Bank of Baroda. This was true of most places where mobs burned entire houses of Muslims but only looted and burned possessions while sparing the house when the house shared a boundary or was too close to a Hindu owned house or establishment. After two days they returned back to their house in an effort to resume their lives. For about 22 days they stayed in the part of their house that had been spared because of its common wall with Bank of Baroda but with little to sustain themselves except onion and *roti* (a kind of bread) as their entire shop with provisions and most of their possessions had been burned. The situation, however, was so tense that their son suggested that they move to Modassa, a town with Muslim concentration and stay on rent for a while. Their move to Modassa however, turned out to be longer than they had ever imagined as the effort to find alternative means of livelihood and recover from their losses led to a permanent relocation for the family.[46]

Muslims in the Panchmahal region control a sizeable chunk of the

---

46 Abbasbhai Dawoodbhai Mansoori (resident of row house, Akram Park, Modassa, Sabarkantha) interview by author, 20 March 2009. The family succeeded in establishing a grocer's shop in Modassa.

moneylending business. The *Dawoodi Bohra* community, known for their business skills, have for generations run shops in remote villages especially in the district of Panchmahal. Soon after the burning of the coach in Sabarmati Express, curfew was clamped in Godhra town and in surrounding areas as a result of which those Muslim shopowners in remote areas could not return to their homes that day. One businessman whose shop was in a tribal village in Baroda district drove all the way to Alirajpur, Indore in Madhya Pradesh, before he could return to his house in Godhra. Another *Dawoodi Bohra* businessman who had a shop in Dhadia, a tribal village spent upto three days hiding in the forests before his family payed 40,000 rupees to have the police escort him home.[47]

At least in the districts of north and central Gujarat that were most affected by the violence no class or segment of society among Muslims was unaffected. In Anand every shop in a chain of bakery stores called Everfresh belonging to a Muslim family was burned down and the family themselves had to move out of their plush apartment in an upmarket area of the city and take shelter in a Muslim village called Hadgood outside city limits.[48] Other small time businessmen and shopkeepers of Anand left with their families to stay with friends and relatives who have homes in 100 feet road near Ismail Nagar, a pocket of Muslim concentration on the periphery of the city. A Muslim journalist then working with a reputed national daily, who covered the riots herself, had to move with her family on the 11 March from their home of more than 15 years in a mixed middle class locality in Baroda to a friend's house in an area of Muslim concentration. They moved house very quickly and put green curtains on the windows of the car so it looked like an ambulance.[49] Even a well known personality such as retired Professor of· Physics in MS University Baroda, Professor Bandukwala who is an active member of PUCL escaped his house, and tellingly, without involving the policeman on guard at his house shortly before a mob attacked and burned it. In Ahmedabad, even two judges of the High Court, one sitting and the other retired were compelled to leave their homes because of the atmosphere of violence (National Human Rights Commission, 2002b, p. 11). In case of the retired judge of the High Court who lived in the upmarket Paldi area of Ahmedabad a mob threw *kakdas*

---

47 Fakruddin Najmuddin Mandalowala and Nuruddibhai (Businessmen from Godhra) in discussion with author, 25 February 2009.

48 Everfresh Bakery functionary, Anand (name withheld on request), interview by author, 9 March 2009.

49 Ayesha Khan (then a journalist with the *Indian Express*), interview by author, 13 December 2008.

(burning rags) into his house. No amount of official and personal contacts with people in high places in the state machinery (otherwise a gaurantee of security) could ensure safety during that time even for middle class and rich Muslims.[50]

During the violence migrant Muslim workers[51] as well as those who had made Gujarat their home for up to three generations, fled the state to find refuge in other states. For instance in Naroda Patiya Muslims who originally hailed from Gulbarga in Karnataka fled to their native villages after they had witnessed the violence and found themselves in camps. Some of these families eventually returned and have once again settled in Ahmedabad.[52] The Bangladeshi press also reported that nearly 200 Muslims from Ahmedabad had made their way to Bangladesh.[53] Houses of Hindu families, who lived on the periphery of Hindu areas as well as those that were in the middle of Muslim areas, were also burned forcing their residents take refuge in a camp near Kankaria lake.[54]

In the case of working class neighbourhoods of Ahmedabad the curfew and continuous violence had left some Muslims trapped in their houses for several days. Yunusbhai Sindhi lived right in front of Nutan Mills in Ahmedabad where he worked before the mill shut down after which he became a casual labourer selling shirts on the street side markets. Although in previous years whenever violence broke out, his family would leave for his village in Degam, Gandhinagar district only to return after tensions had cooled down, during the violence in 2002, with the violence that seemed to be everywhere, he and his family stayed put in their house in Ramanlal Dayalalni Chawli, a *chawl* that had only Muslim residents but was surrounded by chawls of other communities. Mobs had surrounded their house and miscreants would try to provoke them but they expected to hold fort like other places in the walled city and working class neighbourhood where turfs had to be defended by the residents themselves in pitched battles between the two communities till the violence cooled down. Since all the residents of the *chawl* were Muslim, instead of fleeing they could hold off attackers and prevent

---

50 Resident of Paldi (name withheld on request), interview by author, 29 January 2009.

51 'Exodus Begins as Violence Starts to Taper Down', *Times of India,* 4 March 2002.

52 Rukaiyaben Sheikh (resident of Asim Park, Juhapura, Ahmedabad), 23 October 2008.

53 '200 Indian Muslims flee to Bangladesh: Officials,' *Times of India,* 18 May 2002. It was reported that a group living in the slums near Chandola Lake in Ahmedabad were illegal Bangladeshi migrants who fled Ahmedabad for their lives.

54 Monica Wahi (Founding Member of Himmat, an NGO of widows of Naroda Patiya), in discussion with author, 10 October 2008.

them from entering the *chawl*. However, given the fact that they were the only *chawl* with Muslims surrounded by those of Hindus, they could only hold off the attackers till 24 March when they were rescued by the military and escorted to a camp. Each riot that the city of Ahmedabad witnessed in the past had produced some amount of demographic change with people migrating within the city and the concentration of communities in certain localities. In 2002, a large number of *chawls* like this in mixed working class areas got 'cleaned out.' Yunusbhai Sindhi articulates the dispossession of many unfortunate Muslims,

> In these 15–20 years the possessions I had set up got completely cleaned out, everything completely, only the clothes that we were wearing we ran away with...the clothes that we are wearing no, they just put us in the vehicles with them. *Jo maal milkat banaya sab saaf ho gaya* (All the possessions that we had set up all got cleaned out).[55]

Camps and other temporary dwellings

Those who had the means and who had relatives or acquaintances in places that were less affected by violence took refuge with them. But a large number of poor people who had fled with nothing but the proverbial shirt on their back '*pehnele kapde*' and sometimes without even footwear, as well as the traumatized survivors of mass carnage and gruesome incidents of violence including women who had been raped and people who had suffered serious burn injuries found safety with others who suffered similarly and had taken refuge in open spaces in between Muslim dominated localities, *dargahs*, *madrasas*, fields and even graveyards. These places then turned into 'camps'. On 28 February, as many Muslim houses were torched in Vatwa, Ahmedabad in an offensive that went on for 72 hours, its residents fled to 'safe' places, i.e., places in the middle of pockets of Muslim concentration.[56] The men fought with stones and bricks and whatever came into their hands. Eventually the residents of Jehangir Nagar turned their attention to the families whose houses had been burned and who were 'just

---

55 Yunusbhai Sindhi (resident of Imarat-e-Shariya, Juhapura, Ahmedabad), interview by author, 30 October 2008.

56 Altafbhai and Afroze Sayyed (camp organizers Vatwa, Ahmedabad), interview by author, 15 December 2008.

sitting on the *maidan'*(playing field) in the middle of the locality.[57] Some of the young people then decided to give them some tea and water. Soon the numbers increased, and by night time they realized that the people who had gathered there needed food, so again they took a collection from the locality of Muslims who were predominantly poor themselves but who gave for those who were left with no possessions. Some elders also came forward to help organize, and once people realized that there was some help available the numbers swelled 'from 500 to 5000' and the *maidan* became Jehangir Nagar camp, one among the many camps in the city[58] in sites like *maidans* or unused buildings, *dargahs, madrassas,* schools and even graveyards in the middle of Muslim dominated areas or in villages of Muslim majority. Muslim camps were run mainly through the support of community leaders and organizations, NGOs, missionaries and other private sources including some political organizations that made significant donations.[59] After a month of violence according to one estimate there were 97,998 people in 101 relief camps across the state.[60]

A pocket of Muslim concentration in the northwestern periphery of Ahmedabad at Ranip, a place recently included in the Ahmedabad municipality with an old animal slaughter house *Bakrao ni Mandi* (meat market) surrounded by a Muslim settlement of about 2000 families living in shanties, during the violence transformed into a Noah's ark of sorts where women and children took shelter and cooked in the *mandi* (market) area with its high walls for days together while the men in turns fought pitched battles with the attackers. During the violence the *mandi* became a fortress for people and then a camp for those whose houses on the 'border' had been damaged and destroyed.[61] Kinship networks sometimes played a role in camps as well where for instance nearly 500 refugees, many of them relatives from neighbouring villages had gathered from a radius of up to 50

---

57 As Altafbhai explained, 'safety' was in the middle of the locality, as the houses on the periphery were being burned by the attacking mobs and defended by the Muslims. This is why those who fled came to the middle of the locality.

58 *Ibid* and *Times of India,* 13 April 2002 and *Times of India,* 30 April 2002.

59 'Ethnic Cleansing in Ahmedabad: Preliminary Report', SAHMAT Fact Finding Team to Ahmedabad, 10–11, March 2002.

60 Bharat Desai, 'Fear Still Stalks Gujarat, *Times of India,* 27 March 2002, http://articles. timesofindia.indiatimes.com.

61 Ghulam Nabi Mohammed Sheikh (resident of Bakrao ni Mandi, Ranip, Ahmedabad) interview by author, 10 December 2008.

kilometres at Ramayan in Sabarkantha. Unlike other camps where the displaced sought shelter in common public places like cinemas or schools or in a *maidan* where they put up a tent, Muslim families there took shelter in the homes of extended kin members and gathered in a large hall only for meals where they were fed from a common kitchen.[62]

After a few days of relative calm, violence broke out again in parts of Ahmedabad, Vadodara, Bharuch and in smaller towns of Kheda district with VHP's *Ram Dhun* programme on 15 March where mass prayers, processions, beating of drums and bursting of fire crackers were organized.[63] Pamphlets calling for the economic boycott of Muslims were found circulating in Ahmedabad. While on the one hand the sight of teeming Muslims in relief camps led to suggestions that land be given to resettle the victims by a visiting member of the National Commission for Minorities, on the other hand first time camp organizers like Altaf, never imagined that people would stay for more than three days. Altaf and his sister Afroze got involved in helping those gathered in their midst as part of the youth group of their locality and gradually got pulled into what became a task of feeding and providing relief to 5000 people. Initially they took donations from people in the locality and even compelled a grocer to lend his supplies. Only after a little over a week did the government step in to provide basic essentials like grain along with an additional ₹ 5 per person daily. The provision of grains by the government provided relief for camp organizers from having to collect supplies from people in the locality however, that was just the beginning as all the other arrangements such as large vessels, cooks etc. that go into converting raw material into edible food for so many thousands had to be made by camp organizers themselves. In the walled city and working class areas of eastern Ahmedabad as well, those in areas of Muslim concentration that had previous experience of managing displaced population during the time of violence like local leaders (*agevan*), strongmen and youth groups managed to provide food for the thousands of displaced in their midst. In the initial chaos after the violence, for about 10–11 days after thousands of people had been huddled in camps under tents there was shortage of the most basic aid such as blankets, clothes, medicines and sanitation.

---

62 Fact Finding by a Women's Panel, 2002, *How has the Gujarat Massacre Affected Minority Women: Survivors Speak,* Citizens Initiative, http://cac.ektaonline.org/resources/reports/ womens report.htm (accessed 10 March 2011).

63 'Ram Dhun Drums up Feverish Pitch,' *Times of India,* 16 March 2002, http://articles. timesofindia. indiatimes.com.

In Shah Alam for instance there was only one mobile toilet with four chambers for nearly 9000 people.[64] Camp organizers in different camps had arranged for some shelter from the sun by putting up a tent, but the teeming number of displaced cramped inside the tent created unhygienic conditions causing health problems. Although some Muslims in localities where camps came up initially allowed the displaced to use their bathroom and toilet facilities, given the prevailing chaos many also used open spaces around the camp to relieve themselves which created more unhygienic conditions.

Another pressing issue was the problem of missing persons. Those who found themselves in such camps either walking from their village for kilometres over jungles or on the bank of a river in the case of rural areas or who were dropped there by the police with little other than their lives to hold on to were dispossessed and impoverished. On reaching 'safety' the next concern was locating family members who had got separated when they were fleeing. Amidst persisting communal tension and curfew it took up to two to three days for some survivors from Naroda Patiya and Chamanpura in Ahmedabad as also for Muslims from villages in Sabarkantha and other affected districts to be united with the rest of their families in camps and some while waiting even feared that their family members who were missing were dead. Says, Yunusbhai Sindhi, those days were such that 'it was like a father would not save his son but get away himself. It was such a time that you wouldn't get to see where your mother or wife was.'[65] Ayyubbhai Sindhi who was driving one of the two tempos carrying Muslims fleeing from Kidiad village when it was shot at and attacked by a mob forcing him to flee for his life, for more than a week believed that his wife Arjoobibi may have been killed along with others.[66]

In the chaos after the violence for days, many even did not know that they could register an FIR (First Information Report) or a *panchnama* (preliminary documentation and evaluation of crime scene). Besides ignorance, some did not even see the point of making an FIR given that they were convinced that the police

---

64 'Ethnic Cleansing in Ahmedabad: Preliminary Report', SAHMAT Fact Finding Team to Ahmedabad, 10–11, March 2002.

65 Yunusbhai Sindhi (resident of Imarat-e-Shariya Relief Colony, Juhapura, Ahmedabad), interview by author, 30 October 2008.

66 Ayyubhai Sindhi (resident Al Falaha Relief Colony, Sabarkantha) interview by author, 22 March 2009. It was only after she was traced to a hospital and they spoke did he know that she had survived because the mob took her to be dead.

was not on their side.[67] Such was the alienation towards the state that some didn't even register an FIR saying *'police bhi unki sarkar bhi unka'*, (the police is theirs and the government is also theirs). Even among those who did go to register an FIR for other crimes committed against them, only a few were able to register the names of the accused. In some places the police eventually went to camps to take down FIRs of affected people. However, only a few FIRs had the names of the accused, the rest only had mention of a mob attacking. This was because in a large number of cases, when it came to putting down the names of the accused, the police, who were writing the FIR simply wrote that the attackers were 'mobs' as a result of which a large number of cases had to be summarily closed for lack of evidence. Moreover, a vast majority of affected people possessed only a photocopy of a *'samooha'* collective FIR that has a mention of the locality where they were attacked in their homes, but this proved to be of little use as it is almost impossible to successfully prosecute a case where the perpetrators are not identified. Also in a large number of cases the displaced were in relief camps or had fled elsewhere for safety when the police made the *panchnama* of their destroyed homes in their absence. So in most cases the losses estimated by the officers of the collectorate or district officials were far below the actual losses, which meant the compensation they received was also far below what was due to them.

After isolated incidents of violence broke out again, by the end of March i.e., a month after the violence started, the population of the already overcrowded camps was still increasing. At camps in Himmatnagar and Sabarkantha, where thousands of Muslims from neighbouring villages had gathered, camp organizers tried to bring a semblance of order by creating partitions within the large tent with the names of different towns and villages that the displaced had fled from. Camp organizers also drafted women among the displaced to help in the huge task of making food by asking them to do jobs like sifting the grain or rolling out the *rotis*. In some camps women were given flour so they could make their own *rotis* while the camp organizers arranged for cooks, sometimes among the displaced to make the vegetables etc. However for most of the men who were rendered jobless during the course of the violence there was little to do in camps other than to wait. *Chootak major* (casual labourers) such as electricians and painters, pavement hawkers and such other daily wage labourers and self employed were prevented from going out to work and thus deprived of their means of livelihood. These workers and

---

67 Maqsoodabano Firojbhai Sheikh (Jehangirpura, Hadgood, Anand) interview by author, 23 March 2009.

their families were therefore forced to rely on the camps for food. The presence of 500–9000 people in camps for an extended period, most of whom were jobless meant that sometimes fights would break out among people within the camp.

Some Muslims who had fled their homes found the conditions in the camps too overwhelming to live there, *'Wahan rehne jaisa nahi tha'*.[68] This is why some people who had the means lived on rent by drawing from their savings or borrowing rather than in the tents of the camp. Some would live on rent but go to the camps to eat as it was very difficult to find livelihood in those days of uncertainty. Many among those who could afford it simply stayed with relatives or friends. For most of those who lived in camps although the conditions did get squalid and unliveable, they were grateful for the fact that when they were completely dispossessed they got refuge and were provided basic necessities by members of their own community. One aspect of camp life that they had to get used to was waiting in lines, for food, for going to the bathroom, for receiving aid, medical attention or whatever else came in through charitable organizations. What the camps turned out to be however was some kind of official recognition of the condition of being a person affected by the violence *asargrast*. Those who stayed in camps got a *Rahat Chavni Card* i.e., a relief camp card for ration supplies and in the case of all camps, they were the site of disbursal of *ghar vakhri* or cash assistance for loss of household goods of ₹ 2500 in two instalments of ₹ 1250. Cash doles of ₹ 2500 were a paltry sum that in most cases got used up in getting food but they served as evidence of being a riot affected person in later years when the UPA government initiated additional *ex gratia* compensation. Camps, therefore, were an important site of encounter of the displaced with the state.

Although gradually medical aid for the victims of violence was arranged and doctors and nurses regularly attended to people in the camp, hygiene continued to be an issue. In Ahmedabad and few other cities local authorities eventually set up portable toilets but that fell far short of the requirement with one toilet for an average of 400 people.[69] Due to these conditions there was the threat of malaria, gastroenteritis and other water borne diseases. Psychiatrists who visited the relief camps estimated that at least nine out of 10 persons in camps had one or the other symptoms of post traumatic stress disorders, fear, insomnia, and depression and other mental health problems. There were cases of people who were afraid of crowds and of going out of the house. The trauma of watching loved ones being

---

68 Sabina, (Resident of Asim Park Relief Colony, Ahmedabad), interview by author, 21 October 2008.

69 Shyam Parekh, 'Bleak Life in Relief Camps', *Times of India*, 18 March 2002, http://articles. timesofindia.indiatimes.com.

killed, raped or burned was so serious that according to one estimate there was a danger of up to 30 per cent of the population developing serious problems if immediate psychiatric help was not provided.[70]

Incidents of arson and stabbing kept Ahmedabad tense and those displaced stayed put in camps in other parts of Gujarat as well. The National Commission of Minorities at the time sought to draw the then prime minister's attention to the displaced in camps that according to one estimate included '53,000 women, men and children huddled in 29 temporary settlements'.[71] Camps however were not entirely safe havens for the displaced (Bunsha, 2006, pp. 83–84). On 18 March the Odhav camp in Ahmedabad was approached by a group of people who threw stones and petrol bombs within its confines.[72] The then state civil supplies minister even asked three camps including the Shahibaug camp in his constituency to be shifted because they posed a security risk for Hindus around the camp area who felt insecure among so many riot victims.[73] In April one of these camps Daria Khan Ghummat camp, which at that time had 6,052 displaced, was even attacked and two tear gas shells lobbed into the camps starting a near stampede among those within.[74] A mob demanding for the Daria Khan camp to be shut down turned violent at the police commissioner's office in the presence of the police commissioner himself.[75] In Chhota Udepur town of Vadodara district, according to the police, tribals from the surrounding villages who had been instigated for creating trouble tried to enter the town, which had the only relief camp in the area

---

70 A. Deepa, 'Mental Disorders on the Rise in Gujarat', *Times of India*, 20 May 2002, http://articles.timesofindia.indiatimes.com. Dr R. Srinivasan Murthy, Professor of Psychiatry at National Institute of Mental Health and Neurosciences, Bangalore, cited in the article talks about serious repercussions if the riot affected people are not given immediate psychiatric help.

71 Harsh Mander, 'Cry, the Beloved Country,' *Outlook*, 19 March 2002, http://www.outlookindia.com.

72 Amnesty International, 28 February 2002, *A Memorandum to the Government of Gujarat on its duties in the Aftermath of the Violence*, www.amnesty.org/en/library/info/ASA20/005/2002 (accessed 4 December 2009).

73 'Relief Camps Trouble Spots', *Times of India*, 22 March 2002, http://articles.timesofindia.indiatimes.com.

74 Sourav Mukherjee, 'Misguided Teargas Shells Add to Fear,' *Times of India*, 25 April 2002, http://articles.timesofindia.indiatimes.com.

75 'Mob on Rampage at Police Chief's Door,' *Times of India*, 24 April 2002, http://articles.timesofindia. indiatimes.com.

with more than 2000 Muslims affected by the violence.[76] Even at Sureli village in Anand, where the Muslims of Ode had fled to after 26 people had been burned alive, Yusufbhai who had lost members of his own family in the incident recalls how they would take turns to guard the camp and keep a watch for miscreants and mobs who turned up to intimidate the people in the camp. By the end of the month the number of displaced persons in the relief camps had gone up to one lakh persons[77] and there were 101 camps across the state that were run by members of their own community with the help of NGOs.[78] This was probably because it was not just those who were rendered homeless because of an attack on their houses who made their way to camps, but in the five to six districts where rioting was the most intense, most Muslims who lived outside areas of Muslim concentration or on the periphery of such areas made their way to camps if not to homes of relatives or rented accommodation in 'safe' areas. In the debate in the state legislative assembly about people in camps BJP MLA Atmarambhai Parmar said

> who are the people in camps? Who are their supporters who are their admirers? These are the people who are disturbing the peace of Gujarat , but their supporters and admirers are in camps that is why Gujarat is peaceful.[79]

Gendered violence

A striking aspect of the 2002 violence was the high incidence of sexual violence against Muslim women. According to historian Tanika Sarkar (2002) and reports by various women's groups that interviewed victims who had suffered rape such as *How has the Gujarat Massacre Affected Minority Women: Survivors Speak* and *Threatened Existence: a feminist analysis of the genocide in Gujarat,* rape functioned as the central plank of the sexualized violence that took place in Gujarat. There were other forms of sexual violence such as verbal abuses, molestation, taunts, hitting the stomachs of pregnant women, hitting women on the breasts[80] in addition to

---

76 Human Rights Watch, *We Have No Orders to Save You: State Complicity in Communal Violence in Gujarat,* Vol. 14: 3(C), http://www.hrw.org/reports/2002/india/.

77 'CM Wants Refugees with Houses Intact to Return,' *Times of India,* 31 March 2002, http://articles. timesofindia.indiatimes.com.; *Times of India,* 27 March 2002.

78 Gujarat government in its reply to NHRC quoted in *The Indian Express,* 28 March 2002.

79 Gujarat Vidhan Sabha Debates, 10th Vidhan Sabha (15 March 2002), 52 (Atmarambhai Parmar).

80 International Initiative for Justice in Gujarat, 2003, *Threatened Existence: A Feminist Analysis of the extent of the Genocide in Gujarat,* Bombay.

instances of rape, gang rape and their private parts of women being mutilated and pierced with objects. Kallol taluka in Panchmahal district reportedly had the most extreme brutality against women.[81] There were incidents of rape on girls as young as 12 and even on pregnant women.[82] Derogatory language was also used against women and abusive language was scrawled on burned houses and shops as a warning and reminder. In places that were experiencing tension but had not erupted into violence bangles, an accessory worn by women, signifying effeminateness and therefore for right wing activists, cowardice, were sent to provoke the men into violence.[83]

Having seen the effects of 1969 riots, Noorjahan Kalumiyan Shiekh decided to send her daughter in law away first before the rest of the family proceeded to the railway station where she says each woman headed for the safety and comfort of her own *pier,* mother's home.

> If we get surrounded then the woman will get trapped. For a woman then there will be nothing else to take. If we don't take her and leave then if she stays here she will be in trouble.

Unfortunately such as Bilkis Bano could not make good their escape. Bilkis Yacoob Rasool who was then pregnant and fleeing her village Randhikpur along with other women and her child was gangraped by people she knew from her own village. The group killed her daughter and those with her and she herself was thought to be dead. When she regained consciousness and borrowed clothes from a nearby tribal village and eventually made it to the police station, the police refused to record her compliant of rape and in the FIR mentioned only seven of the 15 murders she said had taken place.[84] Other women who had been raped and needed urgent medical attention did not even get medically examined, which is crucial in order to initiate legal action.

---

81   Fact Finding by a Women's Panel, 2002, *How has the Gujarat Massacre Affected Minority Women: Survivors Speak,* Citizens Initiative, http://cac.ektaonline.org/resources/reports/womens report.htm (accessed 10 March 2011).

82   Neera and Rafi (Social activists who worked with women in relief camps of Ahmedabad), in discussion with author, 16 February 2009.

83   Trupti Shah (Activist for PUCL and Shanti Abhiyan, Vadodara), in discussion with the author, 28 February 2009.

84   AIDWA Fact Finding Team quoted in Fact Finding by a Women's Panel, 2002, *How has the Gujarat Massacre Affected Minority Women: Survivors Speak,* Citizens Initiative, http:// cac.ektaonline .org/ resources/reports/womens report.htm (accessed 10 March 2011); S. Anand, 'Bilkis Bano's brave fight,' *Tehelka,* 5(4), 2 February 2008.

Their case was worsened by the fact that in the case of anonymity afforded by mobs, some women were not even in a position to identify their rapists. In the case of women who were sexually abused and who survived to find their way to a relief camp, recording a complaint was a difficult task. Even among some women who did file an FIR, rather than the specific term 'rape' colloquial phrase such as *'bura kaam'* (bad deeds) were used. [85] In a large number of cases of sexual violence, FIRs were not recorded, not only because of the social stigma, but also because of the police's insensitive questioning. Families of victims who had been sexually abused were often not willing to admit that someone in their family had been sexually abused due to the humiliation and social stigma associated with rape.[86]

The overcrowded conditions of camps were especially trying on women and children where according to one estimate as many as 55 children had lost both their parents in the violence. Children who had witnessed violence suffered from post traumatic illnesses and needed urgent counselling. Women who had been sexually abused also needed urgent care and counselling. The camp conditions were especially trying for women who were pregnant, and a number of deliveries were conducted in the camps themselves. While volunteers from NGOs tried to address these needs through counselling and organizing activities[87] among the measures resorted to by Muslim organizations at that time of intense vulnerability was to conduct mass marriages of young men and women in camps.

While pitched battles continued in the walled city of Ahmedabad and in parts of Vadodara and Anand, Kutch which had not witnessed a single instance of violence till then despite having the highest proportion of Muslims in the state at 19.64 per cent, also witnessed sporadic incidents of violence on 2 April. Another case of mass murder that occurred at that time was in Abasana village where six members of a Ghanchi family were murdered on 3 April. In the next ten days no incident of violence was reported in most parts, however contrary to expectations that numbers in camps would come down as the violence scaled down, the numbers in camps remained stagnant at one and a half lakh in April.

---

85 Fact Finding by a Women's Panel, 2002, *How has the Gujarat Massacre Affected Minority Women: Survivors Speak*, Citizens Initiative, http://cac.ektaonline.org/resources/reports/womens report.htm (accessed 10 March 2011).

86 Sohail Tirmizi (lawyer representing the victims of the Gulbarg case), interview by author, 3 March 2009.

87 Neera and Rafi (social activists who worked with women in relief camps of Ahmedabad), in discussion with author, 16 February 2009.

Attempts at return

In Ahmedabad, after a few days of no report of untoward incidents at the end of March, some among the displaced from camps went to check on their shops themselves when an angry mob surrounded them and they had to run for their lives again.[88] In parts of Sabarkantha and Vadodara, the administration took some initiatives to help Muslims return because of which some of them could return.[89] However after a lull violence broke out again in parts of Ahmedabad from the 21April and went on till the end of the month. Parts of Vadodara, Kheda, Kaira and Mehsana districts also saw violence. Fresh violence pushed at least 4,700 people back to camps.[90] The administration was eager for people in camps to go back to their homes and camp leaders even tried to help some of those who were displaced to return back to their homes but they seemed to bounce back every time in greater numbers either with fresh violence or with rumours.[91] In Sabarkantha district according to one estimate, 24,000 Muslims villagers from 207 villages who fled because of arson and attack refused to return home. While the poor lived in ten registered camps and other unregistered ones, those who could afford it lived with their relatives in six villages of Muslim majority or on rent in the periphery of towns with sizable Muslim population such as Modassa, Idar and Himmatnagar. Even in early May parts of Ahmedabad, Vadodara, Jamnagar, Ankleshwar and Viramgam saw incidents of communal violence. 400 victims in Sanjiri Park camp in Ahmedabad for instance, did return home at the end of April, only to return a day later when violence erupted in this locality.[92]

Besides such repeated outbreaks of violence that created insecurity among Muslims, one reason why the number of people in camps remained stagnant for more than a month, despite their overcrowded and squalid conditions, was because there were several instances of people being attacked when they tried to return to their homes. At Makarpura, Vadodara two persons were lynched by a mob when they returned to their homes to get their belongings despite being

---

88 'CM Wants Refugees with Houses Intact to Return,' *Times of India*, 31 March 2002, http://articles.timesofindia.indiatimes.com.

89 Sourav Mukherjee and Leena Misra, 'Refugees Refuse to Leave Camps,' *Times of India*, 12 April 2002, http://articles.timesofindia.indiatimes.com.

90 *The Indian Express*, 26 April 2002.

91 *Times of India*, 30 April 2002.

92 *Times of India*, 30 April 2002.

accompanied by police protection.[93] In another instance when four out of 450 Muslims returned to check on their houses at Panvad village, Vadodara on two occasions they were attacked by a mob and later *adivasis* threatened to kill them if they tried to return.[94] The villagers had a list of demands, which ranged from asking the returning Muslims to withdraw all cases against them to asking them to refrain from raising slogans. The same resistance was seen from villagers across the state barring a few isolated instances where families had actually returned.[95] Thus, despite a great scaling down of violence and the stifling heat in summers, by the month of May there were still 50 odd camps in Ahmedabad alone and a large number of displaced continued to stay in them many of which had only a tent for a shade.[96]

In the month of May however, the state government wanted to close down camps. The government also drastically reduced the amount of food supplied to the camps. Although in some camps, due to aid from NGOs, camp organizers could continue to keep the camp afloat, by the end of June, according to official estimates '80 per cent inmates' had left the camps and 'some 15,433 inmates remained in 15 camps' mostly in Ahmedabad[97] when violence broke out in the communally sensitive places of Vadodara city again.[98] The subsequent onset of monsoon presented another problem for the relief camps, which were housed in cloth tents. The administration directed some camps to be shifted to *pucca* buildings[99] (made of brick and mortar) like municipal schools and some NGOs along with camp organizers built rain proof shelters but they were hardly adequate to keep wind and rain out. In relief camps on the outskirts of Himmatanagar, Sabarkantha, among the thousands of displaced some took shelter in an unfinished Road Transport Office (RTO) near the camp while others like Abbasbhai humour

---

93 Raja Bose, 'In Gujarat, Khaki isn't Awe-inspiring', *Times of India*, 19 March 2002, http://articles.timesofindia.indiatimes.com.

94 Sachin Sharma and Robin David, 'Rehabilitating Victims Unsettles Government,' *Times of India*, 22 April 2002, http://timesofindia.indiatimes.com.

95 *Ibid.*

96 Supreme Court Writ Petition No 530/2002, 33.

97 Government of Gujarat's reply to the proceedings of NHRC of May 31 2002 in letter No. SB.11/COM/1 02002/514/Part-I dated 30 June 2002, 17.

98 *Times of India*, 25 June 2002.

99 Government of Gujarat's reply to the proceedings of NHRC of 31 May 2002 in letter No. SB.11/COM/102002/514/Part-I dated 30 June 2002, 16.

intact, recall the time when they simply got wet and waited to dry off.[100] In a large number of those in camps however, especially in north Gujarat and in some districts of central Gujarat that were worst affected, people had moved out of the camps but into rented accommodations in places of Muslim majority and not their original homes while others had begun to make their way back to their burned and looted homes. Those who left relief camps that were closed down received two months ration and some received a relief camp ration card that entitled them to supplies from a fair price shop for up to six months and a kit of basic essentials like a few vessels, soap etc. from the state administration.

The return to their earlier homes however was a continuing ordeal from the camp for many of the displaced. For Yunusbhai's family that had to be rescued from their *chawl* in Saraspur, Ahmedabad by the military, the return to their house which had been burned, defecated on and the walls filled with obscene graffiti was a difficult experience. For a few days, after their return to their earlier homes, the impoverished residents of the *chawl* would cook meals together by pooling in with supplies they had received from the camp and cooking in large common pots quite like the camp.[101] Even though the violence had scaled down by May when Yunusbhai's family and other members of the *chawl* returned, the prolonged situation of conflict had ruptured social relations to the extent that Muslims were warned against using certain roads in the locality.[102]

There were also instances where people who went back did not meet any untoward incident on return.[103] In many villages of north and central Gujarat however, the violence had affected a complete breakdown of communication among the two communities. These were villages dominated by *Patidars* that had benefitted from the Green and White Revolutions. At Mogri village, Anand district, on the Muslim villagers' attempts to return to the village from camps there was stone pelting and the threat of violence again because of which as late as 2009 only one Muslim family had returned. In many cases however, particularly those among displaced who had seen carnages where mobs had committed great

100 Abbasbhai, Kifayatnagar (resident of Relief Colony, Himmatnagar, Sabarkantha), interview by author, 8 April 2009.

101 Yunusbhai Sindhi (resident of Imarat-e-Shariya, Juhapura, Ahmedabad), interview by author, 30 October 2008.

102 *Ibid.*

103 Former tenant in Doctor Gandhi ki Chali, Chamanpura, Ahmedabad, interview by author, 29 October 2008 and Khatunbibi Sayyed (resident Siddiqabad Relief Colony, Ahmedabad) interview by author, 23 October 2008.

atrocities in the localities of their former homes, like those from Gulbarg Society, Sardarpura, Ode, Kidiad etc., returning to their earlier houses did not seem to be a solution as far as restoration of their lives was concerned. Even villages where no deaths had occurred, hostility towards the Muslims remained.

In Ahmedabad, Muslims from the walled city and working class neighbourhoods that had witnessed much violence like Chamanpura, Bapunagar and Gomtipur had just begun to return to their houses under Central Reserve Police Force (CRPF) or SRP protection since May 2002,[104] when it was time for the annual *rath yatra* in Ahmedabad. The *rath yatra* is a popular tradition in Ahmedabad where once a year, a chariot with the revered idol from Jagganath temple winds its way in a procession down the narrow by lanes of the old city of Ahmedabad. The *yatra* attracts huge crowds of devotees and the procession passes through areas of Muslim concentration as well. Although in previous years, such a large movement of people in congested places had posed law and order challenges for the authorities, in 2002 given the high insecurity, Muslims from these areas who had just returned home from relief camps a few weeks back, left their homes for relief camps or homes of friends and relatives in Muslim dominated areas again for a few days to pre-empt trouble.[105] The *rath yatra* led to riots in parts of central Gujarat where pitched battles between the two communities were witnessed in Petlad and Kheda towns so that curfew had to be clamped in these areas. In Ahmedabad however, violence did not break out because of strict measures taken by the police as the Modi administration did not want hurdles in the assembly elections that were due in the state and it passed peacefully. However, the next month on 24 September two terrorists claiming revenge for the communal violence attacked Akshardham temple and fired indiscriminately with their AK 56 assault rifles and lobbed hand grenades killing 33 people and wounding an estimated 80 persons before National Security commanders gunned them down.[106] This led to fresh tensions among communities.

The Election Commission after a visit to a few camps and areas that had witnessed long periods of curfew was not convinced that conditions in the state

---

104 'Rath Yatra Instills Fear among Muslims,' *Times of India*, 7 July 2002, http://articles. timesofindia.indiatimes.com.

105 'Reprisal Fear Triggers Exodus Again,' *Times of India*, 26 September 2002, available at http://articles.timesof india.indiatimes.com.

106 'Akshardham Terror Case: Acquitted Demand Compensation', *Times of India*, 26 May 2014.

were conducive to hold elections to the state assembly that were due. According to the Election Commission at least 154 of the 182 assembly segments in the state had been affected by the riots and that almost one lakh voters had been disenfranchised. Nearly 992 villages and 151 towns under 225 police stations had been direct victims of the communal riots.[107] The Supreme Court also ruled in favour of elections being pushed to the end of the year in 2002. In July, according to official figures, there were 12,524 people in 10 relief camps across Ahmedabad city, even as in camps that were declared closed there were an estimated of 4000 people. Shah Alam, the largest, still had about 3500 Muslims, and most of them who were residents of Naroda Patiya, Naroda Gam and Saijpur Patiya.[108] That the situation was far from normal was evident from the fact in places like Ahmedabad, displaced persons who had returned to their homes, once again left for relief camps when the VHP declared a national *bandh* in September. The violence had left 1,169 people dead according to official figures and injured 2,548 although unofficial sources put the toll of death and injury as much higher.[109]

While camps were folded in most places and the villagers told to return, very few returned home and many who were too sacred to return or to wait on voluntary organizations to provide them shelter had settled down in Muslim dominated cities, towns and villages in north and central Gujarat. Moreover, till the end of the year, communal clashes continued to break out during religious festivals, and almost any altercation, even motor accidents threatened to turn communal. What has now come to be known as the post Godhra violence had gone on for about three months with sporadic incidents of violence continuing in the tense atmosphere in the state right up to the end of the year. An analysis of interviews with victims, newspaper reports, reports of constitutional bodies and independent reports on the events that followed the burning of the railway coach of Sabarmati Express in Godhra on 27 February till June reveals that the violence took place in phases. From 28 February till 6 March when the violence continued unabated the worst

---

107 Leena Misra, 'IB Says Gujarat Not Normal', *Times of India*, 12 August 2002, available at http://articles.timesof india.indiatimes.com.

108 *The Indian Express*, 20 July 2002.

109 '2002 Riot Hit Await Promised Jobs', *Times of India*, 26 August 2013, http://articles. timesofindia.indiatimes.com.; Gujarat HC Asks Centre to Compensate 2002 Riot Victims, *The Indian Express*, 23 September 2010, http://www.indianexpress.com. and Syed Khalique Ahmed, 'Life after '02 riots: A Long Wait for Help, *The Indian Express*, 3 March 2007, http://www.indianexpress.com.

carnages took place leaving 500 dead.[110] After a few days of apparent abatement, even as the magnitude of violence in *moffusil* areas, towns and villages began to sink in, violence erupted again from 11 March to 3 April with incidents of violence spreading to newer areas like Kutch, which had till then been an island of peace. There were a few days of tense calm with school children wary of stepping out to take their final exams when violence erupted once again from 13 April and went on till the end of the month spreading to Saurashtra while renewed violence went on in walled city areas and main streets of Ahmedabad and Vadodara. Even as the central government announced a package for victims of the communal violence on the first of May, Jamnagar saw its first serious incident of communal violence and sporadic incidents of stabbing, arson and rioting by mobs continued to be reported from places like Ankleshwar, Viramgam and Ahmedabad through May and June.[111]

In the violence of 2002, it emerges that while 16 districts in Gujarat had been affected the violence was most intense in six districts of north and central Gujarat. It is important to note that in places like Surat and even Kutch, which saw incidents of arson initially, there were no further reports of violence neither was any displacement reported from there. However, it was in the worst affected districts of north and central Gujarat that all classes, sects and elements of social organization among Muslims were affected. Estimates of the death toll in the violence that has become a much debated and controversial issue have varied by the official versions of the government of Gujarat as well as central governments. By conservative estimates of the government of Gujarat, there were 1,169 deaths and more than 2500 injured in the violence[112] to which were added the figure of 223 missing persons who were not found for seven years and, therefore, declared dead. The violence had left an estimated 2,548 injured, 919 women widowed and 606 children orphaned.[113] Unofficial figures, however, place the death toll as much higher and not less than 2000.[114] According to one estimate,

110 Matt Frei, 'Hundreds Die in Gujarat Violence', BBC News, 4 March 2002, http://news. bbc.co.uk/2/hi/south_asia/1848843.stm (accessed 20 January 2010).

111 *Times of India*, 3 May 2002.

112 Figures reported to the Rajya Sabha by then Union Minister of State for Home Affairs, Sriprakash Jaiswal, in May, 2005 in response to a question by an unnamed MP; 'Gujarat Riot Death Toll Revealed', BBC News, http://news.bbc.co.uk /2/hi / south_asia/4536199. stm (accessed 11 May 2005).

113 *Ibid.*

114 Human Rights Watch, *We have No Orders to Save You: State Participation and Complicity in Communal Violence in Gujarat*, April 2002, 14 (3(C)), http:// www. hrw.org/legacy/ reports/ 2002/india/.

at the very least, 300–400 women were victims of sexual violence during the 2002 violence.[115]

Given the fluidity of the situation where those displaced continued to negotiate with their changed reality and given the difficulty of arriving at estimates for population movements there are varying estimates about the number of displaced. According to official figures the violence of 2002 rendered at one time more than an estimated one and a half lakh people homeless in around 121 camps across the state at the end of March and the beginning of April,[116] some of whom took shelter for up to six months and some even a year in camps. According to a report by Harsh Mander and Kiran Nanavati, referring to an unpublished government of Gujarat report to the National Human Rights Commission (NHRC) where the state claimed to have provided relief for 1.6 lakh persons in camps and cash doles to 41,844 persons who were not in camps the estimated number of displaced should be 2 lakh during the peak of the violence.[117] Following an NHRC order that took *suo moto* cognizance of the inadequate rehabilitation of the displaced, the study by the Centre for Social Justice, Ahmedabad in collaboration with the Monitoring Committee constituted by NHRC 2004, which surveyed a sample of 4,382 families living in relief colonies estimated that the number of internally displaced families at that time would not be less than 10,000[118] suggesting a population of up to 50,000. In 2007 the Antarik Visthapith Hak Rakshak Samiti (AVHRS) i.e., Committee for the Rights of IDPs held that five years after the violence 25,000 Gujarati Muslims lived scattered across seven districts in Gujarat in approximately 69

---

115 The Citizen's Committee for Extraordinary Report on Gujarat (May 2003), 'Submissions to the CEDAW Committee for Seeking Intervention on Gender-based Crimes and the Gendered Impact of the Gujarat Carnage', cited in India: Five Years on - The Bitter and Uphill Struggle for Justice in Gujarat, Amnesty International. Viewed on 30 March 2011. www.amnesty.org/en/library/asset/ ASA20/007/2007.

116 Figures quoted by then Minister LK Advani who claimed that this number had come down to 19 camps sheltering 18,500 people. Manas Dasgupta, 'More Relief Camps Ordered Closed', *The Hindu*, 18 July 2002.

117 Harsh Mander and Kiran Nanavati, 2006, *Surviving State Hostility and Denial: A Survey of Relief Colonies for People Affected by Mass Violence in Gujarat 2002– A Report*, Nyayagrah and Oxfam, Ahmedabad, 26.

118 Centre for Social Justice, Ahmedbaad with the Guidance of Monitoring Committee constituted by NHRC, 2004, *Status Report on Rehabilitation of Victims of Communal Violence in Gujarat in Year 2002: A Study based on the UN Guiding Principles of Internally Displaced*.

colonies entirely constructed by NGOs.[119] The Government of Gujarat that finally undertook a survey of these relief colonies in response to the queries of the NCM held that 86 'resettlement' colonies existed across 10 districts of Gujarat that housed 3990 families with a population of 20,940.[120] This does not include displaced Muslims who do not live in relief colonies that the AVHRS called *chootachavay* or scattered around areas of Muslim concentration and in the upcoming ghettos of Ahmedabad, Vadodara, Anand and Sabarkantha.

As this account of the events of 2002 indicates, demographic and topographical aspects of a site were the main factors that affected displacement. During the violence of 2002 in the onslaught of mobs and the lack of state protection, the only place of security was among greater numbers of their own community. Even in this, topographical aspects come in to play as there were instances of smaller concentrations of Muslim residences surrounded by Hindu neighbourhoods that found it harder to hold up against the mobs and had to be rescued by the army. It was only places of large Muslim concentration, such as Juhapura in Ahmedabad, or Tandalja in Vadodara where mobs could not penetrate, that were successful in withstanding violence. In pockets of Muslim concentration that were already divided by 'borders' in previous riots, Muslims could hold off attackers in pitched battles while only the houses on the 'border' of both sides were damaged.

Muslim organizations constructed relief colonies for those displaced who could not return to their original homes and continued to remain in camps well after they were declared closed by the government. While some Muslims returned to their original homes, the number of Muslims in villages and places of Muslim concentration in towns and cities has shot up since 2002, an indication that they have moved in here due to the violence. What makes migration displacement is that it is migration induced by coercion (Penz, 2002). The element of coercion in the movement of Muslims since 28 February is clear in this presentation of events of the violence of 2002. The journey of Muslims from being *vatanis* to being identified as *visthapit* is therefore a clear case of displacement as described by the UN Guiding Principles on Internally Displaced Persons. The existence of pockets

---

119 AVHRS Press notes, Response to the Gujarat Relief Package Announced by Central Government, 23 March 2007.

120 Government of Gujarat, *Second Report on the Status of the Identified Resettlement Colonies of the 2002 Riots Affected in Gujarat*, presented to the National Commission for Minorities, New Delhi, 9 August 2002, No. RTI-102008-Information-18-A1, Social Justice and Empowerment Division, Sachivalaya, Gandhinagar, August 2008.

of concentration of Muslims described as ghettos in India's most urbanized state of Gujarat whose population has shot up since 2002 has been dismissed as not very different from migration within cities that has always taken place[121] while the government of Gujarat held that those in relief colonies had moved their of their own volition.[122] However, as one middle class Muslim illustrating the predicament of those who moved without any organizational aid put it, 'just because we have the means does it does not mean we have the choice.'

121 Yamal Vyas (BJP Spokesperson for Gujarat) in discussion with author, 10 February 2009.

122 Government of Gujarat, 'Status Report of the Displaced Families in Gujarat with Reference to NCM Delegation visit on 15/10/2006,' file RTI-102008-Information-18-A1, Social Justice and Empowerment Division, Sachivalaya, Gandhinagar, August 2008. While Muslim organizations, NGOs and the media referred to these colonies as relief colonies, the Government of Gujarat in its report to the National Commission for Minorities refers to these as 'resettlement colonies'.

3

Relief Instead of Rights
The Governance of Communal Violence

The violent events of 2002 inevitably bring up the question of the role of the state. During times of violence, how does one analyse the entity called the state that in Max Weber's famous formulation has the legitimate use of force and is constructed as the neutral arbiter of public interest? Although there was national and international outcry against the events of 2002 as the preceding chapters illustrate, neither displacement nor communal violence is without precedent in Gujarat. This chapter argues that the distinctive feature of communal violence in 2002 was the response of the state more than the violence. It examines the governance of communal violence by the complex of ideas and institutional practices, called the state, through the examination of relief and rehabilitation for those affected by communal violence. The history of violence on caste and communal faultlines in the state, particularly in 1969, 1980s and 1990s, afford much analytical visibility to the governance of communal violence and shifts therein.

The official account

The burning of the coach of Sabarmati Express took place in the early hours of 27 February 2002. By the BJP-led state government's revenue minister Haren Pandya's account given in the legislative assembly two weeks later, the information of this incident was given to the Godhra Control Room by 8:05 am and ambulances from Godhra, Lunawada and Kalol were immediately dispatched to the spot while the district administration organized a medical team. By 10 am, an indefinite curfew was clamped in Godhra and companies of the Rapid Action Force stationed at Ahmedabad and the police superintendent from Vadodara range, along with two more forces, left for Godhra immediately.[1] Even while the legislative assembly was in session that day chief minister Narendra Modi also left for Godhra and reached at 2 pm in the afternoon of the very same

---

1   Gujarat Vidhan Sabha Debates, 10th Gujarat Vidhan Sabha (13 March 2002), 148–54 (Gordhanbhai Zadaphia).

day. As the remaining coaches of the Sabarmati Express were on their way to Ahmedabad, there were incidents of violence at Anand and Baroda in which two people were killed.[2] The dead bodies were brought to Ahmedabad on the same day in a motorcade. 43 people were taken to the Civil Hospital and 21 to other hospitals, while 54 bodies that could not be identified were sent to Sola Hospital, Ahmedabad.[3] Large crowds collected to receive the charred bodies at Ahmedabad railway station and were taken in a public procession.[4] The VHP, the World Council of Hindus, a part of the Sangh Parivar (the family of right wing outfits) declared a *bandh* (strike) for the next day and the state government announced its support to the *bandh* on the very same day.

As violence inevitably broke out on the morning of 28 February in Ahmedabad and other cities and for the first time in rural areas many of which had no previous history of communal violence, chief minister Narendra Modi convened a meeting in the afternoon of that day where a decision was taken to ask the union home ministry, then headed by the BJP-led coalition of the National Democratic Alliance (NDA) for the army. While the army was deployed within 24 hours and curfew was clamped in about 35 towns/cities including night curfew in Ahmedabad, Baroda and Rajkot cities[5] by 1 March, the first day of violence on 28 February had already left more than 140 dead. The Magistracy and police authorities were asked to implement the Riots Control Scheme and the chief minister, had through television, appealed to people to maintain communal harmony,[6] but he also made his now infamous statement that every action produces an equivalent opposite reaction[7] and that,

---

2   Government of Gujarat, Case No. 1150/6/2001–2002, *Preliminary Report of the Government of Gujarat to National Human Rights Commission (NHRC)*, 8 March 2002, 4.

3   *Ibid.*

4   Dr Kamal Mitra Chenoy, S. P. Shukla, K. S. Subramanian and Achin Vanaik, *Gujarat Carnage 2002: A Report to the Nation by An Independent Fact Finding Mission*, www.urdunet. com, (accessed on 5 May 2010).

5   'Gujarat Riots: The story so far', *Times of India*, 2 March 2002, http://articles.timesofindia. indiatimes.com and Manas Dasgupta, 'Callousness after the carnage', *The Hindu*, 31 March 2002, http://www.hindu.com.

6   Government of Gujarat, Case No. 1150/6/2001-2002, *Preliminary Report of the Government of Gujarat to National Human Rights Commission (NHRC)*, 8 March 2002, 6.

7   ' "Newton" Modi has a lot to answer', *Times of India*, 2 March 2002, Delhi edition, http:// articles.timesofindia.indiatimes.com.

'the five crore people of Gujarat have shown remarkable restraint under grave provocation.'[8]

In the state legislative assembly that was in session there was uproar in the house as members of the opposition led by Congress raised slogans asking for the resignation of chief minister Narendra Modi who had failed to protect the lives of *rambhakts*, devotees of Ram, killed in the Sabarmati Express fire. Leader of the opposition and former chief minister Amarsinhbhai Chaudhary said those caught by the government, who were responsible for the Godhra carnage, should be hanged but quoting an article by Professor Dipanker Gupta sought to draw the attention of the house to even bigger incidents that had taken place after the Godhra incident where the police had failed to discharge its duties to protect its citizens.[9] While Narendra Modi had more to say on the rules of discussion on the floor of the house rather than clarify his government's stand, minister of state for home and security with independent charge of police and housing, Gordhan Zadaphia defended his government from the opposition's allegation of the failure of the police administration. According to the then home minister 273 preventive arrests had been made with regard to the Godhra incident, 5579 rounds were fired, 7944 tear gas shells were used, four policemen and home-guards had lost their lives, 100 people had died as a result of police firing and a total of 667 people had died as a result of which he claimed that within 72 hours riots occurring in the entire state had been stopped.[10] Zadaphia argued that it was impossible for any government whether in India or around the world to stop five crore people, who had come out on the streets with a force of 60–61,000 personnel and yet his government, he asserted, had stopped the violence within 72 hours.[11]

A week after the violence had led to thousands of Muslims fleeing their homes and seeking refuge in camps, the Modi government according to precedent supplied food relief to camps on the scale of wheat flour 400 gms, rice 100 gms, pulses 50 gms, oil 50 gms, sugar 50 gms and milk powder 50 gms

---

8   PTI, 'Text of joint appeal for peace', *Times of India*, 1 March 2002, Delhi edition, http:// articles.timesofindia.indiatimes.com.

9   Gujarat Vidhan Sabha Debates, 10th Session, 13 March 2002, 221. (Amarsinhbhai Chaudhary).

10   Gujarat Vidhan Sabha Debates, 10th Session, 13 March 2002, 150. (Gordhanbhai Zadaphia)

11   Gujarat Vidhan Sabha Debates, 10th Session, 15 March 2002, 71–72. (Gordhanbhai Zadaphia).

per person, initially depending upon the number of people registered in the relief camps. The government provided food rations to camps in Ahmedabad, Anand, Dahod, Kheda, Mehsana, Panchmahals, Sabarkantha and Vadodara.[12] According to precedent ₹ 7 per head per day in cash was also provided by the government to the camp organizers, which was increased to ₹ 15 per day per person for five persons per family for a period of 15 days. The government through the Director Voluntary Agencies coordinated the efforts of these relief agencies but the government provided help primarily through cash and kind.[13] In the first week of March the Modi government announced relief on the same scale formulated in 1991 of payment of ₹ 1 lakh in case of death to the heir of the dead person. In case of injury, the injured would be liable for immediate cash assistance for up to 10 per cent disability to ₹ 2000–5000 depending on the extent of disability. In the case of more than 40 per cent disability, persons would be entitled to immediate disbursement of ₹ 10,000 and an additional ₹ 40,000 after permanent incapacitation was duly certified.[14] The then relief commissioner held that that assistance of ₹ 1 lakh announced for the riot victims was in accordance with the relief manual in operation in the state where the same amount was given to the victims of the 1992 riots.[15] However, in another policy that raised serious questions of discriminatory treatment, the government had announced that the legal successors of those who died in the fire in Sabarmati Express would receive ₹ 2 lakh as relief according to the precedent in the state where since 1992 the state government was paying ₹ 2 lakh to any victim linked to the Ayodhya movement, in spite of the fact that not all of the deceased on the train were *karsevaks*.[16] Subsequently this decision was altered so that even the kin of those who died in Sabarmati Express were to be given ₹ 1 lakh. This decision however was not so much influenced by considerations of parity but

---

12   Government of Gujarat, *The Response of the State Government on the Recommendations of the National Human Rights Commission dated on 01/04/2002*, 13 April 2002, 24.

13   Government of Gujarat, *Reply to NHRC Report of 31ˢᵗ May 2002*, 1 July 2002, 16–17.

14   The following orders were precedents for this relief: Government of Gujarat, Revenue Department Order No/RHL/1090/1031/S4, 4 January 1981; Government of Gujarat Revenue Department Order No/RHL/1092/41801/S.4, 26 December 1992; Government of Gujarat, Revenue Department Order No./RHL/232002/513(1)S4, 28 February 2002; and Government Revenue Department Order No./ RHL/ 232002/513/ S4, 23 April 2002.

15   Manas Dasgupta, 'No discrimination in compensation in Gujarat', *The Hindu*, 6 March 2002, http://www.hindu.com.

16   'Modi puts state money where biased mouth is', *The Indian Express*, 5 March 2002.

as Narendra Modi, then the chief minister clarified, because the *karsevaks* had offered to accept ₹ 1 lakh for those deceased.[17]

As those who had been displaced had also been dispossessed, an amount intended as relief for reestablishing one's own household after the loss of household goods called *gharvakhri* of ₹ 1250 was given to those in camps,[18] which in the case of a few camps in Ahmedabad was distributed just in time for prime minister Vajpayee's visit to the city.[19] By a subsequent office order this amount was increased to ₹ 2500.[20] However, only those affected people who stayed in camps received this amount. Those displaced who found the unhygienic and overcrowded conditions of camps unlivable missed out on this small amount as camps were the point of whatever administrative contact there was with the *asargrast* (affected people).[21] At the conclusion of his visit on 4 April 2002 the then prime minister Atal Bihar Vajpayee had announced an additional *ex gratia* assistance to the legal heirs of people who died through substantial contribution from the prime minister's relief fund and the government of India towards the relief and rehabilitation measures of the state government. Thus the amount to be given in case of death was increased from 1 lakh to 1 and half lakh. According to a government order it was decided that of this ₹ 1.50 lakh that was to be given to the legal successor of the deceased person, ₹ 30,000 would be given from the government fund cash relief of ₹ 10,000 from the chief minister's relief fund, ₹ 50,000 from the relief fund and ₹ 60,000 was to be deposited in Sardar Sarovar Narmada Srinidhi bond, the interest from which would be paid for the stipulated period. At the end of the stated period, at the time of maturity, the total amount would be given to them.[22] Pursuant to the announcement made by the prime minister scales of assistance to be paid to the injured also were increased so that for 10 per cent disability persons were entitled to ₹ 5000 relief, more than 10 per cent

---

17 National Human Rights Commission (NHRC), *Suo motu* Case No. 1150/6/2001–2002, *Proceedings* of NHRC, 1 April 2002, 12.

18 Government of Gujarat, Revenue Department, RHL/232002/51 (5)/S4, 5 March 2002.

19 'Gujarat officials work overtime to present clean image to PM', *Times of India*, 3 April 2002.

20 Government of Gujarat, Revenue Department, RHL/232002/51 (5)/S4, 20 March 2002.

21 *Times of India*, 8 June 2002. The administration purportedly made attempts to reach out to those affected who didn't live in camps, but such people would have to get undertaking from people of repute living in the area. This vague criterion did not stipulate who these persons of repute were.

22 Government of Government Revenue Department Order No./RHL/232002/513 (Part 1) S4, 23 April 2002.

and up to 30 per cent disability ₹ 15,000, more than 30 per cent and up to 40 per cent disability ₹ 25,000.[23] In accordance with the existing revenue department's resolution from 1992, relief for damaged/destroyed residential houses was fixed for assistance from ₹ 5000–₹ 50,000.[24] After prime minister Vajpayee's visit the state government even decided to come up with a new housing scheme with a view to facilitate rehabilitation of affected persons at their old and usual place of residence called Sant Kabir Awas Yojana.[25] However, while the government claimed that the modalities of the scheme were still being worked out, the scheme never really took off.

While in the past, the government had two categories in relief for revival of economic activities, for the relief of moveable and immoveable assets, this time the government merged the two categories and in a government order dated 11 March 2002, it was decided that in cases of damage to livelihood sources and property and petty *(parchuran)* businesses *ex gratia* relief of ₹ 10,000 depending upon the actual damage, would be given. The BJP led state Government also announced assistance for the loss of earning assets such as hand cart *lari*, stalls *galla*, cabin, small and big shops etc. The industries and mines department had also come up with a scheme for loan for property and business of affected persons. However, the affected persons who wanted to claim relief had to choose between the provision of the revenue department or the schemes of the industries and mines department and accordingly inform the survey team, which came to assess the damages. The government however offered no schemes for those who were employed but were forced to leave their employment after the riots due to communal tension. The six months of violence had caused enormous losses to the state's economy. A preliminary first sights' assessment by the district industries centre held that a total of 462 industrial units had been affected with an estimated damage of ₹ 60–65 crores. The industries and mines department of Gujarat came up with a package of assistance for affected industries and businesses like shops, hotels, restaurants and big stores, commercial units and self employed entities. This package provided subsidy at four per cent flat rate to affected units and loans

23   Government of Gujarat, *The Response of the State Government on the Recommendations of the National Human Rights Commission dated on 01/04/2002*, 13 April 2002, 29.

24   Government of Gujarat, Revenue Department, RHL/ 1092/4077/S4, 19 December 1992.

25   Response of the State Government on the Proceedings on 1/4/2002 of the National Human Rights Commission, at 31.

sanctioned by banks or financial institutions.[26] The Reserve Bank of India, which has stepped in on previous occasions of communal riots, announced a package for those affected by the violence, which Dena Bank was to implement on 8 March 2002. However, the state government refused to accept aid from international organizations and private agencies for those affected by the violence in 2002 even though it had received substantial amount in aid from international agencies and other countries for victims of the 2001 earthquake. Even help offered by private banks, like HDFC were not taken up.[27]

The then prime minister Atal Bihari Vajpayee announced an additional ₹ 150 crore rehabilitation package for victims on 1 May in the lower house of the Indian Parliament, the Lok Sabha, to help revive normal economic activities, which included assistance for reconstruction and repair of damaged houses and shops, and to self employed categories who lost their earning assets and financial support for recommencing business, commercial and industrial activities. The package also included a programme to assist those widowed and orphaned in the violence. Prime Minister Vajpayee also announced that the relief package would be supplemented by loans and assistance on a liberal basis by banks and financial institutions.[28] Out of the ₹ 150 crore package ₹ 50 crore was earmarked for revival of economic activities and over 45 crore was set aside for rebuilding and repairing damaged houses.[29] Banks agreed to dispose of an application within 15 days of its receipt. Four public sector non-life insurance companies were also inundated with complaints.[30]

The language of the office orders used to disseminate these government resolutions (GRs) in the 2002 violence however is particularly insightful. Official communications for relief for those affected by the violence that came to be referred to as the post-Godhra violence that went on for four months in 2002 constantly invoked the incident near the train station in the town of Godhra. For instance, the intimation of the Collector Office, Vadodara to announce death relief, starts with,

---

26 Government of Gujarat, Response of the State Government on the Proceedings on 1 April 2002 of the National Human Rights Commission, 31.

27 'Who does Gujarat belong to?', Communalism Combat 8 (76), March-April 2002, http://www.sabrang.com.

28 Economic Times, 2 May 2002, Ahmedabad edition.

29 TNN, 'Bankers discuss disbursement of relief to riot victim', Times of India, 13 May 2002, http://articles.timesofindia.indiatimes.com.

30 TNN, 'Insurance firms flooded with claims', Times of India, 6 May 2002, http://articles.timesofindia.indiatimes.com.

On 27/2/2002 when the Sabarmati Express train was stopped and a mob from Godhra city burned a coach and burned the passengers alive, after which riots broke out, in these riots, in Vadodara Municipal Corporation limits incidents that caused deaths have taken place,[31]

As if in keeping with the logic of retribution, a policy that announced relief for those who died from communal violence had to reiterate the preceding incident of the burning of the train. The report of the judicial commission appointed by the state government as early as 6 March 2002 to investigate the violence headed by Justice KG Shah and Justice G. T. Nanavati was also tellingly titled the

> Report by the Commission of Inquiry into the facts, circumstances and all the course of events of the incidents that led to the setting on fire of some coaches of the Sabarmati Express train on 27.2.2002 near Godhra Railway station and the subsequent incidents of violence in the state in the aftermath of the Godhra incident.

After protests about the proximity of Justice K. G. Shah to the chief minister the government appointed Justice Nanavati to also head the commission. After the death of Justice K. G. Shah in 2008 he was replaced by another retired judge, Justice Akshay Mehta.

In the debates in the legislative assembly as well, allegations of failure of the state administration in maintaining law and order and combating communal violence were strongly refuted by drawing attention to the incident of the burning of the coach of the Sabarmati Express. The constant sloganeering by members of the opposition led by Congress and demands for the resignation of Narendra Modi were met by counter allegations by the chief minister who claimed to have evidence of the involvement of certain people in the violence whose names he said he had not revealed in the interests of propriety. When concern for the loss of lives in the communal violence that had racked 154 out of 182 constituencies in the state was expressed, it was expressed by the Home Minister Gordhan Zadaphia who pointed out that due to the carnage at Godhra station and in the circumstances that it engendered due to which hundreds of innocent citizens in the state had lost their lives and livelihood, the government of Gujarat had experienced deep hurt and pain.[32] The communal incident of

---

31   Collector's Office Vadodara, Disaster Branch, N.disaster/DeathRelief/E.doc/2083/2002, 10 May 2002.

32   Gujarat Vidhan Sabha Debates, 10th Vidhan Sabha, 13 March 2002, 189. (Gordhanbhai Zadaphia).

the Godhra carnage that involved Muslims were said to be caused by 'terrorist type of communal elements'[33] and was placed alongside previous terrorist attacks on the Indian Parliament[34] and the September 11 attacks on the twin towers in New York.[35]

In the logic of the state ruling party's cultural nationalism, the communal incident involving Muslims in the Godhra carnage was a grave act of terrorism against the majority community, its rightful citizens while the violence against Muslims that followed were communal incidents or *kaumi toofaan*, the storm of natural anger against the attack on Hindus that unfortunately swept some away. In defence of the government's failure to check communal violence it was argued that just as George Bush was not called a failure by the people of America when five of their planes were hijacked and two of their towers were broken, the government of Gujarat could not be held to be a failure in the face of a terrorist attack.[36] Terrorism invokes concerns of internal security and security is a powerful political tool often used to trump all other considerations in policy making in that in the competition for government attention, security concerns claim priority. Moreover, the labelling of an issue as such establishes a consciousness of its importance in the minds of the population at large (Buzan, 1991, p. 370). In the extreme nationalist logic the burning of a coach of a train after an altercation at the station in a Muslim locality was a 'terrorist attack' on the collective body politic of Hindus. The suspects from the Muslim locality in Godhra were therefore imprisoned as they had been arrested in the more stringent Prevention of Terrorism Act (POTA), which is used for internal security purposes in the context of terrorists. The failure to protect the lives of thousands of Muslims in the reprisal that followed, when weighed against this background, was no failure of governance as what mattered for governance in this scheme of things was the 'terrorist attack' on the majority community. In fact tribal communities that for the first time participated in the violence in 2002 were praised by BJP MLA Atmaram Parmar for participating in responding to the attack on Hinduism. The 'decisive governance' of government structures operating in this logic was demonstrated by the fact that soon after the tomb of Gujarat's classical

---

33 *Ibid.*

34 Gujarat Vidhan Sabha Debates, 10th Vidhan Sabha, 15 March 2002, 53 (Atmarambhai Parmar).

35 Gujarat Vidhan Sabha Debates, 10th Vidhan Sabha, 15 March 2002, 72 (Gordhanbhai Zadaphia).

36 *Ibid*, 59.

Urdu poet Wali Gujarati was razed to the ground by rioters while a police station stood barely 50 meters away from the spot, the Ahmedabad Muslim Corporation promptly constructed a road over it.

Other official accounts

Meanwhile the National Human Rights Commission (NHRC), that was receiving emails and faxes from Muslims being attacked in their homes, sent a team headed by its chairman to visit the state from 19–22 March. The team found that there was a pervasive sense of insecurity prevailing in the state, which extended not only among those vulnerable Muslims such as the poor or those who lived in densely populated and those classified as communally 'disturbed areas' but to Muslims of all classes and sects including two judges of the High Court of Gujarat who were compelled to leave their own homes in Ahmedabad because of the violent atmosphere. The NHRC noted that there were some instances of timely and courageous action by district collectors, commissioners and superintendents of police.[37] In Surat for instance, the fact that police acted on preliminary reports when there was a fire in an industrial area and trouble was anticipated after which there were no further reports of violence[38] from there is indicative of the capacity of the state functionaries to diffuse a potentially violent situation. However, these instances were more the exception than the norm. In a large number of complaints received by the NHRC, both in rural and urban areas of north and central Gujarat, Muslims complained of police inaction to their calls for rescue when they were surrounded by mobs. Even NGO reports held that police directly told Muslims of Naroda Patiya that they had no orders to save them. In many instances police were also seen as abetting the perpetrators of the acts of crime.[39] At the time of

---

37 National Human Rights Commission (NHRC), *Suo motu* Case No. 1150/6/2001–2002, *Proceedings* of NHRC, 1 April 2002, 10.

38 *Ibid*. Also, *The Hindu*, 5 March 2002.

39 Among others Human Rights Watch, *We have no orders to save you: State Participation and Complicity in Communal Violence in Gujarat* (Vol. 14 No. 3(C)), April 2002, http://www. hrw.org/legacy/reports/2002/india/ (accessed on 12 May 2010); Citizen's Initiative, PUCL, June 2002, *Violence in Vadodara*, http://www.onlinevolunteers.org/gujarat/ reports/pucl/index.htm (accessed on 5 July 2010); PUDR, 2002, *Maaro! Kaapo! Baalo!: State, Society and Communalism in Gujarat*, New Delhi: Secretary, Peoples Union for Democratic Rights.

the violence only cases that referred to mob attacks were being registered.[40] After reports in the newspapers and the NHRC's notice, more than 40 days after the incidents the police went to the camps to register FIRs. The application of the stringent law of POTO (Prevention of Terrorism Ordinance) to the first incident of fire in the coach of the Sabarmati Express to Muslims from the locality who were immediately arrested but not those involved in the subsequent violence, the NHRC noted, 'raised serious questions of discriminatory treatment and led to most adverse comment both within the country and abroad.'[41]

Acting *suo motu* on the basis of several complaints of Muslims in Gujarat about the communal situation, as well as of inaction by the police force and the highest functionaries in the state, the NHRC asked the Gujarat Police to reply within three days of the measures being taken to prevent escalation of the situation and the violation of human rights.[42] To this the government replied on 8 March 2002 that 'barring a few sporadic incidents in the rural areas, near normalcy has been restored' within 72 hours and that the state government had appointed a judicial inquiry on 6 March to inquire into the Godhra incident and subsequent incidents in the state. This was the first among government assertions of normalcy in the state about the violence, which went on for three months after that.

The organization of setting up of the camp tents, arranging cooks, enumerating the people in the camps and other logistics for cooking and managing so many thousands of people was all done by the camp organizers themselves along with the help of NGOs. Moreover, till NHRC's visit, three weeks after the camps had come into existence let alone the chief minister, not even a higher ranked political or administrative functionary had visited the camp.[43] It was after NHRC's intervention that the government of Gujarat accepted its recommendation and appointed senior officer of the rank of secretary with the responsibility of overseeing and supervising the relief camps in the district.[44] By 20 March there

---

40 Amit Mukherjee and Radha Sharma, 'Police no helping hand in village', *Times of India*, 25 March 2002, http://articles.timesofindia.indiatimes.com. This issue was raised in the Lok Sabha by a Congress MP. 137 petitioners had moved to High Court claiming that the police had not recorded their FIRs.

41 National Human Rights Commission (NHRC), *Suo motu* Case No. 1150/6/2001–2002, *Proceedings* of NHRC, 1 April 2002, 12.

42 National Human Rights Commission (Law Division), Case No. 1150/6/2001–2002, *Notice to the Director General of Police*, Government of Gujarat, 1 March 2002.

43 National Human Rights Commission (NHRC), *Suo motu* Case No. 1150/6/2001–2002, *Proceedings* of NHRC, 1 April 2002, 13.

44 Government of Gujarat, *The Response of the State Government on the Recommendations of*

were 20,000 people in camps, with more being added to their number daily till there were an approximate 1,50,000 Muslims in 121 relief camps run entirely by their own community across the state in April.[45]

Dispensing with relief

Dispossession was the major fallout of the violence for the *asargrast* or affected people. For a lot of women, the dowry they brought from their maiden home in terms of clothes, jewellery, furniture, brass vessels and gifts given to a new couple to help them establish a home counted as wealth. For many of the poor and especially those from rural areas some of whom had no notion of saving and accumulation of capital in a bank, the loss of their home and possessions meant a loss of their life's savings. Within the first three months itself most affected people who had taken shelter in camps received an amount for the loss of household goods called *gharvakhri* of 1250. However, considering that the displaced in camps were dispossessed, most of this ₹ 2500, which was given in installments of ₹ 1250 each went in buying food and in some cases clothes since people had fled to the camps with just the clothes they were wearing. In the case of relief amounts in other categories verification was required and there were allegations of delay in assessment of damages and payment of relief[46] and arbitrariness in fixing the amount of relief to be given especially in the case of damage to house and property. Besides cash doles, other relief was given in cheques, which in the case of those without bank accounts, especially in rural areas created additional problems. In the case of death, relief of ₹ 1 lakh, which was later increased to ₹ 1 and a half lakh to be given to the legal successor of the dead person required that the successor produce on a ₹ 20 stamp paper, details of the name of the dead person, the date of death, the cause of death, name of the police station, date of the postmortem and the name of the hospital. In cases of mass carnages such as those in Naroda Patiya, Gulbarg Society, Pandharwada etc. dead bodies were buried *en masse*, and hence death certificates could not be issued without producing the body of the dead person.[47] According to the rule, a missing person was not declared dead

---

the *National Human Rights Commission dated on 01/04/2002*, 13 April 2002, 24.

45   Bharat Desai, 'Fear still stalks Gujarat', *Times of India*, 27 March 2002, http://articles. timesofindia.indiatimes.com and Dionne Bunsha, 'The crisis of the camps', *Frontline* 19 (8), 13–26 April 2002, http://www.frontline.in.

46   *Ibid.*

47   *Ibid.*, 51.

until seven years had passed. This created great difficulties for those whose family embers had gone missing in the chaos that prevailed at the time of the violence. NGOs, as well as NHRC, suggested to the government that the procedure for declaring a person dead be reviewed in those circumstances and a procedure be developed based on affidavits by the next of kin and their neighbours or other reliable persons.[48] According to official figures 277 people were missing as of June 2002.[49] In the case of the victims of Kidiad village, out of the 74 people who were killed when they were fleeing their homes packed in two tempos, 62 people's bodies were not found and were declared missing for up to seven years.[50]

The BJP led state government offered bonds in the case of death of a person where of the total amount of ₹ one and a half lakh, 90,000 were given in cash but of the remaining 60,000 was invested in Srinidhi bonds in order to have some long-term deposit for the legal successor of the dead person. The successor of the deceased was therefore given Sardar Sarovar Narmada Nigam Limited's Srinidhi fixed deposit receipts, which were supposed to mature in five years and carried an interest of 10.75 per cent per annum,[51] which in effect meant that only ₹ 360 per month as interest would be available to the successor. The fixed deposit was initially intended to be for the maximum period of three years, which can be renewed thereafter. However, in the case of Srinidhi bonds, victims were left waiting after successive renewal of the bonds which meant that they only got a monthly interest of ₹ 360 for ten years and more.[52] Noorjahan Abdul Kadir who lost her husband in the carnage in Naroda Patiya, preferred that the bond be matured and the lump sum of ₹ 60,000 be given to successors like herself. Being widowed in the violence, and having lost her means of livelihood, she found little help in ₹ 360 per month from the bonds, which she had to go the Collector's office on the other side of the city to encash.[53] In case of loans towards reconstruction of property, businesses and industries, schemes varied from area to area and

---

48   Ibid., 31.

49   Government of Gujarat, Home Department Reply to NHRC Report of 31st May 2002, No. SB.II/COM/102002/514/Pat–I (Sachivalaya, Gandhinagar: 30 June 2002).

50   Salimbhai Sindhi (ex Sarpanch Kidiad village, Sabarkantha) interview by author, 22 March 2009. Figures mentioned here are according to his account.

51   Shefali Nautiyal, 'Government doles out bonds but riot victims can't cash in', The Indian Express, 23 June 2002, http://www.narmada.org.

52   Ibid.

53   Norrjahan Abdul Kadir, interview by author, Faizal Park, Vatwa, Ahmedabad, 19 December 2009.

were for a limited period. Using the Gujarat Small Industries and Development Limited's Bankable Scheme for Riot Affected Persons Fakhruddin Ibrahimbhai Vohra managed to set up his shop at Gamdev in Anand city again after the violence, except that this time to play it safe, he chose to rename his shop that was earlier Ifsa Stores, a evidently Muslim name, to FM Stores.[54]

The government resolution referred to relief in cases of disability or permanent disability and due to this victims who had not been disabled but suffered burn injuries, injuries due to bullets or stabbing were unable to get any medical assistance for a long time.[55] Moreover, injured were also required to produce proof of injury from a hospital according to which relief would be given. However, during the time of the violence when even the medical community seemed to be divided, some injured due to stone pelting or even shrapnel from police firing refused to go to the hospital if they couldn't find one nearby among members of their own community and, therefore, ended up without any written proof for their injury and therefore without relief.[56]

Government assistance also paid the costs of only structural damage to houses during the riots. According to an estimate prepared by the district collectorate, in case of Ahmedabad there were only 900 *pucca* houses i.e., those with concrete ceiling that were damaged during the riots, the rest were shanties, which were not worth more than ₹ 20,000.[57] Also, the amount for household assistance was given to the owners, and so many displaced who had lived on rent and lost all their belongings, got no assistance amount. For instance Shiekh Pikumiyan Rasoolmiyan who owned farmland but whose family had set up home in an uncle's house, the entire assistance money went to the uncle and not to the family that had been dispossessed.[58] Further, regarding the survey of damaged property that was undertaken, by officials often in the case of homes or property that were considerably if not completely burned down, estimates were arrived at by the

54   Fakruddinbhai Ibrahim (shop owner in Gamdevi, Anand) interview by author, 13 March 2009.

55   Mahasweta Devi, Writ Petition Civil No 330/2002, 63.

56   Radha Sharma, 'Docs told to stay off minority areas', *Times of India*, 11 April 2002, http:// articles.timesofindia.indiatimes.com.; Zakia Jowher (Indian Social Institute) interview by author, April 2009.

57   *The Indian Express*, 27 May 2002.

58   Pikumiyan Rasoolmiyan Shiekh, interview by author, Sahara Colony, Modassa, Sabarkantha, 22 March 2009.

government by surveys conducted by engineers in consultation with the local *talati* (village accountant) or *sarpanch* in the midst of ongoing hostilities where there were even instances of attacks on the survey team and where in a large number of cases owners were displaced and away in relief camps or among relatives or staying on rent in places of Muslim concentration.[59] Since the violence broke out repeatedly after periods of lull, some homes were burned and destroyed again after the first survey. Therefore, according to reports received by the NHRC as well as most of the displaced interviewed, the relief announced for damage to houses and property was arbitrarily fixed and much lower than what the affected people claimed it was.

In case of relief for earning assets the procedure to access *ex gratia* payment up to ₹ 10,000 required details and proofs such as copy of earning asset, loss assessment, rent receipt if the asset was rented, electricity bill, registration number under the Shop and Establishment Act, receipt of the taxes paid to the municipality, ration card number and its copy, FIR number etc. However, many affected people especially the displaced had been dispossessed and lost all documentary proof as their houses had been burned or looted. A revised GR allowed a waiver of some of the above mentioned documents or proof by allowing affidavits of the person and an indemnity bond to access *ex gratia* amount up to ₹ 5000. In Anand, the collector employed the services of a photographer and videographer to carry out the survey of damaged shops and houses and weed out bogus claims.[60] In the Mahashweta Devi and Others vs. Union of India and Others (Writ Petition Civil No 330/2002, pp. 42–44) the petitioners held that many claims were not being considered due to the fact that in group FIRs individual losses were not shown and the police were not inclined to register a second FIR regarding the loss of property, loss of livelihood etc. Even in cases where affected persons had *panchnamas* that is the first hand report of the scene of crime, they received less than the relief they had applied for. For instance, a rickshaw driver who applied for Rs. 10,000 relief received only ₹ 700. Even in the case of household assistance, which allowed claims between ₹ 5–50,000, people were given amounts less than even ₹ 5000, such as ₹ 3,450, ₹ 2000, ₹ 1250 for their houses.[61] In case of relief given for housing assistance

---

59 Rajiv Shah, 'Bhandari wants survey of riot–hit areas completed', *Times of India*, 6 May 2002, http://articles.timesofindia.indiatimes.com.

60 Ayesha Khan, 'District relief panel takes lead, records riots damage,' *The Indian Express*, 26 April 2002.

61 *Ibid.*, 45, 46. TNN, 'Paltry compensation not for the weak–hearted', *Times of India*, 5 May

and for losses to commercial establishments, small shops etc. the compensation was nowhere near the actual losses as estimated by an independent technical team of architects and engineers.

Closure of camps

Despite the state government's declaration of the return of 'normalcy' within 72 hours of the outbreak of violence, the very presence of such a large number of people in camps even four months later in June was evidence that raised questions about the government's claims. The immediate goal therefore was to do away with 'camps' – the obtrusive visual presence of the displaced that spoke volumes about the existing hostility and insecurity between the communities and the fact that things were not 'normal' yet. The then home minister L. K. Advani stepped in to demonstrate that the administration was taking measures to rehabilitate the victims. 'At one time in the state, there were over 1.5 lakh riot victims in 121 camps' he said, 'but with no untoward incident taking place, people have returned to their homes. And now, in 19 camps, there are just 18,500 people. In the last week alone, over 12,000 people had gone home.'[62] This in fact can be considered as the central government's first allusion to the situation of displacement in the state without actually naming it as such.

Since April, people in camps had been trying to return. However with the continuing violence and atmosphere of insecurity, a large number of Muslims continued to remain in camps and by the end of May there were 50 camps in the city of Ahmedabad alone. This number dropped to about 27 relief camps in Ahmedabad by the end of June and further down to 20 in July 2002 when only the very poor were staying put.[63] The state government in its response to NHRC on 12 April 2002, as well as in media reports, reiterated that people would not be asked to leave the camps till relief and rehabilitation measures were complete and they felt assured of their safety to return home. However, in its 31 May report to the government of Gujarat, NHRC stated that it had received reports of 'pressure

2002, http://articles.timesofindia.indiatimes.com/2002-05-05/india/27136405_1_ relief-camp-compensation-shahibaug.

62   'Cornered Modi gets a clean chit from Advani', *The Indian Express*, 17 June 2002.

63   Mahashweta Devi and Others vs Union of India and Others, Writ Petition Civil No 330/2002, 29, 33 and 'Paltry compensation not for the weak-hearted', *Times of India* 5 May 2002, http://articles.timesofindia.indiatimes.com.

being exerted on inmates or conditions in some camps being so inhospitable, that inmates have felt compelled to leave the camps and seek refuge with family and friends.'[64] There were instances of displaced in camps being coerced to leave. A GR dated 6 March, which permitted all the camps to function until 6 March, was invoked at official district level meetings to implement a plan of action to shut down the camps.[65] Minister of state for home, Gordhan Zadaphia said that the administration expected all camps to be shut down within a week.[66] Following a Public Interest Litigation (PIL) in the state High Court filed by the Citizens for Justice and Peace through journalist Anil Dharker and lawyer-activist Teesta Setalvad that contended that the government might close the camps on 31 May and the appeal that they should not be closed till rehabilitation work was over, the state government assured the High Court that the relief camps would not be closed till those in camps were rehabilitated.[67]

According to government figures, as of 26 June there were only 15,433 people in 15 camps out of which 13,865 were in Ahmedabad alone[68] but officials alleged that the number could be much lower than this as camp organizers projected a much high number of people in camps than those that they found on verification.[69] The government, in the meanwhile, provided those who were leaving camps with rations for two months and a relief camp ration card, which would entitle them to rations for six months.[70] While the government held that it had not exerted any pressure to close the camps and that people were returning to their homes because of the return of normalcy, district and municipal officials used various tactics to exert pressure on camp organizers to close the camps. In May when temperatures

---

64 National Human Rights Commission, *Suo motu* Case No. 1150/6/2001–2002, 31 May 2002, 53.

65 '4 refugee camps in Dahod closed', *Times of India*, 29 April 2002, http://articles.timesofindia.indiatimes.com and 'Walkout in LS over Gujarat', *Times of India*, 7 May 2002, http://articles.timesofindia.indiatimes.com.

66 *Ibid.*

67 'Govt not to close relief camps', *Times of India*, 27 June 2002, http://articles.timesofindia.indiatimes.com.

68 National Human Rights Commission, *Suo motu* Case No. 1150/6/2001–2002, 31 May 2002, 16–19.

69 Sanjay Pandey, 'Numbers being changed in riot camp', *Times of India*, 9 June 2002, http://timesofindia.indiatimes.com.

70 Government of Gujarat, Revenue Department, Order No. RHL 23/2002/513 (part-2)/ S-4, 9 May 2002, quoted in Mahashweta Devi, Writ Petition, 34.

were soaring and the heat became stifling in camps which only had a cloth tent for a covering, people would go to rest in neighbouring houses of friends or relatives or under a tree or go to check on their properties or look for work, the collector's staff would surround the camp and the number of people in the tent at that time were counted. The state administration then alleged that the camp had far lesser number of inmates than what camp organizers were claiming and reduced the supply of rations to the camp drastically. In May the government even stopped rations to camps.[71] The government claimed that those who had voluntarily left the camps were provided two months' ration on the existing scale, which was provided to them daily in the camps.[72] However, camp organizers were told that rations would be given only if they gave it in writing that the camp was closed. After the government stopped supplying rations, a collective of NGOs like Citizens Initiative, Red Cross, Action Aid, St. Xaviers Social Society etc. continued the flow of food supplies to relief camps.[73]

The next month of June however also brought with it monsoons and camps which were by and large shelters made of cloth tents and were flooded with rain water as the collector's office had not responded to all representations made for provision of rain shelter in camps. NGOs again pitched in to provide shelters in some of the camps that continued to run. Already the reduction of daily rations to camps had brought down the number camps for instance in Ahmedabad from 60 to 10 officially. Citing reasons of monsoon, the administration asked to shift people to the bigger camps such as Qureshi Hall in Vadodara, Shah Alam camp or Dariya Khan Gummat camp in Ahmedabad. In rural areas, such as in Panchmahal district a minister wanted to shift Muslims in camps to village schools or *panchayat* buildings till their damaged houses would be made inhabitable.[74] In Ahmedabad, 11 municipal schools were converted into relief camps, after the collectorate requested the municipal corporation to provide infrastructure.[75] People were

---

71   Altafbhai Sayyed (Jehangirnagar camp organizer) interview by author, 15 December 2008.

72   Government of Gujarat, Reply to National Human Rights Commission, *Suo motu* Case No. 1150/6/2001–2002, 31 May 2002, 18.

73   Mahashweta Devi and Others vs Union of India and Others, Writ Petition Civil No 330/2002, 29, 33.

74   *Times of India*, 3 May 2002.

75   Sanjay Pandey, 'Officials in a fix over sifting refugee camps from school', *Times of India*, 12 May 2002, http://articles.timesofindia.indiatimes.com/2002-05-12/ahmedabad/27125487_1_municipal-schools-relief-camps-school-buildings.

reluctant to leave their earlier camp for various reasons such as proximity to original place of residence or work. After lakhs of people had been in camps and thousands continued to remain in the them even after four months, the state government held that normalcy had been restored, that it had completed payment of assistance and confidence building measures because of which 'more than 80 per cent of the camp inmates have willingly left the camps and have gone back to their original place of dwelling.'[76] Approximately 15,000 people continued to stay in relief camps that were officially declared as closed by the administration as many of them had either not received state relief or the relief amount received was too meagre to set up a new house or earn a livelihood.[77] The government further reduced the number of recognized relief camps in the first week of July from 10 to four in Ahmedabad.[78] By the end of June, the government also declared 'closed' all the 40 camps that existed in these districts of north and central Gujarat. Some of the camps however, in Ahmedabad, Modassa and Himmatnagar however continued to run for more than a year after that because the displaced, especially the poorest of the poor, would not leave the camps.

'Rehabilitation'

Rehabilitation strategies varied from area to area. Since April 2002 the state administration in Vadodara and Sabarkantha took some initiatives for the return of those displaced but incidents of violence broke out again. The National Commission for Minorities however held that the BJP led state government was concerned only with relief and not rehabilitation. From the following month in May that year the administration provided escorts of the Central Reserve Police Force (CRPF) and State Reserve Police (SRP) to those among the displaced in camps who had decided to return to their homes from the camps. Muslim traders at Naroda fruit market in Ahmedabad and Bakraoni Mandi in Ahmedabad were also given protection to return to markets where they used to ply their wares. SRP and CRPF companies also manned some areas where Muslims had returned. Police and revenue department officials held meetings with the *panchayats* in

---

76 Government of Gujarat, No. SB.11/COM/102002/514/Part-I, Reply to the Proceedings of NHRC of 31 May 2002, at 18 (30 June 2002).

77 *Ibid.*, 33, 59, 61. Shefali Nautiyal, ' "Closed" camps have 15,000 inmates', *The Indian Express*, 4 June 2002.

78 *Times of India*, 8 July 2002.

many places, however, social tensions were not as easily diffused as village elders and *sarpanches* imposed conditions for returning Muslims, such as the withdrawal of specific names of villagers from FIRs filed by the Muslims. At Panvad village in Vadodara district displaced Muslims were attacked twice when they went to the village. The district administrators wanted to send the displaced Muslim villagers back to the village under heavy police protection by the 1st of June but in successive meetings district administrators were unsuccessful in convincing the villagers who said they did not want Muslims to return to the village.[79] Muslim men from these villages were finally successful in rebuilding their houses under heavy police protection. The administration itself acknowledged that in some cases it was not advisable to bring in women and children even six months since the violence took place. In one case police picked up men from Maretha village from different parts of Vadodara where they had taken shelter and sent them to the village under heavy police protection after they had already warned the villagers to let the displaced in.

In case of Sayla village in Panchmahal district, district officials held meetings with the *panchayat* as well as the *panchayats* of surrounding villages to allow Muslims to return but in the same night the villagers were threatened with dire consequences, which forced them to return to the camp.[80] In case of victims of carnages like those at Kalol camp in Panchmahal district where relatives of 50 people who were killed from the villages of Delol, Boru and Eral, the problem of rehabilitation was even more complicated. The camp had 28 orphans, 13 widows and women who were sexually abused who on return would have to face the men who had raped them as those men were not arrested and continued to roam free. The fact that even in some of the major cases of mass murder, not a single arrest had been made until then and the perpetrators roamed freely was another major reason why Muslims in camps did not feel safe enough to return.[81] The government however, refused to allot any separate plots of land for those displaced who felt unable to return to their original homes.[82]

---

79   Sachin Sharma and Robin David, 'Government Finds it Difficult to Build Bridges', *Times of* India, 23 April 2002. Also, *The Indian Express,* 21 May 2002 and *The Indian Express,* 18 August 2002.

80   Rajiv Shah, 'Government bent on closing down refugee camps by May 31', *Times of India,* 2 May 2002, http://articles.timesofindia.indiatimes.com.

81   Rajiv Shah, 'Govt bent on closing down refugee camps by May 31,' *Times of India,* 2 May 2002, http://articles.timesofindia.indiatimes.com.

82   Rajiv Shah, 'Gujarat Riot Victims Plea for Resettlement Sites Goes Unheard', *Times of India,* 5 May 2002.

Although the government had got its numbers of camps closed and disbursed relief, many Muslims from north Gujarat and some districts of central Gujarat like Panchmahal, Vadodara, Kheda and Anand who were affected by the violence had not returned to their original homes. Those who had fled their homes at the time of the violence took up houses in rent in Muslim dominated villages, and in towns with sizeable Muslim population. In Sabarkantha, Anand, Panchmahal and Kheda, minority dominated villages like Kesarpura, Haripur, Sureli etc. and Muslim localities in towns with significant Muslim population such as Idar, Modassa, Himmatnagar, Godhra, Hallol etc became places of refuge. In both cities and rural areas of north and central Gujarat, a large number of Muslims moved to areas of Muslim concentration.

History of state practices in dealing with communal violence and displacement

Displacement due to communal violence however is not entirely without precedent in Gujarat. Riots in 1969 left more than 1000 people dead mostly in Ahmedabad, injured over 1,084 persons and displaced thousands of persons.[83] The violence had also spread to other districts such as Baroda, Kaira, Mehsana, Sabarkantha and other districts. According to the Commission of Inquiry headed by Justice Jagmohan Reddy, (henceforth Reddy Commission Report) appointed by the Hitendra K. Desai-led Congress government in the state to assess the causes for the violence and government action, there was a delay in the imposition of curfew and there were also instances of police inaction and its failure to rescue those trapped in the violence that were brought to the notice of the commission of inquiry by various organizations that deposed before it (Reddy Commission Report, 1970, p. 575). Ghanshyam Shah also noted police inaction and the role of Congressmen in colluding with rioters directly or indirectly and even misguiding the administration while ageing Gandhians in the party although disturbed by the violence, did little more than pray in safety (Shah, 1970, p. 199) quite unlike Gandhi who himself in his lifetime personally intervened in some riots. The ruling Congress government was indecisive in taking important decisions such as calling the army however according to the Reddy Commission after a delay, when it was evident that it had become a major conflict, the police rescued thousands of Muslims

---

83 Government of Gujarat, 1970, *Report of the Commission of Inquiry: Ahmedabad Communal Disturbances (1969)*, Chapter XVIII, 211, Ahmedabad.

when they found them stranded, or in response to calls for help escorted them to places of safety or to the relief camps that had come up (Reddy Commission Report, 1970, p. 201).

While the Hitendra Desai government dithered in acting effectively and decisively during the violence, it was more proactive in measures of relief and rehabilitation. The government had then opened four relief camps apart from which there were seven private relief camps in Ahmedabad. In about four days the collector and district collector took charge of a government run camp at the Police Stadium in Ahmedabad in which 12,000 Muslims had taken refuge. According to government estimates the four government run relief camps housed a total of 20,500 people that it referred to as 'refugees' while private relief camps had 7,250 people, bringing the total number of displaced, excluding those in several unaccounted for private camps and those who left the city, to 27,750. Railway authorities testified to the fact that a large number of people had left the city. Officers and staff of the state government worked to run the camp where two very basic meals a day were provided. The Public Works Department (PWD) along with local contractors constructed large tents and the joint director of public heath visited government camps to check sanitation and health facilities. While the government provided ration supplies to private camps as well, if the joint director of public health's deposition is an indication, then it is not certain that the officers ensured the provision of health and sanitation facilities in the private camps as well (Commission of Inquiry, 1970, p. 181). As the violence had rendered them homeless and with very little or no possessions, those leaving the camps were provided a household kit that included a set of utensils, blankets, cloth, bed spreads etc. to help them rehabilitate themselves. Transport facilities were provided for those who wanted to leave the camp for their homes or the houses of their relatives. Also, a large number of the camp inmates who were from other states and who wanted to return to their native states were given travel fare for the journey to their native places. Officers of the Hitendra Desai-led state government, according to the report, also went directly to the affected areas and made on the spot payments of the amount that was sanctioned for cash doles as immediate relief after oral inquiries (*Ibid*, p. 208). The camp was closed officially on 15 October, which means in effect it ran for about 15 days.

The state government then had also set up a full time administrative agency to provide what it called 'long term relief' measures for rehabilitation. According to the Reddy Commission's account, the city was divided into five zones based on municipal wards and each zone was put in charge of a Deputy Collector for relief operations. Officers worked on an urgent basis irrespective of government holidays and went out to deliver relief in cash to the affected people (*Ibid*, p. 208). As a part of the 'long term relief and rehabilitation' efforts of the state to provide food and shelter to the 'needy', the government also announced subsidy of up to ₹ 250 depending on the extent of damage for repairs to houses and huts and loans up to ₹ 5000 depending on the extent of the damage. For the reconstruction of huts a subsidy of ₹ 350 was authorized. Moreover this cash relief was given after engineering staff attached to the office of rehabilitation work assessed the properties of those who had applied for the same but with regard to loans, they were released only after the applicant produced necessary title papers and security.

As a part of the rehabilitation efforts, some government housing facilities for lower income groups such as those built by the Gujarat Housing Board and Municipal slum rehabilitation quarters were reconstructed in the same site that they were earlier using brick, cement and Galvanized Curved Corrugated (GCC) roof regardless of whether the earlier houses were *kuccha*. The government gave 385 such applications a sanction of ₹ 172,360 for repair and reconstruction to houses where subsidy was found to be inadequate and 700 huts, which were damaged, were reconstructed in 42 different localities (*Ibid*). Subsequently the Ahmedabad Municipal Corporation allotted temporary accommodation to the mainly Muslim displaced in vacant plots in New Bapunagar, which subsequently became one of the settlements of Indira Garibnagar Slum (Shani, 2007, p. 123).

The displacement of thousands of Muslims due to the violence in 1969, which the camps bore testimony to, also meant a loss of livelihood and even the means of livelihood for thousands as those who had been rendered homeless had lost all their possessions that included their tools, instruments and other means of livelihood. According to one account, the entire Muslim Chhipa community living near Astodia Gate, Abdulwada, who specialized in block printing, was wiped out from their trade there.[84] Khan Abdul Gaffar Khan or 'Badshah Khan' who had visited Ahmedabad then was informed that 1500 artisans had left Gujarat. The Congress government's 'long term relief and rehabilitation' measures to help those who had lost their means of livelihood was to announce a subsidy of ₹100 for purchase of tools and equipment not exceeding the extent of original loss

---

84   Professor Abid Samshi (retired Professor at St. Xavier's College, Ahmedabad), interview by author.

or damage. In a similar measure state government orders provided subsidy and loans to Maldhari, cattle breeders etc. who had lost their animals. A committee was also appointed for advancing loans to shopkeepers and industrial units, which had suffered damage. The then state government also provided monetary assistance to an organization called Bazme Khatoon, which took on the care of widows and orphans who were rendered destitute. It is important to note that after depositions and representations by several civil society organizations regarding the damage to places of worship, the then state government gave subsidy and loan for reconstruction of places of worship that were damaged at the same rate that was given to private buildings. However, in comparison to the large scale destruction caused by the violence, as pointed out by the Reddy Commission, the amount spent by the Hitendra Desai government on relief though large, was insignificant when compared to the damage done and suffering undergone by the victims (*ibid*, p. 211).

In the next major communal riot, which took place in 1981 during the upper castes' movement against the reservation system where violent clashes that started in Ahmedabad and spread to 18 out of the then 19 districts in Gujarat for up to six months and in many villages of north and central Gujarat, Dalit homes were burned displacing them for a while. The government had then come out with an order that fixed the assistance for death at ₹ 1 lakh per person.[85] In 1985 when violence broke out in Ahmedabad again over the Madhavsinh Solanki government's decision to extend the reservation system to more backward communities, and eventually took a communal turn, hundreds of houses were burned down and thousands of people, mostly Muslims, were displaced and forced to take shelter in relief camps (Shani, 2007, p. 123) as strikes, curfews, school closings, *bandhs* ('shutdowns' of businesses, shops and offices), and tight restrictions on public transportation disrupted life for six consecutive months in the city, far longer than any of the previous riots (Spodek, 1989, p. 766). '*Ahmdavad ma nagrik bhaybhit banyache*' (the people of Ahmedabad have become fearful) – that fear among citizens in Ahmedabad city was palpable and many persons were leaving Ahmedabad due to the violence[86] was discussed in the legislative assembly for serious consideration and strict action by the

---

85 Government of Gujarat, Revenue Department, Order No/RHL/1090/1031/S4, 4 January 1981.

86 Gujarat Vidhan Sabha Debates, Part II, Book 7, July 1985, 428–33.

government.[87] In Sabarkantha district, at places like Idar and Prantij, houses and shops were set on fire.[88] What started as protests by upper and middle castes against the government's reservation policy had led to a situation of increasing lawlessness where anti social elements were also emboldened to indulge in looting. In the state legislative assembly concerns were raised about the security of the citizen and the restoration of the feeling of safety of the citizens of Gujarat *gujratne nagrikone salamatino bhavana*.[89] In the Report of the Commission of Inquiry (henceforth Dave Commission Report) headed by Justice VS Dave, which was appointed to inquire into the riots, testimonies of both Hindus and Muslims mentioned that their hutments were set on fire in the presence of the police. According to testimonies of those that deposed before the Commission in Bapunagar not only did the local police take sides in the clashes, they also helped to organize the violence. The government acknowledged that 25,469 people were affected by violence in Godhra, Bharuch, Rajkot, Jamnagar, Ahmedabad, Viramgam, Nadiad, Kadi, Mehsana, Visnagar, Patan, Siddhpur, Vadodara, and Surat.[90] According to one estimate, the violence had left some 275 people dead, thousands injured, tens of thousands homeless, and a loss of property and trade estimated at ₹ 2,200 crores.[91] The Dave Commission Report held that Muslims were the main victims of the riots, 2,500 of their houses had been damaged, 1,500 shops had been burned or looted, approximately 100 Muslims had been murdered, 400 stabbed and hundreds severely injured. Around 12,000 Muslims had been rendered homeless and 900 had been arrested.[92]

In a practice that came to be followed until the 2002 violence, victims in relief camps were given a cash dole of ₹ 5 per day per head and a total assistance including household kits was limited to ₹ 650.[93] The government maintained that ₹ 20,000 had been given as relief in case of death and ₹ 5000 was given in case of

---

87   Gujarat Vidhan Sabha Debates, Part II Book 52, 18 Feb 1991, 727–28. (Chimanbhai Patel)

88   Gujarat Vidhan Sabha Debates, Part II, Book 5, July 1985.

89   Gujarat Vidhan Sabha Debates, Part II, Book 9, January 1985, 571.

90   Gujarat Vidhan Sabha Debates, Part 2, Book 10, January 1986.

91   Quoted in Spodek, *Ahmedabad 1985 Riots*, 60 and 119.

92   Government of Gujarat, *Report of the Commission of Inquiry: Into the Incidents of Violence and Disturbances which Took Place at Various Places in the State of Gujarat since February, 1985 to 18th July 1985* by Justice V. S. Dave, Ahmedabad, April 1990, Vol. III, annexures XXXVII and XXXVIII, 439–40. (Henceforth cited as Commission of Inquiry 1990).

93   Government of Gujarat, Response of the State Government on the Proceedings on 1/4/2002 of the National Human Rights Commission (Sachivalaya, Gandhinagar), 29.

injury or permanent disability although there were allegations of discrimination in the disbursing of relief.[94] In the case of injury however a little over ₹ 500 per person was given (*ibid*). Moreover, the existing rules of assistance to those who sustained injuries in communal riots involved a cumbersome procedure for reimbursement of expenditure incurred on medicines after bills were duly certified by a proper authority.[95]

In 1986 the violence triggered by caste-based reservations suddenly turned communal. Given the already volatile situation, the annual procession of the chariot carrying the revered idol of the Jagganath temple thronged by massive crowds through the narrow streets of Ahmedabad during the annual *rathyatra* turned violent and led to communal riots that continued for three months from March to May 1986 spreading to places such as Vadodara, Veravan (Junagad), Junagad, Palanpur (Banaskantha), Amreli, Borsad (Kheda), Jamnagar, Godhra (Panchmahal), Devgad Bariya (Dahod), Svarkunkala (Bhavnagar) as well[96] killing an estimated 80 persons, wounding hundreds, rendering thousands displaced and causing losses to business amounting to an estimated ₹ 150 crores in one week of violence (Spodek, 1989, p. 777). The then minister of state for internal security, P Chidambaram pulled up Congress MLAs and councillors for not visiting their constituencies during the riots and a police inspector who connived in the violence in 1986 was transferred later by the then chief minister Amarsinh Chaudhary. The home minister also threatened the police with drastic action if violence was not brought under control (Engineer and Tanushri, 1986, p. 1346). However, sporadic incidents of violence continued even after that from June 1986 to June 1987 in a number of places with the highest number of incidents i.e., 12 in Ahmedabad, nine in Baroda and seven in Bharuch.[97] In Ahmedabad, Malek Saban Stadium at Bapunagar, which was the site of a camp in 1969, was turned into a camp again and ran for close to seven months in 1986 while a camp in Juhapura on the outskirts ran for a month.[98] According to the Congress-led state government, for those affected by the violence from

---

94   Gujarat Vidhan Sabha Debates, Part 2, 22 July 1987.

95   Response of the State Government one the proceedings on 1 April 2002 of the National Human Rights Commission *Suo motu* Case No. 1150/6/2001–2002, 1 April 2002, at 28.

96   'The names of the districts to which these towns belong have been mentioned in parenthesis and in places where they have not, the names of the district headquarters match those of the cities.' Gujarat Vidhan Sabha Debates, Part II, Book 19, August 1986, 7.

97   Vidhan Sabha Debates, February 1988, 859.

98   *Times of India*, 30 April 2002.

1984–87 ₹ 20,000 was given for death of a person and ₹ 5000 for injury. In 1986, through a resolution dated 21/7/1986, assistance for loss of moveable properties depending on actual loss was increased incrementally from ₹ 2000 to ₹ 3000 while the *ex gratia* assistance for loss of earning assets was increased from ₹ 5000 to ₹ 10000 in case of earning assets.[99] The Rajiv Gandhi-led central government in 1985 had also launched the Indira Awaas Yojana (IAY) as a sub-scheme with the purported intent of meeting the housing needs of the rural poor that included a provision for riot affected victims. However, the scheme was primarily aimed at people in rural areas who were below the poverty line belonging to SCs/STs, freed bonded labourers and non-SC/ST categories in the construction of dwelling units and in the upgrading of existing unserviceable *kutcha* houses by providing grant-in-aid and was to be allotted according to the *panchayat*, with only five per cent of the allocation for those affected by exigencies including riots.[100] Given the scale of the displacement and communal violence in Gujarat this scheme had negligible relevance.

By this time, the many riots experienced by Ahmedabad had led to its reputation as a *samvedansheel shahar*, which means sensitive or disturbed city.[101] With prevailing tensions and riots breaking out repeatedly in prolonged instances of violence, Muslims and Hindus had begun to sell their houses in neighbourhoods where they once lived side by side to buy houses in areas that had a concentration of members of their own community, and were therefore considered 'safe'. Such processes of people preferring to live among their co-religionists have been noted in other cities such as Mumbai as well. However, given the persistent social and political instability in Gujarat that didn't seem to let up during the 1980s and 90s, coupled with the Gujarati culture of emphasis on profit and business, the buying and selling of property under these pressures led to intense land speculation (Khan, 2012) so that initially Muslim properties in areas of concentration of Hindu population received much less than their worth and the same was the case with property owned by Hindus in areas of Muslim concentration. Distress selling of houses from people in both communities led to partition of areas of mixed living like Bapunagar (Shani, 2007, p. 214), Gomtipur, Gupta Nagar etc. into distinct Hindu and Muslim *ilakas* areas separated by a 'border' marking where the Hindu area ended and the Muslim area began.

---

99 *Ibid.*

100 *Ministry of Rural Development*, n.d., http://rural.nic.in/rh.htm (accessed 13 May 2011).

101 Gujarat Vidhan Sabha Debates, Part II, Book 9, January 1985, 571.

Following a representation by a few Muslims to the then chief minister Madhav Sinh Solanki, the Congress-led state government, through an ordinance, enacted 'The Gujarat Prohibition of Transfer of Immovable Property and Provisions for Protection of Tenants from Eviction from Premises in Disturbed Areas Act', 1986 under which certain areas of Ahmedabad, which were riot prone were declared as disturbed areas, where property could not be bought or sold without the permission of the collector. In effect it meant that Hindus and Muslims could not sell or buy land from each other in these places. This act was limited to certain areas of some police stations of the Ahmedabad Police Commissionerate and District Superintendent of Police (Rural) Ahmedabad areas that the government declared as disturbed. A disturbed area was defined as follows,

> The state government, having regard to the intensity and duration of riot or violence of mob and such other factors in an area is of the opinion that public order in that area was disturbed for a substantial period by reason of riot or violence of mob during the period commencing from 18th March, 1985 and ending on the day immediately before the commencement of this act, it may, by notification in the *Official Gazette*, declare such area to be a disturbed area. (The Gujarat Government Gazette 1986, pp. 42–1).

The act was to ensure that people got a fair value for the property and that distress sale was prevented. In effect, the Act made it more difficult for Muslims than Hindus to buy property as those who wanted to live in middle class localities that were more serviced on the western side of Ahmedabad and not in 'ghettoes,' i.e., Juhapura on the periphery of the city or areas of Muslim concentration such as Jamalpur in the walled city, had very few choices such as Paldi or a handful of colonies around Muslim Society in Navrangpura for which they had to pay astronomical amounts as the demand for these houses increased. Hindus on the other hand could make a huge profit by selling their houses in these areas and buying a house anywhere in the city for less than half the price.[102]

Just a few years later when BJP leader L. K. Advani launched his *rathyatra* which sparked communal riots in several places *en route* in Gujarat, in Ahmedabad the violence went on for four months as Dalits and Muslims clashed in industrial neighbourhoods and houses of upper class Muslims were attacked in the city.[103] In the atmosphere of communal tensions and mistrust even the most mundane

---

102 Zakia Jowher (Indian Social Institute), interview by author, 4 April 2009.
103 *Ibid.*

of fights and conflicts such as the unavailability of movie tickets in Patan had the potential to spiral into breakdown of public order and where people were emboldened to undertake antisocial activities and where *khoonani koshish, vyatha, irja pohochvadna dhad ane, loot* attempts to murder, injure and loot were witnessed in Patan as well as Mehsana. The issue of fear spreading through this was again deliberated upon in the state assembly[104] as people from communally sensitive areas started to flee their homes for camps. A camp in Shah Alam *dargah* ran for a little more than three months while camps at Juhapura remained for about a month.[105] The chief minister (Madhavsinh Solanki) then responding to a question in the legislative assembly about what measures the government had taken after six months of communal rioting to assuage the fear and insecurity among the minorities replied that the *hijrati* (displaced) are returning to their original dwellings but have also been given police protection. The government had then committed to setting up 'fixed points' for police in sensitive areas, responding to calls for help immediately through special control rooms and setting up peace committees. The then chief minister Chimanbhai Patel had, on the floor of the house, claimed to have issued instructions to government functionaries such as district magistrate (DM) and police commissioner to meet community leaders, to take up their complaints, remove their fears and constantly be in touch with minority community leaders. To create an atmosphere of trust among the minorities, his government claimed to have taken the help of NGOs as well.[106] The Congress government had then declared a relief of ₹ 1 lakh for each of the deceased persons 'as per rules', which meant that like in the past, the heirs of the deceased had to produce proof of being an heir. Of this 1 lakh the government decided that, ₹ 30,000 cash would be given from the government's relief fund, ₹ 60,000 would be given in the form of Sardar Sarovar Narmada Nigam bonds, and ₹ 10,000 cash would be given from the chief minister's relief fund.[107]

With repeated occurrence of riots in Vadodara especially in Wadi, Panigate, Machipeeth and other such old city areas of Vadodara that had acquired a reputation of being communally sensitive areas, there were demands for the government to come out with stringent schemes to check communal

---

104 Gujarat Vidhan Sabha Debates, Part II Book 53, March 1990, 189.

105 *Times of India*, 30 April 2002

106 Gujarat Vidhan Sabha Debates, Part II Book 52, 18 February 1991, 727–28.

107 Gujarat Vidhan Sabha, 8th Gujarat Vidhan Sabha, 4th session, Gujarat Vidhan Sabha Secretariat (Gandhinagar: March 1991).

violence in 1991. In addition to the usual measures of peace committees in the neighbourhood, combing operations to search for weapons, the government set out strict conditions for taking out religious processions, which were often a trigger for outbreak of violence especially in narrow streets of old city areas. The coalition government led by Chimanbhai Patel also extended the 'The Gujarat Prohibition of Transfer of Immovable Property and Provisions for Protection of Tenants from Eviction from Premises in Disturbed Areas Act' in 1991. However, the Act proved to be ineffective as people would conduct transactions on property in disturbed areas by bribing authorities for an exemption, by renting it out through an agreement on stamp paper or by manipulating the clause of power of attorney. Moreover, the Act did not seem to have much effect because processes of polarisation were already in full sway on the ground.

Once again during the chief ministership of Chimanbhai Patel who in 1992 led the government of a Janata Dal (G) and Congress alliance, Gujarat witnessed some of the worst communal clashes in the otherwise peaceful Surat, which accounted for 190 deaths that was more than half the deaths in the entire state of Gujarat during that riot (Yagnik and Sheth, 2005, p. 264). His government had then announced an assistance of ₹ 5000–50,000 to affected persons whose houses were destroyed in the violence.[108]

The relief conceived by the government since then has been faithfully adhered to in scale with very negligible increments. In what can be considered as immediate relief the government provided food for relief camps, cash doles which till 2002 were ₹ 5 per day and were increased to ₹ 7 per day and *gharvakhri* or assistance for household goods given to people in camps ostensibly to help those dispossessed to start anew but which through the 1980s and 1990s was as little as ₹ 1250 and was increased to ₹ 2500 in 2002. Assistance offered in case of death and injury were also low and as arbitrary as in 1969 when a distinction was made of assistance of ₹ 500 for an earning member and ₹ 250 for any other member of the family. The state also provided assistance for loss of earning assets, which provided assistance to self employed but not to those employed wage earners who lost their livelihood. Assistance for housing was also purportedly intended only for structural damage of four walls and ceiling and not loss of household goods, which eventually worked out to much less than even that, and assistance for the losses in commercial or industrial establishments. The analyses of categories of 'relief' or 'assistance' to

---

108 Government of Gujarat, Revenue Department, GR No.RHL/1092/4077/S-4, 19 December 1992.

victims of communal violence given gratuitously sometimes varied according to the government of the day. However, there was an overall adherence to existing categories of assistance with very little increase in the scale of assistance. The question of those displaced by violence although framed differently as *hijratis* or through questions on *gharvakhri ane gharote nuksan* dispossession and damage to houses came up in the 1990s.[109] However, far from being compensation for the losses, both personal and material, suffered due to violence, the paltry amounts doled out by the government under various criteria was intended only as *rahat* 'relief' for those *asargrast* who were affected by communal violence and had been dispossessed and displaced.

Relief instead of rights: The language of relief

In government practice relief for riot victims is treated as emergency relief, which has been allotted as a subject of the revenue department, where the commissioner of relief coordinates relief at the secretariat level and the district collectors and district development officers at the field level. The office of the commissioner of relief implements relief work through line departments like the health department for medical examination of camp inmates, deworming, pregnancy cases etc., civil supplies department for obtaining food for camps, women and child development department etc. Administrative mechanisms in case of relief for natural disasters on the other hand have been developed, after developments at the national level for the same, under the Gujarat State Disaster Management Authority (GSDMA). GSDMA also operates only through line agencies/departments and particularly through the collectors and district development officers.

In 2001, when Gujarat suffered a massive earthquake in Kutch that claimed up to 13,000 thousand lives and destroyed an estimated 900 villages, the government was faced with a mammoth humanitarian challenge. The GDSMA was set up soon after the earthquake in 2001 on 8 February, headed by the chief minister Narendra Modi to implement relief, rehabilitation and reconstruction work while agencies such as World Bank, Asian Development Bank and many international NGOs had also set up camp in the area. The government accepted aid from within and outside the country, which came in significant contributions along with the help of secular NGOs and faith-based relief organizations such as the Islami Relief Committee and Evangelical Fellowship of India Commission on Relief (EFICOR) for rebuilding villages,

109 Gujarat Vidhan Sabha Debates, Part II, Book 52, September 1991, 92–93.

while among the first to volunteer and make their presence felt particularly in helping with the last rites of the dead were volunteers of right wing groups such as the RSS. Many leaders of the ruling BJP were also intimately involved with relief and reconstruction work as were members of Congress Party (Simpson and Corbridge 2006, p. 574). Initially there was much criticism of the government given the massive scale of destruction left behind by the earthquake that exposed bureaucratic inadequacies, leading to policy changes and several transfers. Eventually, despite the criticism, the government's involvement in relief and rehabilitation enabled by the aid that poured in through sympathizers within and outside India, GDSMA became, even if by the Narendra Modi government's own assessment, a model for other states in disaster management. However, the response of the state in relief, rehabilitation and reconstruction efforts for those displaced by the earthquake stands in stark contrast to its response for those affected and displaced by the violence in 2002.

In 2002 in the light of the humanitarian situation when according to official figures there were more than one and a half lakh people seeking shelter in camps,[110] for lack of a better framework, the NHRC, as well as other civil society members had recommended that GSDMA, which had received substantial aid both nationally and internationally for the management of relief work for the victims of the 2001 earthquake, take up relief work for those affected by the violence as well.[111] The government, however, declined to accept the suggestion to involve the GSDMA citing reasons of the small staff that was already being engaged in rehabilitation of earthquake victims.

The recommendation for relief efforts to be taken up by the GSDMA was made as the scope of its authority covers both natural and man-made disasters and in it, administrative mechanisms had been recently put in place to deal with relief, rehabilitation and reconstruction efforts. However, as far back in 1969 the Reddy Commission Report had held that relief and rehabilitation of those affected by communal violence 'should not be tackled on the footing of the relief afforded on the basis of natural calamities.' The Commission had even suggested that punitive tax should be levied on the community which instigated the riots and the tax be used for relief of persons in the affected community (Reddy Commission Report, 1970, p. 222). The point the Reddy Commission Report seemed to be

---

110 See note 56.

111 Government of Gujarat, *Response of the State Government on the Proceedings on 1/4/2002 of the National Human Rights Commission*, 33.

making was that relief and rehabilitation in case of communal violence should not be handled as in the case of natural disasters where the government could at best take pre-emptive measures to warn and evacuate people, to ameliorate the inevitable, unavoidable consequences of nature[112] but rather that society should be held responsible. The issue of creating accountability, however, is crucial but it requires more than just fixing responsibility vaguely on society as the Reddy Commission suggested, to the exclusion of the state.

Riots in Gujarat are often referred to as *toofaan* or storm. Notions that place communal violence as man-made disasters *manav sarjit mushkilo* (man made disasters) on par with natural disasters *kudarat sarjit mushkilo* (natural disasters) are not uncommon in political parlance,[113] in state practices, among civil society groups, and even in academic understandings (Parsuraman and Unnikrishnan, 2000). During the debates in the legislative assembly on the communal turn that the movement for reservations had taken in the prolonged period of caste based violence in 1985–86, the comparison of riots as man-made disasters along with natural disasters was made, a comparison that continues to have much currency to date. In the Indira Awas Yojana, the only central scheme that mentioned housing for those affected by communal riots, they find a share among five per cent of the central allocation for meeting exigencies arising out of natural calamities along with 'other emergent situations like riot, arson, fire, rehabilitation etc.'[114] The many GRs that the Government of Gujrat came up with for the *asargrast* (riot affected persons) in 2002, in keeping with the GRs in previous instances of communal violence all used the language of 'assistance' that was 'gratuitous', which literally means given as a favour rather than as any legal requirement, which belie the understanding of communal violence as being on par with other exigencies such as fire, arson or natural disasters.[115] This

---

112 Modern technocratic and managerial notions of disaster management however have also been challenged. For instance in A. Oliver-Smith, 2006, in 'Theorising Vulnerability in a Globalised World: A Political Ecology Perspective', in *Mapping Vulnerability: Disasters, Development and People*, edited by G. Bankoff *et al.*, 10–24 (London: Earthscan) argues that among pre modern Andean people there was a cultural tradition of disaster awareness reflected in territoriality and settlement patterns.

113 Gujarat Vidhan Sabha Debates, Part II, Book 9, January 1985, 788; Gujarat Vidhan Sabha Debates, 10th Gujarat Vidhan Sabha, 13 March 2002, 148–49; Gujarat Vidhan Sabha Debates, 10th Vidhan Sabha, 15–16 March 2002, 21 (Amarsinhbhai Chaudhary).

114 See note 99.

115 Joya Chatterjee has argued about state practices towards displaced in the partition of the subcontinent employing the language of charity. (Chatterjee, 2001, 37).

has been the practice of the state governments across India including Gujarat. Recent normative developments such as the UN guiding principles on IDPs in 1998 have sought to disseminate the notion of state responsibility towards rehabilitation and repatriation of displaced persons.[116]

Both the terms compensation and reparation refer to the payment of an amount to make amends for wrong done. However, far from being compensation for the losses, both personal and material suffered due to violence, the paltry amounts doled out by the government under various criteria are at best as the word suggests 'relief' or 'assistance'. Moreover, even applying the framework of relief for natural disasters to situations of prolonged communal violence such as those witnessed in Gujarat where there is a breakdown of law and order and targeted violence against a particular group, would tantamount to equating the victims of communal violence, which involves larger and political issues, with other exigencies, and absolves the state of any responsibility.

When as chief minister of Gujarat Narendra Modi expressed sympathy regarding the violence of 2002 in public address for the first time, albeit 10 years after the violence, he placed it alongside natural calamities, such as the massive earthquake in 2001 that Gujarat 'became a victim to' since the beginning of this century.

> 21st century did not begin well for Gujarat. In 2001, the devastating republic on our republic day, took a very heavy toll. In the subsequent year, Gujarat became a victim of communal violence. We lost innocent lives, suffered devastation of property and endured a lot of pain. One can visualize what all we have gone through.[117]

The violence in 2002, referred to as a pogrom (Brass, 2003, p. 388; Varshney, 2004) and genocide (Nussbaum, 2007, p. 45; Thapar, 2004, p. 201) and that a number of investigative and independent media reportage alleged his government to be complicit in was thus held as a situation that happened to Gujarat much like an earthquake.

In the governance of communal violence that the many riots in the state of

---

116 United Nations, UN Guiding Principles on Internal Displacement, UN Document E/ CN.4/ 1998/ 53/ Add.2. Principle 29.2. 'Competent authorities have the duty and responsibility to assist returned and/or resettled internally displaced persons to recover, to the extent possible, their property and possessions which they left behind or were dispossessed of upon their displacement. When recovery of property and possessions is not possible, competent authorities shall provide or assist these persons in obtaining appropriate compensation or another form of just reparation.'

117 Narendra Modi, Letter to countrymen on eve of 3 day fast, http://www.narendramodi. in, (accessed on 30 March 2012).

Gujarat afford analytical visibility to, there was at least an attempt by the state to project itself as the secular guarantor of order and security for its 'citizens' even through prolonged periods of communal violence in the 1980s and 1990s. In the debates in the legislative assembly on the issue of communal riots during the decades of 80s and 90s that saw much social and political instability and periods of prolonged communal violence in Gujarat one finds debates characterized by concerns about the minority question 'lagumatino prashno upar vishesh dhyan aapvama aavshe',[118] (we should give special attention to the question of minorities) the extent of disbursal of relief, law and order, the safety and security of citizens regardless of their community and assuaging the feeling of asalamati ane bhayni lagni (fear and insecurity among minorities). During 1985 riots for instance, when Chimanbhai Patel asked the government to take serious note of situation of communal violence because of the fear among the citizens of Ahmedabad, the then Congress chief minister Amarsinh Chaudhari claimed that he himself was paying continuous detailed attention to the situation the whole day till he saw results. Speaking in the assembly he argued that the establishment of peace in Ahmedabad was everyone's moral responsibility. Importantly, the restoration of peace from communal strife was framed in terms of development as Gujaratna vikasna hitma cche (in the interest of development in Gujarat).[119] Just a few years later however, in 1990 when Chimanbhai Patel was in the position of chief minister himself and faced with the question of increasing lawlessness due to communal violence and its coalition partner BJP's involvement in it, he seemed to be arguing that communal violence was endemic to Gujarat when he defended his coalition government by arguing that governments cannot be blamed for riots that have happened even in the past as 'Gujaratma aa vastu cche' there is this thing (communal violence) in Gujarat and the government was alert to it.

Thomas Blom Hansen has argued that the modern Indian state seeks to maintain the 'myth of the state' as sovereign that legitimates itself as the guarantor of order and protection from violence even though this myth was shattered during major communal riots in other parts of India for those in Mumbai during the riots in 1992 (Hansen, 2012, p. 32). During major communal riots in Gujarat, such as in 1969 and 1985–86, the participation of members of the ruling political party in violence, delay of decision-makers in the state machinery, inaction of

---

118 Gujarat Vidhan Sabha Debates, Part II, Book 53, March 1990, 191. (Chimanbhai Patel, chief minister).

119 Gujarat Vidhan Sabha Debates, Part I, Book 85, March 1984, 433. (Amarsinhbhai Chaudhari).

state functionaries such as the police and even instances of involvement of the police have been brought to light through testimonies in Commissions of Inquiry, newspaper reports and academics who studied those episodes of violence (Shah 1970, 1987; Shani, 2007). However, in the debates in the Gujarat Legislative Assembly one also finds the articulation of the commitment to provide security to minorities and the guarantee of protection of the life and property of all 'citizens'. During the violence in 2002 however, despite the furore in the Legislative Assembly over the violence and sloganeering and disruption by members of Congress led by Amarsinhbhai Choudhary to 'stop the violence', there was a conspicuous absence of any commitment or nod in the direction of secularism or citizenship by the head of the administration led by Narendra Modi. In the state where the administration has been noted for the convergence of state functionaries with a majoritarian and nationalist cultural agenda reflected in the bureaucracy, police and the public service providers in sectors such as health and education (Sud, 2012, p. 196), Mayaben Kodnani, MLA, who led and encouraged the mob in Naroda Patiya was elevated to the position of Minister for Women and Child Welfare in 2007 even while the case against her was pending in court. Whereas earlier instances of communal violence were denounced as a blot that lowered the prestige of Gujarat (*komi ramkhan kalankrupi cche*),[120] after the violence in 2002, Narendra Modi chose to campaign for state level elections that were then due through a *gaurav yatra* or a procession of pride.

What is also striking in the state's response, is that the government of Gujarat after 2002, by and large, managed to avoid addressing the issue of displacement and even using the term displacement. Responding to NHRC's notice, which pointed out to the fact of a sitting judge of the high court having to flee his house in the middle of the violence, the government replied that the judge had made the decision to move 'voluntarily' after assessing the situation. A few months later in response to NHRC, while referring to the rape of Bilkisbano the government again referred to fleeing Muslims as those who were 'migrating to safety'.[121] In one of its replies to the NHRC after referring to the role of the media, the government asserted, 'There is no agenda of the ruling party to drive out the Muslims by mobilizing grievances of the tribals.'[122] As late as 2009 the Modi government also appointed

---

120 Gujarat Vidhan Sabha Debates, Part II, Book 9, January 1985, 1260.

121 Government of Gujarat, Response to the National Human Rights Commission, dated 30 May 2002. D.O. No. SB.II.COM/102002/514, 19.

122 Government of Gujarat, Reply to Confidential Report of the National Human Rights Commission, *Op.cit.*, 15.

a commission to inquire into changes in the demographic pattern of Gujarat since independence and to identify reasons behind the 'polarisation' and 'migration' of population. The Commission was to study where people of different religions live, the area and the size of the population, in order to assess the total area in square meters occupied by people of different religious faiths, and where they lived and moved to every year since independence. While the commission's mandate was to give 'recommendations and policies on guidance for stopping polarisation of population in the state' the state government maintained that the allegations made by the court and the media against the state government about the 'polarisation of population on the basis of religion' were unscientific conclusions.[123]

The BJP government of Gujarat returned ₹ 19.1 crore of the central government package for those affected by the violence in 2002 as unutilized amount claiming that full relief had been paid.[124] However, when the United Progressive Alliance (UPA) government came to power in New Delhi, it announced an additional package of ₹ 262.44 crore in January 2007 in fulfillment of its election manifesto promise of relief for victims of the 2002 violence. This package, which was on par with the package given to the anti-Sikh riots of 1984, substantially increased the scales of assistance although it came five years after the violence. The next to kin of the dead were to be given ₹ 3.5 lakh in addition to the *ex gratia* of ₹ 1.5 lakh given by the state government as well as *ex gratia* amount for damage to residential property and uninsured commercial property of '10 times the amount given by the state government less amount paid'. The injured individuals were to be given ₹ 1.25 lakhs each in keeping with government practice however this relief was given gratuitously. The state's offering gratuitous payments to victims who have been displaced and dispossessed, however, is far removed from the logic or terminology of compensation and is indicative of a lacuna in the law that does not hold the state accountable for its responsibility to maintain law and order. In a landmark judgment in 1996 the Delhi High Court asked that 'compensation' instead of the established practice of 'ex gratia payment' be paid to riot victims of 1984 anti-Sikh riots. This verdict by Justice Anil Dev Singh, which ensured that the compensation paid to 2,700 victims of the 1984 anti–Sikh riots in New Delhi was increased from ₹ 20,000 to ₹ 2 lakh held that,

> The state cannot escape the liability to pay adequate compensation
> to the family of the person killed during riots as his or her life has

---

123 *The Indian Express,* 4 July 2009.
124 *The Indian Express,* 15 May 2009.

been extinguished in clear violation of Article 21 of the Constitution which mandates that life cannot be taken away except according to the procedure established by law.

While this judgment did subsequently influence central government decisions on payment of relief in case of victims of communal riots,[125] governments have adhered to established practice of offering this amount as 'ex gratia payment' that is far removed from principles of compensation let alone reparation and can be arbitrary.

The examination of the governance of communal violence through state responses in the many instances of communal riots in Gujarat reveal that while the scale of relief offered in different categories of assistance for the victims of communal violence was increased howsoever variably, the categories of assistance remained the same, even in case of the latest relief package offered by the UPA government in 2007. Successive governments in Gujarat have adhered to precedent and offered 'assistance' to victims, which amounts to precious little per person and is not even intended to compensate victims for the losses suffered due to break down of law and order due to instances of communal violence. However, while successive governments in Gujarat have acted according to precedent with regard to relief for victims of communal violence, there are distinctly discernable differences in other areas of the response of Gujarat led by Narendra Modi in 2002 to the governance of communal violence and its aftereffects. The correspondence of NHRC and the government of Gujarat, independent and media reportage, including several fact finding team reports and investigative journalism, have illustrated the biased role of the state during the violence that was led by cultural nationalist groups such as VHP, BD and other functionaries of the Sangh Parivar that the BJP is a part of. The response of the state in 2002 in comparison with state responses historically further illustrate the distinctive shift in the state in 2002 where there is not even an attempt to project the myth of a neutral state or employ universalizing terms as it had in the past of the security of citizens. While protests from Congress-led opposition, given its own mixed record in the past, were ineffective in providing a constraint to the overwhelming dominance of cultural nationalist forces in the state, it was only bodies such as the NHRC and NCM that compelled the state to reply using the language of rights.

---

125 This payment of relief by the central government in case of Gujarat 2002 post-Godhra violence as well as the 1989 Bhagalpur riots was brought on par with the compensation paid in the anti-Sikh riots. *The Hindu*, 13 June 2008.

Moreover, the state government scrupulously avoided the term displacement or IDPs referring to it as migration which suggests that the movement was voluntary and not under compulsion. This illustrates the state's absence in the complex problem of displacement where a large number of people did not want to return to what was once their homes because it had become a place of vulnerability that was exposed during the violence and in some instances, a site where crimes had occured that after the violence held the probability of legal action and led to continued tensions in neighbourhoods.

4

Reconstruction and Rights through Self Help

Salimbhai Sindhi who lives in Al Falaha Relief Colony in 2009 was a picture of confidence as the owner of a cattle farm, having found a measure of success in rebuilding his life. However, he recalls the time a few years back when he was *sarpanch* of Kidiad village and there was a total sense of chaos and confusion during the violence in 2002 and 'nobody knew what to do.' Salimbhai's wife, son and 18 others from his extended family were among 74 other Muslims from his village who were killed by mobs when they were fleeing their village.[1] Out of the 74 Muslims from Kidiad village who were killed on the highway in Panchmahal district by mobs when they were fleeing their village packed in two tempos, 62 bodies were not found and were declared missing for up to seven years until they were finally declared dead. The violence that had pushed more than one and a half lakh Muslims into relief camps and others to places of Muslim concentration caused increasing polarization of population along religious lines. By 2008 however, increasingly voices from within the community began to urge Muslims[2] to move on from the violence and in the run up to the 2012 assembly elections more Muslims than ever before expressed support in public for the Bharatiya Janata Party (BJP), the party that was in power at the time of the violence in 2002 and that had continued to emphatically win elections in the state.

How does displacement affect the experience of citizenship rights? Displacement with regard to the 'refugee' is understood to create a radical disjunction between a person's familiar 'way of being' that affects the social and the personal (Daniel and Knudsen, 1995, pp. 6, 9) where the new reality of socio-political circumstances also entails altered parameters of daily life. In the troubled waters of the Indian

---

1   Salimbhai Sindhi (displaced from Kidiad, resident of Al Falaha Relief Colony, Modassa, Sabarkantha) interview by author, 22 March 2009.

2   Maulana Vastanvi's comments as Vice Chancellor of Darul Uloom Deoband created an uproar that forced him to step down, http://articles.timesofindia.indiatimes.com/2011-01-27/india/28367708_1_maulana-vastanvi-seminary-resignation-issue (accessed on 28 March 2011).

nation-state however, and in the context of Gujarat in particular that has claimed to have leapfrogged on the path of development since the violence in 2002 that caused displacement of Muslims and where there is public support among a number of Muslims for the same government after a decade, this becomes a pertinent question. According to the government of Gujarat normalcy had been established in the state within 72 hours of the outbreak of violence on 28 February 2002. While the administration of the government of Gujarat went about relief as was established in state practice by giving gratuitous assistance much like in the case of other exigencies, it turned a blind eye to the prevailing situation of fear and insecurity in the violence that occurred sporadically for four months because of which large number of Muslims did not want to return to their former homes where they were attacked. This chapter traces the various coping strategies that came up in response to the displacement of Muslims and the principal actors that emerged in reconstruction efforts. It examines the phenomena of relief colonies, an estimated 86 of which came up in 10 districts of Gujarat[3] and the strategic adjustments and negotiations made to get on with the act of living in the changed circumstances after the violence to gauge the effects of displacement and the agency of the displaced in the milieu of an economically 'vibrant' Gujarat.

Despite the then prime minister Atal Bihari Vajpayee's appeal, the relief that came in for those affected by the 2002 violence, was far less than the outpouring of public sympathy and donations witnessed as a result of the 2001 earthquake in Gujarat. The atmosphere in Gujarat in 2002 was so surcharged by communal tensions and the fear so palpable that even NGOs that were very active in relief and rehabilitation efforts during the time of the earthquake were comparatively restrained in their interventions for the victims of the post-Godhra violence given the widespread anger at the popular perception that the train was deliberately burned by a mob of Muslims and the political implications involved when the state government was so openly partisan.[4] Gagan Sethi, then member of NHRC monitoring committee for the 2001 earthquake relief and subsequent member of NHRC monitoring committee in 2004 had even requested police protection at that time.[5] NGOs did step in to make interventions that proved to be crucial such

3   Government of Gujarat, *Second Report on the Status of the Identified Resettlement Colonies of the 2002 Riots Affected in Gujarat Presented to the National Commission for Minorities*, New Delhi, 9 August 2007, 3.

4   Prasad Chacko (Action Aid, former Director, Behavioural Science Centre, Ahmedabad), in discussion with the author, 17 October 2008.

5   *Also Surviving State Hostility and Denial: A Survey of Relief Colonies for People Affected by*

as documenting what had happened, collecting testimonials of the victims, number of camp inmates, injured, sick etc., counseling traumatized survivors and creating livelihood options. As many as 30 NGOs came together under a collective called 'Citizens Initiative' in order to coordinate relief work amongst themselves. The Behavioural Science Centre (BSC) in St. Xavier's College, Ahmedabad, became a headquarter of sorts for NGOs to collect relief material and for social activists as well as for young students from different parts and of the country who had volunteered in response to an international NGO, Action Aid's online appeal for help.[6] Young students from different parts of India volunteered as *Aman Pathiks* (peace volunteers) to visit camps and help in relief work among the displaced. Among other efforts by NGOs to create livelihood options for inmates in camps were those of SEWA that engaged those in camps in Ahmedabad with paper bag making etc. and Himmat, an NGO started by two volunteers[7] along with the widows of Naroda Patiya to provide them livelihood options by sewing clothes. NGOs also made efforts at building peace between the two communities through initiatives such as arranging meetings between members of different communities and even organizing a camp for youth of a locality outside the communally charged atmosphere in Gujarat. However, these proved to be a drop in the ocean of continuing communal tensions.[8] There was also an instance of an NGO assisting the rebuilding of 168 houses in Boru village.[9] However, in the volatile situation where the state had openly aligned with the majoritarian position, the role of NGOs that had limited resources and could not afford to entirely antagonize the state government was constrained and all camps were run entirely by Muslim organizations themselves.[10]

Mass Violence in Gujarat 2002– A Report, Nyayagraha, December 2006, 29.

6   Monica Wahi (Co-founder, Himmat, Ahmedabad), in discussion with the author, 28 August 2008.

7   Monica Wahi and Zaid Shaikh (who were instrumental in setting up Himmat, Vatwa, Ahmedabad) in discussion with the author, 28 October 2008.

8   Gazalla Paul (Trustee of Samerth NGO, Vejalpur, Ahmedabad) in discussion with the author, 28 January 2009. Also Neera and Rafi (social activists who worked with women in relief camps of Ahmedabad), in discussion with the author, 16 February 2009.

9   There was also an instance of an NGO rebuilding 168 houses in Boru village. *Times of India*, 31 July 2002.

10 According to one NGO practitioner, NGOs that actively participated in relief and rehabilitation of the victims of the violence were subjected to audit and questioning by the state government authorities subsequently. Neera and Rafi (NGO practitioners, Ahmedabad) in discussion with author, 16 February 2009. Also, Prasad Chacko (Action

The transition from camps

'*Tamam buraiyan,* major evils had broken out in the camp', said a leader of one of
the faith-based Muslim relief organizations, riled at the fact that traditional social
norms of propriety and boundaries were thrown to the wind in the urgency of
meeting basic needs for the survival of thousands of people dispossessed by the
violence in camps.[11] This is why by the end of May 2002, organizations like his
were eager, like the state government, for the displaced to leave the camps and
return to their homes. Since April of 2002 itself, organizations from among the
Muslim community such as Jamiat ulema e Hind, Islami Relief Committee, Gujarat
Sarvajanik Relief Committee among others had started repair and rebuilding of
homes in areas like Naroda Gam in Ahmedabad, Gupta Nagar etc and Ode in
Anand. In Panderwada where 26 Muslims were killed, the Islami Relief Committee
managed to rebuild the houses of the displaced who returned. In Naroda Patiya
where 95 people were killed, a number of Muslims returned to houses that had
been reconstructed. In fact, according to one account, the number of Muslims
after the violence seemed to have increased in Naroda Patiya,[12] a fact that can be
ascribed to the perception of safety in numbers, although those that had rented
accommodation there stayed away. The scale of damage and destruction, however,
was too high for these organizations working in their individual capacities to
cover all areas adequately.[13] Moreover, given that this was a private initiative by
organizations of the minority community themselves and the urgency of the
situation and the lack of coordination among the various NGOs and faith-based
organizations working towards rehabilitation, a large number of displaced who
returned had to do so on their own strength. For instance in Randhikpur, the
village from where Bilkis Bano was raped while fleeing with 13 others who were
killed in March, 50 men returned to rebuild their houses after three and a half
months of living in camps despite the fact that not a single arrest had been made.[14]

While the government of Gujarat, on its part, moved towards a closure of relief
camps from May 2002 by stopping food supplies so that by June end all 40 camps

Aid, Ahmedabad) in discussion with author, 17 October 2008.

11   Afzal Menon (Gujarat Sarvajanik Relief Committee, Ahmedabad) in discussion with
     author, 19 December 2008.

12   Noorjahan Abdul Kadir Sheikh (resident, Faisal Park Relief Colony) interview by author,
     19 December 2008.

13   Professor Ansari (Paldi, Ahmedabad) in discussion with author, 11 December 2008.

14   *The Indian Express,* 20 June 2002.

in districts of north and central Gujarat as well as several camps in Ahmedabad were declared closed[15] and by August, by which time it had been six months since when the violence had begun, most of the camps were declared closed, even in the 'closed' relief camps however, a number of displaced families refused to leave. This was despite the fact that rain flooded camps that were in open *maidans* and fields. Sharifaben, a widow among the thousands of displaced from rural areas of Sabarkantha and neighbouring districts who had taken shelter in the outskirts of Himmatnagar, in a large open ground off the highway described how she and other families took shelter from rain in an unfinished RTO building on the other side of the road even as their newly acquired belongings of relief material in the camp bobbed up and down in their water logged camp.[16] In Ahmedabad, there were camps that although declared closed by government, served as a shelter for daily wage earners who supported themselves by going out to find work but returned to the camp in the evening.[17] Even in rural Sabarkantha, of the 81 affected villages in Idar *taluka* Muslims had returned to stay in only ten villages while in some villages they would go for farming in the daytime and return at night.[18] An old primary teacher in a school in Madhepura village in Dhansura *taluka*, Sabarkantha who had been threatened during the violence by people from his own village continued to commute daily from Garib Nawaz Relief camp in Modassa, a town with a large Muslim concentration, to the school in Madhepura.[19]

The government's course of action was for the displaced to leave camps and return to their original homes with the help of district level administration in rural areas and the collectorate in cities along with the police should a situation of law and order arise. Officials of the collectorate and district development officers held meetings between villagers and the displaced. Ramjanishah Gulabshah Diwan, a primary school teacher who happened to be visiting his relatives along with his children while taking a break from the relief camp during vacations found himself to be the sole attendee from among the displaced Muslims in his village at a peace committee meeting called by the Collector.

---

15   *The Times of India*, 31 July 2002.

16   Sharifaben (resident of Kifayatnagar Relief Colony, Himmatnagar, Sabarkantha) interview by author, 30 March 2009.

17   *The Indian Express*, 29 August 2002.

18   *Times of India*, 27 July 2002.

19   Diwan Ramjanishah Gulabshah (resident Sahara Colony, Modasa, Sabarkantha) interview by author, 22 March 2009.

I went there so they made me sit on a seat, and whoever were the *toofan bananewale* (the rioters) they all came with pant shirt and had come and sat down. So *saab* (Sir) and everyone said (in that one press reporter was also there) so they said where are your other people, I said our other people are all in the Modasssa relief camp. So they asked can those people come here? Then I told them that now those people will not come at all, because they are all scared.... Then the meeting got over, then they said, even then you try. I said I will try but we dont like the *mahaul* atmosphere here now. The trust that we had kept on them, that trust they have broken, now how will we trust them. Today they have destroyed even their houses of the people who used to stay here since years, so then again we will come, again they will break it. Again, they will harm them. This time we got saved, again we are not going to be saved are we? Next time they will certainly kill us. How can we trust them? is there any guarantee for them?

So *saab* said we can only guarantee (*your safety*) till our protection is there, ahead of that how can we give guarantee? So from there we came to Garib Nawaz camp.

There were also instances such as Pavagad in Vadodara, Mogri, Sisva, Ode, Karamsad and Vasad in Anand where even if Muslims were willing to return with the help of the district administration, there were instances where the villagers made it clear, in no uncertain terms to the displaced, as well as to the district officials, that they did not want Muslims to return to their houses in the village.[20] In case of Ode village, some Muslim families did eventually return but only those who lived in the area on the periphery of the village where there was a *mohalla* that had to initially face instances of stone pelting before the situation calmed down after the intervention of the police. In Mogri a village in Anand district that has been on the map of the Green Revolution and Milk Revolution, villagers reacted violently when attempts were made by Muslims to return. Two families from the village that dealt in firecrackers returned after the violence but they could only return to their shops outside the village just off the highway and tellingly, not to their houses in the village. They had to first clean up and rebuild their houses, which were mainly extensions of their shops and keep watch while they did that. They give credit of their return to one police sub inspector (PSI)

---

20   *Times of India*, 23 April 2002.

who did the rounds and was serious about not allowing any untoward incident from happening. Only after months of keeping a vigil at night in shifts the father son duo of the family was able to take possession and function on the property as they did before. The village however, was clearly off limits for Muslims who had filed cases against the attackers. Since these villagers refused to compromise and withdraw charges, they were not allowed to return.[21]

In Deshotar village in Sabarkantha an accused in a case of attack on Muslim houses in the village was among the clients getting his farm equipment fixed from a Muslim's shop that he had attacked during the violence, depicts the predicament in many villages where Muslims on return had to interact in quotidian matters and everyday interactions with people who had attacked them at the time of the violence. As activist Ganesh Devy explained, 'You can't hide behind anonymity in a village. Everybody knows everybody, making it very difficult to build bridges. In a city, on the other hand, you can merge with a crowd.'[22] Muslims in this same village had returned to their shops in 2003 gingerly testing the waters each day, amidst threats to leave. Explaining how he returned, one shopkeeper said, 'first we came for an hour. Then the next day we stayed for three quarters of an hour and went, the third day we stayed for one and a half hours, on the fourth day we stayed for two hours. Like that we gained our ground (*humne jamaya*). In this way we sit the whole day now, this is how we gradually came and sat.' They did gradually establish their presence in this way, but this was only with regard to their shops. Their families continue to live in Kesarpura, a village with almost 90 per cent Muslim population from where the men commute to their shops daily. After two years some Muslims with shops got their families to live with them in their houses, which were extensions behind their shop, while others continued to commute to and from their business in the village.[23]

However, for some returning to their original homes was not an option at all. '*Saval hi nahin*', absolutely out of question said Ayyubbhai from Kidiad village from where 74 Muslims were killed while fleeing on the highway when asked

---

21 Shiekh Shamsuddin Gulzar Ali (resident of Mogri Siswa Township, Anand) interview by author, February 2, 2009; Rabiya Ismailbhai Vohra (resident of Mogri Siswa Township, Anand) interview by author, 20 February 2009; Abubakr Umarbhai (Maulana and functionary for Tablighi Jamaat) interview by author, 20 February 2009.

22 Quoted in *Times of India*, 23 April 2002.

23 Abdul Razzak Chand Mohammed (Deshotar village, Sabarkantha) interview by author, 19 March 2009.

about the possibility of return. When Ayyubhai agreed to visit Kidiad along with his wife Arjoobibi for the first time after the violence, there was much warmth and affection between him and a Patel family that he had close relations with. About the apparent bonhomie on his meeting with them for the first time after the violence Ayyubbhai remarked,

> Ayyubbhai: Yes we were very close. Every time I came back from driving, even if it was late in the evening I would first stop by at their place, since its on the way.
>
> Q: So why didn't you come to them then in 2002?
>
> Ayyubbhai: The time was only such. We didn't know what to do.
>
> Arjoobibi: This road that you saw while coming in to the village, our tempo was pelted with stones all along that way on our way to the highway.[24]

Ayyubbhai was driving one of the two tempos from which 74 people were killed by a mob on the highway while fleeing Kidiad. Arjoobibi, his wife survived because when she lost consciousness because of her injuries the mob on the highway took her to be dead. Later a crew of journalists from a TV channel that were passing by saw that she was alive and took her to a hospital. In Kidiad itself there were also two other cases of stabbing of Muslims who did not manage to flee in the tempo. Despite the good relations he has with his old friends in the village, returning to live there even seven years after the violence is simply out of the question for him.[25]

This sentiment was even stronger in 2002 for thousands of Muslims who had gone through harrowing experiences just getting out of their homes to escape to a safer place. They continued to live in camps, which were closed or in a few instances shifted to buildings like school buildings or district administration buildings in July but refused to return home. In Modassa, Sabarkantha district, which turned out to be the district with the largest number of displaced Muslims and remains so to date, after camps were formally closed, around 1400 displaced continued to live in tents on agricultural land on the periphery of the town or in the houses of relatives in Modassa, which has a large Muslim population.

---

24 Ayyubhai Sindhi (resident Al Falaha Relief Colony, Sabarkantha) interview by author, 22 March 2009.

25 *Ibid.*

The feeling of insecurity ran so strong among those displaced that thousands of families who continued to live in camps were waiting not for their houses to be reconstructed but to find an alternative home in a 'safe' area. For a large number of Muslims from rural Gujarat who had seen violence for the first time in their lives, they simply could not bring themselves to go back to their original homes, set up house and expose themselves to the risk of a similar situation breaking out again. A common refrain was, 'we managed to save our lives this time, but what if it happens again? We have a responsibility towards our children. Our lives are over now but for their sake we have to think.'[26] This was especially the case in places where women had been raped, where on return they would have to face their attackers who continued to roam free. Hostilities, therefore, continued long after the violence had ebbed, which made the displaced apprehensive to return. Besides, for a large number of displaced who had been rendered destitute, the compensation amounts were too paltry to help rebuild their completely burned and broken homes in any significant way.

A large number of those who had been displaced wanted an alternate site of settlement rather than to return to their hostile neighbourhood.[27] The then chairman of the National Commission for Minorities (NCM), Justice Mohammad Shamim, had also suggested to the state government that land be given for displaced in camps 'so that they can create a new settlement and get a sense of security.'[28] In response to the request of a delegation of Muslim leaders, Narendra Modi clearly ruled out the possibility of the government allotting land for the thousands of Muslims, who could not bring themselves to return to their earlier homes. The official reasoning being that even for carnage cases like Naroda Patiya this would lead to segregation of the two communities.[29]

Relief colonies: Muslim organizations step in

In this situation of crisis where the state was unresponsive with respect to reconstruction efforts for the displaced, Muslim organizations constructed houses

---

26   Kulsumbano Hasan (from Ode, resident of Relief Township, Anand) interview by author, 19 February 2009.

27   *Times of India*, cited in *The Uprooted Caught Between Existence and Denial: A Document on the State of the Internally Displaced in Gujarat*, Centre for Social Justice and Anhad, February 2007, 88.

28   *Times of India*, 16 March 2002.

29   *Times of India*, 5 May 2002.

in places of Muslim majority with the aim to provide a roof over the head for the displaced.[30] Muslim organizations from places of large Muslim populations such as in Hyderabad, Karnataka, Kerala, Bihar etc. as well as from other countries with Muslim populations such as neighbouring Pakistan made significant contributions for the displaced Muslims. An organization from Bihar Sharief constructed a relief colony Imarat-e-Sharia in Juhapura for displaced Muslims. However, the construction of houses for displaced Muslims was taken up in a big way by three Muslim organizations, namely Islami Relief Committee, a relief wing of Jamaat-e-Islami one of the most active Islamic movements of south Asia; Gujarat Sarvajanik Relief Committee, an initiative of the Tablighi Jamaat, which is a reformist Islamic movement and Jamiat Ulema-e-Hind, a pan India organization, which claims nationalist leanings and has worked with mainstream political parties like the Congress and BJP in the past (Jasani, 2008, p. 436). These organizations constructed relief colonies for displaced Muslims regardless of their sect, doctrinal leanings or *jammat*,[31] while organizations such as the All India Memon Federation constructed colonies for displaced Memon families.

In Modassa, a town where Muslims are known for their hold over the transport business, Babubhai Tada, a local businessman took a lead in efforts to construct houses for the displaced on agricultural land. Under the Sahyog Seva Trust, Tada oversaw the construction of more than 500 houses close to where the tents for camps were put up on agricultural land due to which he has become a household name for Muslims in Modassa and many among the displaced for several years after the violence continued look to him for solutions and even hold him responsible for their problems.[32] Other Muslim organizations also constructed additional houses for the displaced in the adjoining area. The most destitute among these continued to live in tents for up to three years before an Ahmedabad based NGO Jan Vikas and Centre for Social Justice completed construction of houses in a row of houses called Millat Nagar in that same area.

---

30 Dr. Shakeel Ahmed (Trustee Islami Relief Committee, Ahmedabad), in discussion with the author, 27 January 2009.

31 *Jamaats* are composed of people who might share the same occupation, ethnicity or regional origin; or might comprise people who recognize the authority of a particular shrine, or follow a specific school of jurisprudence or doctrinal orientation. E. Simpson, 2004, 'Migration and Islamic Reform in a Port town of Western India', in *Contributions to Indian Sociology, Migration, Modernity and Social Transformation in South Asia*, (n.s.) 37, 1 and 2, New Delhi: Sage Publications.

32 *Times of India*, July 27, 2002 and Yakob Khan Yusuf Khan Pathan (Millat Nagar, Modassa, Sabarkantha) interview by author, 23 March 2009.

Soon Muslim organizations were flooded with requests from displaced and affected persons for allotment of houses. In the chaotic urgency of dealing with a situation where the state refused to be drawn into the idea of resettlement land for the displaced and in the absence of any central leadership planning and guiding their efforts, every organization seems to have done what they thought best. Certain patterns can however be discerned from the continued existence of relief colonies today. The criteria for allotment of houses in some colonies was to first attend to those most destitute such as widows and poorest of the poor, although as in most cases of post-conflict scenarios/humanitarian work allegations continued to fly thick about unfair allotments based on who could pay more for years to come.[33] Before allotting houses to the displaced some organizations under police protection in the midst of continuing tensions undertook their own independent survey in order to determine the extent of losses as the *panchnamas* and FIRs made by the police often understated losses and were made in the absence of the victims themselves who at the time were taking shelter in relief camps or elsewhere in localities of Muslim concentration of population.[34] In some colonies in Ahmedabad, specific categories of affected people were given houses together such as the widows of Naroda Patiya were given houses in a row at Faisal Park in Vatwa while those who were witnesses in court cases related to Naroda Patiya were allotted houses in Ekta Nagar in Vatwa. Some houses in relief colonies, especially in the case of some widows of Naroda Patiya, were given for free. For most houses however, some amount of money was taken from the occupants. The amounts taken from the displaced vary from colony to colony ranging from ₹ 10,000 to 20,000. However, when the houses were allotted the occupants only received a stamp paper, which states their occupancy under the relief colony built by the organization so that with the exception of one relief colony, the occupants in all other relief colonies did not have ownership rights. According to the organizers this was done to ensure that the houses would be used only for the purpose they were created i.e., for the displaced and that they would not be sold again for profit.[35] In one relief colony, the occupants had only received a receipt for the payment they made and that too the receipt said the money was a donation and not payment

---

33 Shafi Madni (Trustee Islami Relief Committee, Ahmedabad) in discussion with author, 17 February 2009.

34 Afzal Memon (Gujarat Sarvajanik Relief Committee, Ahmedabad) in discussion with author, 19 December 2008.

35 Shafi Madni (Trustee Islami Relief Committee, Juhapura, Ahmedabad) in discussion with author, 17 February 2009.

towards the house. The displaced however, who lived in such colonies, have to pay municipal or *panchayat* taxes, which came for water etc. in bills under their names. According to one of the leaders of the Islami Relief Committee, the houses will eventually be transferred to the name of the displaced, but no such move had been made up to seven years after the violence.

According to government of Gujarat estimates prepared in response to the visit of the NCM relief colonies exist at 10 districts in north, east and central districts of Gujarat namely Kheda, Bharuch, Dahod, Anand Mehsana, Vadodara, Panchmahals, Sabarkantha, Gandhinagar and Ahmedabad. Sabarkantha has the largest number of relief colonies followed by Anand and Ahmedabad. According to the Concerned Citizens Tribunal (CCT) that had sought to document the violence during 2002 itself, 78 per cent of people affected had fled their homes for at least three months during the violence and in scenes of large scale violence in Mehsana, Panchmahal, Anand, Dahod and Ahmedabad districts, this has resulted in 'near permanent migrations and shifts of populations' where only an estimated 20 per cent of the population had returned to their original homes (*ibid*, p. 246). Among the districts where some of the worst carnages took place, in Mehsana and Panchmahal there are nine relief colonies each in small towns and villages of Muslim concentration, while Dahod and Ahmedabad, which also saw the worst cases of violence have one relief colony and 11 relief colonies respectively.

Although the large number of relief colonies in Ahmedabad could be attributed to the presence of pockets of Muslim concentration as well as the presence of a large number of *jamaats*,[36] it is Sabarkantha that turned out to be a safe haven for displaced Muslims. This is because relief colonies were made in places of Muslim concentration on the basis of the availability of land and its location, which is why towns like Wadali, Idar, Modassa and Himmatnagar in Sabarkantha district that have large concentrations of Muslim population as well as centres of businesses controlled by Muslims they became places of refuge for displaced Muslims.

Muslim organizations were looking to buy land to resettle the displaced in a safe place, which inevitably meant a place of Muslim concentration even if it was not always regularized land. Work on these houses started on a war footing and by July 2002 itself, 1131 houses for the displaced in Sabarkantha district in Muslim dominated areas of Hasanpura, Savli and Vadali villages as also Himmatnagar,

---

36 Ahmedabad has 41 Shia and Sunni *jamaats*. Rubina Jasani, 2008, 'Violence, reconstruction and Islamic reform: Stories from the Muslim ghetto', *Modern Asian Studies* 42(2–3): 431–56.

Meghraj, Vijaynagar and Idar towns were under construction to enable displaced Muslims to move into them.[37] In Ahmedabad, which was most affected by the violence, and which also has the largest number of relief colonies, such colonies were constructed in areas of Muslim concentration on the periphery of the city such as along the eastern periphery in Ramol, in the industrial suburbs of Vatwa, Bombay Hotel areas and on the western periphery in Juhapura. In the city of Baroda, there are eight relief colonies on the eastern periphery, one of which consists of houses built by the displaced themselves by squatting on government land and also by paying for it in installments to a middle man.

In Anand, just on the outskirts of the city limits six relief colonies were built for those Muslims who had fled from villages in Anand and neighbouring Kheda. In Panchmahal relief colonies were set up in towns like Kallol, Hallol and one on the outskirts of Godhra. Some relief colonies for displaced in Panchmahal have been constructed just a few kilometers away from the original village of the displaced. For instance in Lunawada, a relief colony has been constructed just off the highway near a Deoband seminary a few kilometers away from the village of Anjanwa in Santrampur *taluka* where twelve people were killed on 5 March 2002. Even more than seven years later farmers go to the village in the daytime to attend to their fields but return to the relief colony situated on the periphery of Lunawada. One farmer who lost four members of his family of which three were children while they were waiting for the police to come and pick them up explained that they go to work their fields during the day but they couldn't think of staying back at night in the village where their burned houses still stand.

> When asked why he didnt stay there and spare himself the daily commute he said very matter of factly with much fear in his eyes *dar lagta hai na ben* one feels afraid sister.[38]

As Muslim organizations were faced with the task of sizeable proportions of providing housing for such a large number of displaced on an urgent basis, land was purchased wherever it was easily available in areas of Muslim concentration.

---

37   Shafi Madni (Trustee Islami Relief Commiteee, Ahmedabad) in discussion with author, 17 February 2009; Afzal Memon (Gujarat Sarvajanik Relief Committee, Ahmedabad) in discussion with author, 19 December 2008.

38   Mohammad (farmer, Anjanwa, Panchmahal) interview by author, 18 September 2008.

Housing, security and social rights through self help

Since March 2002, even in the midst of the violence, areas of Muslim concentration on the periphery of cities like Bombay Hotel and Juhapura in Ahmedabad and Tandalja in Vadodara became much sought after places for buying homes in safe areas, which led to the shooting up of real estate prices in these places. It also led to a lot of illegal development and slumming in such areas where in response to the urgent need for housing for a large number of Muslims, many of whom could not afford it, builders and middle men offered plots of land that in many cases they didn't have legal papers for. This was done in instalments so that people could begin to live there by paying ₹ 500 or more a month. During the violence in 2002 upcoming areas of large Muslim concentration such as Juhapura and Bombay Hotel in Ahmedabad, Tandalja in Vadodara, Ismail Nagar in Anand, Idar, Modassa and Himmatnagar in Sabarkantha and even villages of Muslim concentration such as Kesarpura in Sabrakantha or Sureli in Anand[39] were islands of peace due to their location on the periphery as well as the concentration of large Muslim populations by which they were able to ward off mobs more successfully than in those pockets of Muslim concentration in the middle of the city or in the congested old city areas. For the poor these places became the sites of camps and then relief colonies that sheltered the displaced and for those who had the means, these places became safe havens that Muslims of all sects and classes flocked to.

The location of such places on the periphery of cities and towns however has meant that despite its diverse population that includes economically well off Muslims such as doctors, engineers, government functionaries and civil society practitioners, along with the poor and marginalized Muslims, they have limited access to civic facilities such as street lighting, sanitation, educational and healthcare amenities. During the violence itself, a doctors' collective had issued an appeal for Hindu doctors to not go to Muslim areas after one doctor was stabbed in Juhapura.[40] In Juhapura a 260 bed facility was coming up along with other facilities like schools and restaurants with the purported aim to make it self-sufficient so that its residents don't have to venture out especially in the time of riots. An informal

---

39   The size of the concentration of Muslim population also played an important role here. For instance on March 1, 2002 a small village, Nava Station that was Muslim dominated but surrounded by Hindu villages, was surrounded and attacked by a group of 200 people killing more than six Muslims while some were even dragged and killed in the nearby fields before the police arrived to disperse the mob. *The Hindu*, 3 March 2002.

40   *Times of India*, 11 April 2002.

residents association had identified professionals including 80 doctors and blood bank laboratory technicians whose services were to be retained in the area itself. Some Muslims in Juhapura have also taken up the task of establishing schools in the area[41] where the lack of educational facilities is illustrated by the fact that the first municipal school in this area was built as recently as 2013.

The government's argument, with respect to the NCM's observation of the lack of the availability of civic amenities in relief colonies was that the lack of amenities is commensurate to the areas in which they are located, and not specific to what it has described as 'resettlement colonies.'[42] More commonly referred to as relief colonies these make shift houses constructed with the intention of speedily providing at least a roof over the head of those displaced turned out to be little more than that. The relief colonies, which continue to be used as residential areas for those who did not return to live in their original homes, have turned out to be difficult places to live in given that almost all of them are constructed on the periphery of villages, towns and cities on land that is in a large number of cases low lying and not regularized and where makeshift houses were hastily constructed. However, for those displaced who had to move in to these relief colonies or rented or owned accommodations in these places of Muslim concentration, the comparative lack of amenities from their previous places of residence put them at a disadvantage. In Ahmedabad, Muslims who had lived in working class areas like Chamanpura, Bapunagar and even Naroda Patiya had easy access to economical public transport and educational facilities such as schools and healthcare through government hospitals. Majority of houses in relief colonies have access to electricity, which is not uncommon in Ahmedabad with even semi permanent structures being provided with power by the government in collaboration with private providers, the displacement of Muslims from working class areas to to relief colonies in the industrial eastern or western periphery of the city has meant that they didn't have access to government healthcare and education facilities. Although private healthcare and education facilities are available, they now have to pay much more. Even those who lived in slums like Naroda Patiya had better access to sanitation facilities than in relief colonies as over the years residents in large slum areas that act as votebanks secure facilities such as water supply and public toilets through patronage of politicians whereas those who

---

41   Basharat Peer, 'Being Muslim under Narendra Modi', *The New York Times*, 18 April, 2014, http://www.nytimes.com.

42   Status Report of the displaced families in Gujarat with reference to the NCM delegation visit on 15 October 2006.

found themselves in relief colonies had to start all over again in trying to procure these facilities. This comparative deprivation after displacement was even more pronounced in Ahmedabad for those who lived in working class areas that had made incremental advancements over years of struggle through associations such as TLA for their social rights (Breman, 2004, p. 42). The more recent improvement in the cityscape and the new paths of development that Gujarat was alleged to have leapfrogged on since 2002 have also stopped short of these areas of concentration of Muslim population that have come to be referred to as ghettoes (Jaffrelot, 2012) whether it is the state transport services such as in the case of Ahmedabad's bus rapid transit system (BRT) that has mainly benefitted the middle class (Mahadevia, Joshi and Datey, 2013, pp. 60–62), the proposed metro system, gas pipeline or sewage systems. More than anything else however, what raises questions of disadvantage and makes these places a study in contrast in vibrant Gujarat is the presence of marked borders such as in Juhapura where one border with the Hindu locality is marked with surveillance cameras and barbed wires or for instance the relief colony in Himmatnagar after leaving which the road that approaches the city carries a signboard saying 'here begins the Hindu rashtra'.

While the state government administration under Narendra Modi has been lauded for the creation of infrastructure such as roads in the rest of Gujarat, roads are an area where Muslim organizations have been unsuccessful in the endeavour to help themselves because of the high costs involved. Approachability of relief colonies is a major issue that affects the lives of those in relief colonies in more ways than is immediately apparent. Some houses in relief colonies such as Kifayatnagar in Himmatnagar, Sabarkantha stand out from other matchbox like houses due to extensions that have been made and structural modifications that have been added. However, at a cursory glance, the houses numbering more than 500 of various relief colonies that come into view after walking a little less than a kilometer off the Himmatnagar bypass road, belie the fact that during the monsoons the place becomes a veritable swamp, which even the milkman refuses to venture into. The problem becomes particularly critical for pregnant women, school children who have had to skip school, sick, old people and even NGO practitioners and workers of faith-based organizations who have to restrict their movement to the colonies during the monsoons.[43] In another cluster of relief

---

43 Sister Celine (Co-ordinator of self help groups in the relief colony) in discussion with author, 28 March 2009.

colonies built in the middle of farmland on the outskirts of Modassa town, the owners of the field on occasion stop big *shuttles*[44] that people use to commute to and from the colony from going through dirt tracks in between the fields so as to protect their field. During the monsoon these dirt tracks fill up with rain water making the area inapproachable while the stagnant water causes diseases such as jaundice, dengue and stomach related disorders. In Rashidabad relief colony, as NCM had also noted, the collection of rainwater in a pool a few feet deep that submerged the *kuccha* road leading to the colony even led to the drowning of two adolescents.[45] It is the lack of roads in these relief colonies that house 20 to 500 houses that compound the isolation and makeshift nature of the colonies. Residents of the Mogri Siswa Relief Township recall their initial days in the relief colony where there they had to clear up the bushes around the area and keep watch at night in the isolated location to ward off thieves and even visitors from nature such as snakes. For those living in Satnagar Navi Vasahat, a relief colony built by a US based organization called Al Fami for the survivors of what is now referred to as the Sardarpura carnage where 32 Muslims died, in the first few days of the stay a child died of snake bite.

Sanitation is a major problem for the hastily constructed houses in relief colonies especially in those relief colonies where proper toilets were not constructed. In majority of relief colonies there are private arrangements for sanitation where each house or two houses share a shallow soak pit for sewage collection. These small soak pits need to be periodically evacuated at personal expense failing which they overflow and create unhygienic conditions. Given the fact that majority of relief colonies have dirt roads, which have not been concreted, the soak pits that overflow on to the *kuccha* roads add to the squalor of the places where they are located.

Human habitation in a place often leads to the building of much more beyond one's home, through relationships and social networks with those in the neighbourhood. For those who did not return and who continue to be displaced, the loss of their dwelling place accompanied the loss of other such relationships and vital aspects of their existence. For an elderly middle class couple in Vadodara city for instance who had spent more than 17 years in Ellora Park, a locality where

---

44   Shuttles are larger rickshaws that have a total of 3 rows of seats. Even autorickshaws that are shared by people going to different destinations along the same route are referred to as shuttles.

45   Harsh Mander and Kiran Nanavati, 2006, *Surviving State Hostility and Denial: A Survey of Relief Colonies for People Affected by Mass Violence in Gujarat 2002 - A Report*, Harsh Mander and Kiran Nanavati, Nyayagrah and Oxfam, Ahmedabad.

their children grew up and where they had several good relations not the least important of which were the ones with particular vendors, grocers, tailors, the doctor and dry cleaners, the shift to another place in the middle of the violence has not deterred them, since they have the means, from continuing to patronize the same vendors etc even if it means at the additional cost and trouble of commuting. For the poor however, distance snapped the access to some vital aspects of their former existence. In Naroda Patiya a slum on the eastern industrial periphery of Ahmedabad for instance, as is the case with many cities in India where the settlements or slums *bastis* of the poor exist side by side with factories or working units, the *basti* was also home to such small working units, which were the sources of employment for its inhabitants, especially women who could earn some extra money by working in such small scale factories of lace, buttons etc. both within Naroda Patiya and in the factories nearby. The loss of their homes has also led to a loss of income for some in this way given that relief colonies on newly developed land lacked such opportunities.

For those displaced from rural to urban areas, their new existence in relief colonies on the periphery of towns and cities meant a much higher cost of living. Ameena Misumiyan Sindhi from Kidiad village in Sabarkantha who now lives in Al Falaha Relief Colony, Modassa is not as sentimental about her village as she is about the fact that in her village poor people like her somehow had access to water, milk and sometimes even eggs without necessarily paying for them monetarily. In the city however, she complains that one has to even pay for salt. Ayyubbhai Sindhi also from Kidiad, points out that they never had to pay for things like firewood and water in the village that is located near a river, whereas now, during winters he has to buy firewood at the cost of ₹ 20 to heat water. The absence of common property resources like water, firewood and things that are more easily available in Gujarat's rural economy only added to the woes of Muslims from rural areas who found themselves in relief colonies in towns and cities after the violence. Due to the location of relief colonies on the periphery of towns and cities and among places of Muslim concentration displaced Muslims now have little opportunity or reason to interact with Hindus.

The growth of the influence of muslim organizations

'The water comes from the *Masjid*,' said Aishabibi explaining the source for this essential requirement of human existence in Faisal Park, Vatwa in Ahmedabad.

This is the case in most relief colonies where borewells were installed by Muslim organizations that built the relief colonies and continued to manage them. In neighbouring Arsh Colony since water from the borewell is not reliable, the residents have to pay ₹ 10 every half an hour for water from the private borewell of the owner of the land nearby.[46] In Modassa, Sabarkantha for the many relief colonies that have come up in the same place, where tents of the relief camps once stood, the borewell belonging to the owner of the surrounding fields is their source of water for all purposes. The government of Gujarat's report on relief colonies to the NCM mentions the availability of water to all the colonies but what it does not mention is that this untreated groundwater is not always potable. The residents of Citizen Nagar Ahmedabad located next to a huge garbage dump on the eastern periphery in the industrial suburbs have now got accustomed to tea that has a salty aftertaste due of the presence of effluents from surrounding industries in the ground water. Some relief colonies had access to water from regular sources such as the Municipal Corporation or *panchayats*.

With the state's looking the other way when faced with the problem of displacement, the stepping in of Muslim organizations to build relief colonies has greatly increased their influence among the displaced. Besides the fact that many relief colonies have a *masjid* and a resident *maulvi* who subscribes to and prescribes a particular practice of Islam, in some relief colonies even essentials like the supply of borewell water is under the *masjid*. The organizations that built these colonies continue to intervene in the affairs of the colony.[47] In one relief colony for instance, after some elders of the colony had alleged that four widows were engaging in sex work, they were arbitrarily evicted from the relief colony. It was only after the concerned women along with the support of a few NGOs put up a fight that they were allowed to go back after four months.[48]

Increase in religiosity is not unexpected after an event of catastrophic proportions such as a natural disaster or in post-conflict scenarios, and commentators were quick to note an increase in religiosity among Muslims after the violence of 2002. Reformist organizations such as the Tablighi *jamaat* made

---

46   Shamsuddin Babubhai Ajmeri (previously lived in Talod, Sabarkantha, resident of Arsh Colony) interview by author, 16 December 2008.

47   Dr. Shakeel Ahmed (Islamic Relief Committee trustee), in discussion with the author, *Op.cit.*

48   Afroze Sayyed (social activist with Nyayagraha, Ahmedabad), interview by author, 15 December 2008.

inroads in relief colonies that they had built. Their popularity increased not just because they delivered in times of need but also because in coming to terms with what had happened to them during the violence, people were looking for explanations through their faith.

The influence of reformist organizations has increased not just in Ahmedabad but also in parts of rural Gujarat. Muslims from communities like Memons and Bohras who lived and worked in the villages of Gujarat where three or two or sometimes even a single Muslim family lived among other castes or *adivasis* for generations before the violence and who now find themselves in relief colonies see their displacement as judgment from Allah for not living in strict adherence to His tenets. One Memon businessman, who along with his brothers ran a cement business that incurred huge losses during the violence when one of his clients refused to pay up for the delivery of a huge consignment of cement, and who now lives in a relief colony says he is thankful that the Almighty used this incident to draw his family out of living with non-believers into a better practice of the faith among his co-religionists.

Having to live among co-religionists has affected changes in clothing as well. A Mansoori woman from Chiloda village in Ahmedabad district who now lives in Siddiqabad relief colony in Ahmedabad recalled how in the village she used to wear sarees as Mansooris, she explains, are known to live 'as Gujaratis'. In fact, there were rumours of a VHP pamphlet that said only Mansooris could return to their homes. In the relief colony however, the woman changed her attire to one associated with Muslims in the city, *salwar kameez* in order to fit in better.[49] These pressures are felt even by educated middle class Muslims who have had to move into areas of Muslim concentration or Muslim enclaves. A retired engineer of Gujarat Tractor Company who had to leave his house of 30 years in Tarsali in a mixed colony among people of different castes and religions to move to Mariam Park in Tandalja a Muslim enclave in Vadodara in 2002 admitted that he didn't have a beard before but after moving into a Muslim locality, he felt the need to keep one.[50]

However, the influence of reformist organizations has not been such a straightforward one. At Alliance Colony in Modassa for instance, the inhabitants of the relief colony were urged to worship in the *madrassa* built in the colony by the

---

49 Husseinbhai Gafoorbhai Mansoori (previously resident of Chiloda, residing in Siddiqabad Relief Colony, Ahmedabad), interview by author, 30 November 2008.

50 Sikander Basheer Khan Pathan (Tandalja, Vadodara), interview by author, 25 February 2009.

Tablighis and volunteers who would also go around the colony to impart teachings or *taleem* to the children. While, residents of the relief colony welcomed the *taleem* for their children, in order to offer *namaaz* the residents who were Sunni Muslims would go to a Sunni masjid in the village despite being called to worship in the Tablighi masjid on a number of occasions. The situation worsened when on the death of an old woman in the relief colony, the relatives who wanted to conduct her last rites according to their customs were reportedly not allowed to do so in the Tablighi masjid. This led to an altercation and the residents decided to change the masjid to a Sunni one.[51] In some other colonies as well people are open about their disagreements and complaints against the organizers of the colonies.[52]

Reconstruction of livelihood

One aspect of life after displacement that proved to be the toughest to deal with is that of finding means to make a livelihood. In the six months of camp life following the outbreak of the violence, a large number of those in camps had been jobless but after the violence had scaled down, the relief scaled down as well and camps were closed. For a large number of displaced many of whom were still in search of a roof over their head, earning one's daily bread became the biggest question.

There are instances of those among the displaced who have struggled and rebuilt their lives successfully such as Salimbhai Sindhi, the ex *sarpanch* of Kidiad village who now owns a cattle farm and Mansoori Abbasbhai Dawoodbhai who took various loans from Sriram Finance, Nagrik Bank etc. and managed to start another business in the wholesale trade of grain in Modassa similar to the one he had in his native village Shinol in Sabarkantha but such examples are few and far between. The assistance offered by the government and NGOs had little impact in creating livelihood options for displaced in relief colonies particularly those from rural areas who now live in relief colonies in Kheda, Anand, Sabarkantha or Panchmahal.[53]

One of the widely acknowledged effects of displacement is social marginalisation (Cernea 1997, 1569). In the relief colony in Lunawada, which is

---

51   Sirajbhai Gafoorbhai Meghraji (Alliance Colony, Modassa, Sabarkantha), interview by author, 23 March 2009.

52   *Surviving State Hostility and Denial: A Survey of Relief Colonies for People Affected by mass Violence in Gujarat 2002 - A Report*, Nyayagraha, December 2006.

53   Khairunissa (AVHRS or Antarik Visthapit Hak Rakshak, Anand), in discussion with the author, 7 March 2009.

situated close to Anjanwa village, farmers have been able to continue with their former occupation of farming by commuting from the relief colony to their village which is about 5 kms away. In some relief colonies landholding farmers have had to become absentee landlords and rent their farms out to Hindu farmers to till their land in their absence.[54] For Mohammad Pikumiyan Shiekh a driver and farmer from Satarda village who now lives 20 kms away from there at Sahara Relief Colony in Modassa his earning from his 10 *bigha* land for a season has dropped from ₹ 30,000 to ₹ 8–10,000 since he had to find a Hindu farmer in the village to till the land in his absence.[55]

However, besides those displaced who live in relief colonies, even for people who chose to return to their original homes after their stay in camps, with or without the assistance of the state, NGOs or Muslim organizations, their absence from their original place of stay and work for six months had an impact on their livelihood options. Already in the midst of the violence a VHP pamphlet had been circulating calling for a boycott of all Muslim businesses. At Deshotar village in Sabarkantha district, when Abdul Razzak Chandmohammad and his two brothers, who each ran a row of shops in the village, returned after six months but no customers came to their shops for a few months. Abdulbhai says that initially villagers put conditions 'sell here and not there, sit here and not there but we said this is our place and we entered *ghus gaye*.' Eventually customers did start coming to their shops but their profits were greatly reduced because their earlier customers also had access to similar goods from shops that were opened after the 2002 violence by people from other communities.[56]

The self employed and casual labourers among those displaced such as painters who do *colour kaam* (painting) or vendors who go door to door have also had to suffer a serious cut in their earnings both due to the location of relief colonies, which is usually on the periphery and in localities where people have less spending power as well as due to the concentration of so many casual labourers with similar trade in the relief colonies, which increases competition. The same holds true for the self employed in urban areas as well. Sarfarazbhai Abdul Qadar Munshi, an auto rickshaw driver in Ahmedabad who plied his rickshaw in other parts of

---

54 *Times of India* and Sheikh Fakir Mohammad Pikumiyan (farmer's son, resident of Sahar Society, Modassa, Sabarkantha), interview by author, 22 March 2009.

55 *Ibid.*

56 Abdul Razzak Chandmohammad (Deshotar village, Sabarkantha), interview by author, 19 March 2009.

Ahmedabad but not Juhapura despite living in Siddiqabad relief colony in nearby Sarkhej, complained sarcastically that in Juhapura there were more autorickshaws than people. Another hurdle for the self employed to begin to earn livelihood from a new place was that new customers and clientele had to be established all over again.[57] For some displacement has meant a complete change of profession. Shamsuddin Babubhai Ajmeri for instance was a shopkeeper who dealt in eggs on a wholesale basis. His business did well in Talod, Sabarkantha where the village had a population of around 35,000 people and he could get a good price for his eggs among the villagers there. After having relocated to Vatwa's Arsh Colony besides the fact that in a locality of Muslims where there were a dozen vendor's of meaty snacks and eggs every few feet he had to opt for another *dhandha* (business) also because he didn't have capital to invest in anything more than an iron and so he started a stall for ironing clothes, which also meant that his income dropped drastically. For salaried employees the location of relief colonies in the periphery created additional hardships for them. Before their house in Meghaninagar was attacked in the 2002 violence, Rukhsanabano Ayub Sama's husband used to commute daily from there to a mill in Naroda where he worked the night shift. After living in various temporary accommodations as well as a camp when they finally got a house in Siddiqabad relief colony in Sarkhej near Juhapura, her husband who eventually died of health complications had to cycle daily for two hours from their house in the relief colony on the western periphery of the city to get to the factory where he worked.[58]

The impoverishment that displacement had brought about due to the problems of finding livelihood was nowhere more evident than in the case of a family of Memons living in Kifayatnagar relief colony in Sabarkantha that were shopkeepers in a remote tribal village before they found themselves in camps. However, in 2002 when this family of shopkeepers was attacked by *adivasis* they fled with only their lives and no possessions and eventually managed to find a place among the many other contenders in Kifayatnagar relief colony. While they didn't have a large bank balance at their original village in the remote hinterland, they didn't lack anything and had led a comfortable existence as shopkeepers in the village of tribals, in the relief colony on the outskirts of Himmatnagar however, the lady and her daughters

---

57 Sarafarazbhai Abdul Qadar Munshi (previous resident of Chamanpura, at the time of interview, residing in Siddiqabad Relief Colony, Ahmedabad), interview by author, 30 November 2008.

58 Rukhsanabano Ayyubbhai Sama (previously resided in Meghaninaga), interview by author, 29 November 2008.

who had seen better days were forced to work as housemaids in an effort to make ends meet while the husband struggled to get a steady source of income.[59]

In 2004 the NCM, as a constitutional body intervened specifically for displaced persons in Gujarat. After visiting 17 relief colonies in the districts of Ahmedabad, Panchmahal, Dahod and Sabarkantha in 2006, the team of NCM members held that the situation of displaced persons in relief colonies was very difficult. Pointing to the lack of even basic amenities like potable water, sanitation, electricity or ration cards in the colonies and to the government's responsibility to provide for these displaced, NCM suggested that a larger policy should be formulated to address the plight of those displaced due to communal violence.[60] The NCM even suggested that a relief package be formulated on par with those affected by the 2001 earthquake, which was rejected by the state government.[61] In its October 2006 report the NCM recommended granting them the status of IDPs and a fair monetary compensation.[62] The state government, however, continued to maintain that there were no IDPs in Gujarat and those who stayed in relief colonies did so voluntarily.[63] However, a petition under the right to information act made public the government of Gujarat's response to the NCM report in which the state government detailed the names of the relief colonies, which it estimated at being 81 in number along with the list of amenities in them.[64] The state government, however, questioned the legality of these constructions and whether they actually housed riot victims. The Supreme Court's committee of commissioners, in its report however, citing the NCM October 2006 Report, held that had the Government of Gujarat had misrepresented the situation to the court-appointed commissioners by denying the existence of these colonies and

---

59 S. Memon (resident Kifayatnagar Relief Colony, Sabarkantha) in discussion with author, 30 March 2009.

60 ENS, 'NMC seeks better amenities for riot-hit', *The Indian Express*, 18 October 2006, http://archive.indianexpress.com.

61 Seema Chrishti, 'Modi govt returns riot rehab funds, minority panel says victims suffer', *The Indian Express*, 24 October 2006, http://archive.indianexpress.com.

62 National Commission for Minorities, 2006, *Status Report of National Commission of Minorities Delegation visit on 15/10/2006 in the districts of Ahmedabad and Sabarkantha*, New Delhi.

63 Syed Khalique Ahmed, 'Two months after study, riot-displaced await Centre's special package', *The Indian Express*, 27 January 2007, http://expressindia.indianexpress.com.

64 Social Justice and Welfare Wing, Secretariat, RTI No. 102008, Information 18-A.1, Gandhinagar.

that a contempt notice should be issued to the chief secretary and other officials concerned.[65] In response the state government came up with another report, which identified the existence of 86 such colonies where 'people affected by riots have been staying'.[66]

To be or not to be displaced

The number of those displaced, however, remains fluid as victims of the violence continue to negotiate their changed circumstances since the violence. In Kidiad village that lost 74 of its Muslim villagers, no one wanted to return till 2007 when Shamim Sindhi's father who lost his wife, four daughters and his son to the mob while trying to save his brother, returned to the village and built his house again but this time not in the *mohalla* in the village which had been razed the ground, but in his field itself. As late as 2009 another family put up a tent where their house once stood in the empty land that was once their *mohalla* with a few of their possessions that amounted to little more than a *charpayee* (cot made of ropes) and a few vessels to wait and see how things worked out. With little success in creating a livelihood after four years in the relief colony, Shamim's father had remarried and returned to till his land with his wife and surviving daughter Shamim, who still carries the mark of a sword across her forehead. Children from Shamim's school nearby and Hindu women from the village come to Sindhi's field to use water from his borewell which to an outsider would convey the impression of a restoration of normalcy in the relations but Arjoobibi, Ayubbhai's wife who was severely injured and taken to be dead by the mob in 2002, says you like it now, but you won't be able to stay at night.

Two years after the violence Karimbhai Rasoolbhai Vohra's family returned to the ruins of their burned and broken home in the center of Ode village in Anand district where a total of 24 Muslims were burned alive in two separate houses the dilapidated remains of which continue to remain among the homes of their neighbours in this NRI village of prosperous Patels. However, when most of the family members were away from home Karimbhai Rasoolbhai Vohra then in

---

65   Supreme Court of India, Writ Petition (Civil) No. 196 of 2001.

66   Government of Gujarat, *Second Report on the Status of the Identified Resettlement Colonies of the 2002 Riot Affected in Gujarat,* presented to the National Commission for Minorities, at 60, New Delhi, 9 August 2007.

his 50s claims that he was pulled out of his house by a mob that poured petrol on him. Some in the mob were ready to set him on fire but others intervened and Karimbhai managed to get away with his life. Some villagers threatened the family with dire consequences if they did not withdraw the case against them. In response to the intimidation, the family went on to file another court case on the attack on their father.[67]

According to Misuben Panjamiyan Sindhi, who had been elected *sarpanch* of Prantij village in Sabarkantha for five years in 1999, the Muslims from her village didn't have any skills to be able to hope to survive in the relief colonies and so they had no choice but to return to their village.[68] There were 50 Muslims families among 400 Hindu households in the village, some of whom were farmers who collectively owned 700 *bighas* of land. All of them returned to the village. Initially villagers refused to talk to the Muslims, who had returned there since some of those involved in the attack had been arrested. However, after negotiations eventually a *samadhan* compromise was effected where the Muslims withdrew charges. Misuben holds that the *josh*, or zeal, at the time of the violence has now worn out and that relations between the two communities have returned to normal. This is besides the fact that the police have to make rounds at every Muslim festival to ensure that there is no trouble.[69] In the new 'normal' (Gupta, 2011) that was alleged to have returned within 72 hours of the first instance of violence, *samadhan* or compromise with changed circumstances was vital.

At Kifayatnagar relief colony in Sabarkantha, Muslims who had some bank balance and so were not rendered completely destitute when their homes were burned and destroyed have even invested in renovating and rebuilding the hastily constructed 10 by 10 houses of the relief colonies. The presence of *laris* (handcarts) in the evening and people congregating around tea stalls has given this cluster of relief colonies a semblance of a *basti* (habitat), which is not always the case with other relief colonies. However, for some of the displaced like Sayeda Meghraji from Itadi village, the feeling of having settled into the house in the Alliance Relief Colony, Modassa after seven years is a fleeting one.

---

67 Karimbhai Rasoolbhai Vohra (returned to Ode, Anand), interview by author, 12 March 2006.

68 Misuben Panjamiyan Sindhi, interview by author, *Op.cit.*

69 Misumiyan Punjamiyan Sindhi (ex *sarpanch* of Hanmaitya village, Sabarkantha), interview by author, 23 March 2009.

Q: Do you feel now that you have got set here?

Sister in law: Yes now we feel. *Abhi dil lagta hai* (now our heart feels like being here) earlier we used to not feel that way.

Q: For how long did you feel that way?

Sayeda: Like that many years it went on, (laughs) even today, if something happens, we feel like we should not stay here.

Sister in law: when difficulties come, when monsoon comes, then water fills up, children fall sick, so then we feel that in such a place what is there for us, in the village only when we were there it was good.

While court rooms and seminar rooms echoed international human rights language and grieving victims of the violence such as a woman whose husband committed suicide in the relief colony wished revenge on Narendra Modi, by 2008 there were also a few voices of support among other Muslims who believed that while violence and the lack of justice was nothing new, Modi had worked for the development of Gujarat evident in the creation of infrastructure such as roads and streetlights.[70] As a Muslim advocate from the upmarket Paldi locality in Ahmedabad argued, BJP was going to be in Gujarat for certain for at least next ten years in which case he thought it futile to waste his vote on a candidate of Congress who he knew would lose in a locality like Paldi where there were very few Muslim residential areas. Instead, when there was the possibility of obtaining a few sops such as a park bench or even amenities like water supply, one would rather support the party most likely to win.[71] Zafar Sareshwala, who went on from being a critic of Modi after the violence in 2002 to be the Muslim face for BJP praised the chief minister's accessibility and decisiveness as a result of which he was able to set up a BMW showroom at the heart of Ahmedabad in which he counts wealthy Hindus, as well as Muslims, as his customers.[72] In the 2009 elections to the lower house of the national parliament, the Muslim vote consolidated against BJP and the support for the party in terms of vote share declined to three per cent in 2009 from seven per cent in 2004 according to the National Election Survey.[73]

---

70   Mohammad Yakub Rangrez (resident of slum in Ramol), interview by author, 29 October 2008.

71   Resident of Paldi (name withheld on request), interview by author, 29 January 2009.

72   Madhu Purnima Kishwar, *Modinama: Work in Progress*, Madhu Purnima Kishwar, Manushi Trust, http://www.manushi.in/docs/Modinama-ebook.pdf, 46.

73   Some results of the National Election Survey conducted by the Centre for the Study of

In the 2012 state assembly elections where BJP won clear majorities an increasing number of Muslims showed vocal support for the party. Narendra Modi claimed that over 30 per cent Muslims had voted for him and so did feminist scholar Madhu Kishwar.[74] Calling attention to the serious methodological challenges involved in estimating actual vote share of a community in an election given the secret ballot, a Hindu Policy Studies report based on booth level data, however, held that while vocal support among Muslims was unprecedented in the 2012 state assembly elections, the actual vote share was much less at not more than 10 per cent, the contradiction in public support and electoral support being attributed to absence of space for dissent (Dhattiwala, 2014, p. 31).

Among the casualties of the violence of 2002 for Muslims was trust that effectively altered the parameters of reasonable expectations of the state. During the uncertainty created by the events of 2002 and the deficit left by the state's governance of the aftermath of the violence the principal actors that emerged in reconstruction efforts were Muslim organizations that hastily constructed makeshift homes and whose influence in relief colonies has continued long after they built the houses. From this account of reconstruction after the violence in 2002 it is not just the long-term effects of displacement that are illustrated but also that the phenomena of displacement is not a 'one time set of events' bounded in time and space (Peteet 1995, p. 171) but can continue long after violence as those affected negotiate the uncertainties in their changed realities. In Gujarat these negotiations have included the assertion of their rights through recourse to litigation and self help for security, housing and social rights as well as through different forms of settlements or compromise to avoid conflict. These shifts gleaned from grounded analysis reflect changes in the larger political universe that further need to be unpacked.

Developing Societies or CSDS were published by *The Hindu* in the following 'The Muslim Vote and where it went' in 'How India voted: Elections 2009', *The Hindu*, 26 May 2009.

74 Madhu Purnima Kishwar, *Modinama: Work in Progress*, Madhu Purnima Kishwar, Manushi Trust, http://www.manushi.in/docs/Modinama-ebook.pdf.

5

Violence and Good Governance

Violence in Gujarat in 2002 can be described as the most commented upon and analysed period of communal violence in recent times. It resulted in citizens groups aided by media attention launching a sustained and emphatic campaign for those affected by the violence that invoked constitutional provisions for protection of all citizens and employed the language of human rights to produce a significant body of independent and media reportage on the violence. It is not uncommon for groups such as minorities, refugees, stateless persons or aboriginals who feel their rights are not guaranteed by the dominant majoritarian vision of the nation-state to make rights claims in the language of human rights (Isin and Turner, 2002, pp. 6–7). This is because despite the historic dovetailing of rights with the nation-state and the entrenched international regime of sovereign nation-states, the intrepid vision of human rights is of the existence of rights that are universal across nation-states i.e., international and, therefore, a sphere above them. However, in a world of sovereign nation-states, howsoever globalized, it is the journey of these claims at the national level that is of much relevance. How did these campaigns for rights of displaced and for justice, reconstruction and reparation for victims of violence that sought to employ the human rights paradigm play out in the larger political universe of the state of Gujarat and at the national level in India?

While it is the democratic tradition of an active civil society, a free press, statutory institutions and the Supreme Court that took these campaigns on board and took the Narendra Modi-led government to task by holding up the plumb line of secularism and human rights, it was that same democratic set up that elevated him to the post of chief minister and prime minister through repeated electoral triumphs in elections in the state and at the national level. This chapter examines this puzzle by examining the journey of these rights claims through the courts and in the larger political universe. Since 2003, allegations of state excesses and human rights violations have been countered by that of economic growth and good governance. While the spirited campaign of civil society activists held up the standard of human rights,

Narendra Modi dismissed these as propaganda and instead held up an alternative benchmark of *sushasan* or good governance reaping rich dividends electorally from a religiously polarised electorate but also by projecting himself as a '*vikas purush*' man of development who delivered results. This chapter thus goes on to examine the emergence of the discourse of governance as *sushasan* after 2002. It argues that these developments are reflective of a paradigmatic shift in the criterion for assessing the state and policy-making from that of more traditional benchmarks such as citizenship and secularism to that of performance and efficiency.

Pursuit of justice after violence: The language of rights

On 6 March 2002, the government of Gujarat had appointed a judicial inquiry headed by Justice K. G. Shah and subsequently G. T. Nanavati whose mandate initially was as indicated by the title to report by the Commission of Inquiry into the facts, circumstances and all the course of events of the incidents that led to the setting on fire of some coaches of the Sabarmati Express train on 27.2.2002 near Godhra Railway station and the subsequent incidents of violence in the state in the aftermath of the Godhra incident' (henceforth Nanavati–Shah Commission Report). Fact finding reports also started to emerge from within ten days of the violence[1] from groups as diverse as feminist groups, professionals such as doctors, psychiatrists and editors, political parties and a delegation of parliamentarians, who sent teams to visit Gujarat to assess the situation. Not satisfied by the Gujarat government's 'perfunctory report' in response to its orders, which asserted the restoration of normalcy within 72 hours of the outbreak of violence while it continued to receive letters and complaints of human rights violations, the NHRC, led by its chairman former Chief Justice of India J. S. Verma, led a team of members that visited Gujarat from 19–22 March to assess the situation itself. In its preliminary report subsequent to this visit the NHRC held that 'most of all, the recent events have resulted in the violation of fundamental rights to life, liberty, equality and the dignity of citizens of India as guaranteed in the Constitution.'[2] Amnesty International was among the first voices to invoke the United Nations Guiding Principles on Internally Displaced Persons on 28 March in a 'Memorandum to the Government of Gujarat on its duties in the aftermath of the

---

1 'Ethnic Cleansing in Ahmedabad: Preliminary Report', SAHMAT Fact Finding Team to Ahmedabad, 10–11 March 2002.

2 National Human Rights Commission, *Suo motu* Case No. 1150/6/2001–2002 dated 31 May 2002, para 64.

violence' for those displaced by the violence while also grounding the principles to fundamental rights already guaranteed in the constitution in the right to life (Article 21), prohibition of discrimination on grounds of religion (Article 15) and equality of all persons before law (Article 14). A collective of retired judges and prominent citizens from different parts of India held a 'Concerned Citizens Tribunal' led by a Mumbai based NGO called 'Citizens for Justice and Peace' that toured three affected cities within two months of the outbreak of the violence and recorded testimonies of affected people. The tribunal, headed by retired Chief Justice Krishna Iyer, included lawyers, judges and academics that collected 2,094 oral and written testimonies and collected documents and testimonies, which were compiled into a three volume report called *Crimes against Humanity: An Inquiry into the Carnage in Gujarat.*

After a visit to Gujarat on the third week of March the international human rights group Human Rights Watch presented a report that documented major incidents of violence. The report held that there was state participation and complicity in the violence.[3] Two other reports, one by a women's rights group and another by a team of independent citizens that visited Gujarat to assess first-hand the effects of the violence collected testimonies of victims who had witnessed burning, rape and killing of people in their family or acquaintances and were living in relief camps. Their assessment after two months of violence was that the violence was nothing short of a genocide against the Muslims.[4] The report by independent citizen's groups highlighted the plight of children who had lost one or both their parents in the violence and those who were traumatized after watching violent acts such as the burning, killing and rape of their loved ones. People's Union of Civil Liberties (PUCL) and Vadodara Shanti Abhiyan documented women's experiences with police atrocities on one hand and mobs on the other as did various feminist groups.[5] NGOs also

---

3   Human Rights Watch, April 2002, 'We Have No Orders to Save You: A Report on State Participation and Complicity in the Communal Violence in Gujarat'.

4   Forum Against Oppression of Women and Awaaz-e-Niswaan, May 2002, 'Genocide in Rural Gujarat: Experience of Dahod District' and Kavita Punjabi and Krisha Bandopadhyay, May 2002, *The Next Generation: In the wake of the Genocide.*

5   Fact Finding by a Women's Panel, 2002, *How has the Gujarat Massacre Affected Minority Women: Survivors Speak,* Citizens Initiative, http://cac.ektaonline.org/resources/reports/ womens report.htm (accessed on 10 March 2011); International Initiative for Justice in Gujarat, 2003, *Threatened Existence: A Feminist Analysis of the extent of the Genocide in Gujarat.* Bombay; Jagori, 'What happened in Gujarat? The Facts', http://www.jagori.org/ wp-content/.

sought to draw attention to the displacement of Muslims.[6] Following reports of the violence writ petitions and (Public Interest Litigations) PILs were also filed by reputed civil society members including writers, artists and journalists such as Mallika Sarabhai, Mahashweta Devi, Anil Dharker and Teesta Setalvad, that in addition to the immediate situation regarding the inability of displaced to return, appointment of an independent national/statutory body to monitor relief and rehabilitation and reopening of camps also sought to draw the courts' attention to suggestions such as entrusting criminal investigation to a body outside the state of Gujarat such as the Central Bureau of Investigation (CBI) at the federal level, constitution of fast track courts to expedite criminal cases, etc.[7] The NHRC after another visit to the state in April – observing the widespread discrepancies in the first step in the justice system, the registering of FIRs, made urgent recommendations with regard to the registration of FIRs in camps and also went on to suggest that in order to ensure independent investigation, five major cases be transferred to the CBI.[8] Mallika Sarabhai, Digant Oza and Indukumar Jani filed a PIL in the Supreme Court, in which the petitioners, accused the then chief minister Narendra Modi of being biased against Muslims and where their senior counsel P Chidambaram, quoting extensively from the NHRC interim report that argued for the need for a special investigation team to be appointed to investigate the various crimes that had occurred in the protracted communal violence, reiterated that need. In a final report on the violence in June, the NHRC reiterated its recommendation to transfer major cases of violence to CBI. Rejecting the contention of the Gujarat government that such transference would discredit the Gujarat police investigation, the NHRC held that it is the central principle in the administration of criminal justice that those against whom allegations are made should not themselves be entrusted with the investigation of the allegations. In an indictment of the government of Gujarat the NHRC also said that the state government had comprehensively failed to control the persistent violation of the rights to life, liberty, equality and dignity of the people of the state and that its actions pointed to complicity in the violence that 'was tacit, if not explicit'.[9]

---

6 Muchkund Dubey and Sayeda Hamid, 'Gujarat Four Months Down the Road' and Harsh Mander, 'Mass Violence in Gujarat: State Impunity and Violation of Human Rights in Relief and Rehabilitation'.

7 Writ Petition (Civil) No. 530/2002, Mahashweta Devi versus Union of India and Others, Supreme Court of India.

8 NHRC, *Suo motu* Case No. 1150/6/2001-2002, *Proceedings* of NHRC, 1 April 2002, 12.

9 NHRC, *Suo motu* Case No. 1150/6/2001-2002, 31 May 2002, http://nhrc.nic.in/gujratorders.htm#no5.

The NHRC's apprehensions were proved right when in October that same year, in a trial of the case involving the killing of 74 Muslims fleeing from Kidiad village in a tempo in Panchmahal district, a trial court acquitted all nine accused. In the same month in two other cases related to the killings at Panderwada in Panchmahal district all the 21 accused in both cases were acquitted. In the face of a barrage of reportage and growing national and international outrage against the violence Narendra Modi dissolved the state assembly prematurely not however as a mark of taking responsibility for the violence but in order to get the people's verdict in the face of 'propaganda'. He launched a campaign called *Gaurav Yatra* (campaign of pride). In a roadshow for the *gaurav yatra* he asked villagers if they had heard the news that 60 *rambhakts* had been burned alive in a train. Using his great ability to work the crowd he prodded them into responding loudly to questions such as:

Narendra Modi: Did anyone of you stab anyone?

The crowd responds: No

Narendra Modi: Did anyone of you behead anyone?

The crowd responded: No

Narendra Modi: Did anyone of you take the honour of any sister/daughter *(rape anyone)*?

The crowd respond: No

Narendra Modi: Even then enemies of Gujarat are only saying that from village to village there were flames, from village to village people were being killed, from village to village people's heads were being smashed. They have defamed Gujarat so much, to give them all an answer, I have undertaken this Gauravyatra.

In another speech in the *yatra* he said,

When I embarked on the Gaurav *yatra* my friends from the Congress said in pride of what? To me that question itself underscores the need for a Gaurav Yatra.

They say in our Gujarat there are rioters, in our Gujarat people have knives, in our Gujarat people are killers, are looters. This is a definitive attempt to finish the pride of Gujarat and in the face of this the BJP is determined to fight it. People may try a million times to malign Gujarat but I have decided to bring out the truth of Gujarat boldly.[10]

---

10 Rakesh Sharma, *Final Solution*, Associated Cinema and Television, 2002, http://scroll. in/article/658119/.

The people's verdict delivered in December that year when the state assembly elections were declared was to give the Bharatiya Janta Party (BJP) an absolute majority of 127 seats from 182 constituencies and to give Narendra Modi a second term as chief minister. Given that the significant body of critical reportage and human rights abuses notwithstanding, Modi's administration was to continue as the popularly elected government for the next term of five years if not more, the search for an alternative verdict and interpretation of the events of violence that took cognizance of those who had suffered shifted to the courtrooms. A number of NGOs invested themselves in the pursuit of justice through sustained campaigns such those of Teesta Setalvad-led Centre for Justice and Peace (CJP), Mukul Sinha led Jan Sangharsh Manch, Harsh Mander-led Nyayagraha and through Jan Vikas of the Centre for Justice.

What propelled the campaign for justice for victims of the violence was the unprecedented intervention of the Supreme Court in what has come to be known as the Best Bakery Case that began in February 2003. In a trial for an incident where 14 people were burned to death on 1 March 2002 in a bakery called Best Bakery owned by Muslims in Vadodara city, a sessions court acquitted all the 21 persons accused after majority of the 73 eyewitnesses including Zahira Sheikh and her mother who lost members of their own family in the incident 'turned hostile' or retracted their statements in a court in Vadodara. The public prosecutor appointed by the government for the case was a sympathizer with the Vishwa Hindu Parishad (VHP), the organization that led, planned and attacked Muslim houses during the violence. There were other cases as well such as the Sardarpura Case where 33 people were burnt alive and the Deepda Darwaza Case involving the killing of 14 people where the district public prosecutor appointed by the government was the general secretary of VHP. Excerpts from statements in the judgment are telling on the rationale of the court for delivering the judgments such as 'The policy of industrialization, following the example of the Soviet Union, helped create conditions for communal riots' or 'It needs to be said that if one's identity and loyalty do not lie toward one's land, one is likely to be destroyed.'[11] Thus at the first three crucial stages of justice namely investigation handled by the police, prosecution by state government appointed public prosecutors and adjudication by a lower court, the fourth being appeal, the functioning of the

---

11 PUCL, Press Release, 7 July 2003, www.pucl.org /Topics /Religion.../2003/best-bakery. htm. According to the PUCL the public prosecutor in the case is known to have a bias against Muslims while his deputy was known to be affiliated with the right wing RSS.

crucial, initial components of the criminal justice system in Gujarat did not function independent of the ruling party's dispensation and affiliation with its associated ideological organizations (Jaffrelot, 2012, p. 80).

With the support and guidance of the Centre for Peace and Justice, Zahira Sheikh and her mother testified before the NHRC that they retracted their statements in court as they were threatened by an MLA of the party in power , BJP. In addition to the Best Bakery Case of the 4,256 cases registered related to the violence, more than 2,108 had been closed including 1,960 under 'A summary' i.e., that those responsible could not be found or that the police did not have enough evidence to file a chargesheet. This was because in an alarming number of cases where victims went to file an FIR, the police clubbed a number of offences that occurred in the area under a single FIR and recorded the alleged offenders as *tola* or mob instead of individual names, which rendered investigation fruitless at the first stage. Drawing attention to the Best Bakery Case that in its assessment had led to the 'miscarriage of justice,' NHRC filed a special leave petition before the apex court of India, the Supreme Court seeking reinvestigation of the case not by the Gujarat police but by the CBI and its retrial outside Gujarat. Shortly thereafter the first conviction in a case of communal violence came in November 2003 where a sessions court in Nadiad convicted 12 people for killing 14 Muslims at Ghodasar village in Kheda district.[12] Following the Gujarat High Court's verdict in the Best Bakery Case that upheld the lower court's judgement of all accused, Zahira Sheikh with the support of Citizen's for Justice and Peace's Teesta Setalvad appealed to the Supreme Court. Despite an earlier dismissal of the plea to hold the case outside Gujarat by the Gujarat High Court, the Supreme Court, in an unprecedented instance of judicial activism, not only upheld Zahira Sheikh's appeal and ordered a retrial of the Best Bakery case but in an indictment of the administration in Gujarat also went on to say, 'When the investigating agency helps the accused, the witnesses are threatened to depose falsely and prosecutor acts in a manner as if he was defending the accused, and the court was acting merely as the onlooker and there is no fair trial at all. Justice becomes the victim.'[13]

---

12 When the accused appealed to the Gujarat High Court, it reversed the conviction of all the accused in the case in April 2012.

13 Quoted in International Human Rights and Conflict Resolution Clinic at the Stanford Law School, May 2014, *When Justice becomes the Victim: The Quest for Justice after the 2002 Violence in Gujarat.*

The case was transferred to the neighbouring state of Maharashtra, its investigation transferred to the state's capital city Mumbai and the Public Prosecutor was also appointed from Mumbai. Zahira Shiekh and some others from her family, however, retracted their statement once again, this time alleging that she was under pressure from Teesta Setalvad while subsequently the investigative journalism of *Tehelka* showed Zahira receiving a bribe from a BJP MLA Madhukar Shrivastav. Zahira Sheikh was eventually convicted of perjury for lying under oath, while the Mumbai trial court in 2006 convicted nine of the seventeen accused and sentenced them to life imprisonment while also mentioning that defence lawyers were in collusion with witnesses who turned hostile during the trial.

Another case whose investigation was transferred by the Supreme Court from the Gujarat police to the CBI and the trial shifted outside Gujarat was the gang rape of Bilkis Bano Yakoob Rasool. During the violence in 2002 a pregnant Bilkis Bano from Randhikpur village in Dahod district was gang-raped by men from her village. She also witnessed the rape and killing of 14 other members of her family. From the very first stage of registering her FIR the Gujarat police obstructed the case by registering 7 instead of 14 murders, recording the bodies that could not be found as missing persons and summarily filed a closure report. This would have been another one of more than a thousand cases that were summarily closed were it not for a vigilant press that exerted relentless scrutiny on the developments in Gujarat for the first few years after the violence and crucially, a broad-based team of people and activists who provided emotional, material and legal support to Bilkis Bano for six years. After the intervention of Supreme Court that asked a central policy agency the Central Bureau of Investigation (CBI) to investigate the case, bodies were found buried in a mass grave. The CBI also arrested 12 persons as well as two police officers and Bilkis Bano, who was receiving threats, was given protection by a central level police force while the public prosecutor was also appointed by the central government. Eventually in 2008, in what is considered to be a landmark case as the first conviction for rape during communal violence in modern India, 13 of the 20 accused were convicted on charges of criminal conspiracy, rape and murder (Anand, 2008).

Fearing a failure of free and fair trial in Gujarat where witnesses were being threatened first the NHRC and then Citizens for Justice and Peace (CJP) filed a transfer petition in the Supreme Court for the investigation of cases to be transferred to CBI and their trial to be transferred outside Gujarat. Supreme Court in November 2003 stayed all proceedings in 14 cases including those involving mass killings such as Naroda Patiya, Naroda Gam, Gulbarg, Ode, Baranpura, Machipith, Tarsali, Pandarwada and Raghovpura pending a decision on whether they should be tried outside Gujarat. In 2004 after a shift in power at the national level when the Congress-led UPA came to power after the defeat of the BJP-led National Democratic Alliance (NDA) in the national elections, it was also suggested that the cases be investigated by the CBI and trials be shifted to the neighbouring state of Maharashtra. The BJP-led Gujarat government's counsel, however, opposed the appointment of any outside agency to conduct the investigation. The Supreme Court appointed the Godhra Riots Inquiry Committee that reexamined 2107 cases that had been closed and concluded that 1597 cases require further investigation and should, therefore, be reopened. In a decision that, in principle, was a mid way between concerns for a free and fair trial, which seemed unlikely in Gujarat, and the need to restore the damaged credibility of the judicial process in the state the Supreme Court in March 2008 instituted the five member Special Investigation Team (SIT) comprising three senior Indian Police Service (IPS) officers from Gujarat, Geeta Johri, Shivanand Jha and Ashish Bhatia; the retired CBI director RK Raghavan; and a retired police officer from Uttar Pradesh – C. B. Satpathy.[14] Thus, although SIT was headed by R. K. Raghavan who came from a federal investigative agency, it was in fact for the larger part composed of functionaries from the Gujarat police force, and was to function utilizing the very judicial administration in the state whose shortcomings had led to its creation in the first place. In some cases public prosecutors appointed by the government of Gujarat continued while some were appointed in consultation with NGOs such as CJP.

The SIT was to conduct a fresh probe and further investigations into the major cases that had been stayed for more than four years and ensure free and fair trial. Shortly after its institution, fresh FIRs were filed in cases where local police had filed closure reports in 2002 citing lack of evidence such as in the case of the killing of 17 Muslims in Delol village, where supplementary charge-sheets were filed and some arrests were made. In May 2009 based on the report of the Supreme Court appointed Godhra Riots Committee and a confidential report filed by SIT chairman RK Raghavan the Supreme Court gave an order according to which the Gujarat High Court appointed nine judges for nine fast track courts, four of which would be located in Ahmedabad, two each in Mehsana and Anand and one in Sabarkantha district respectively to conduct trials on a day to day basis. Although

---

14 'Probe afresh 14 Gujarat Cases: Court', *The Hindu*, 26 March 2008.

with the coming of the SIT little had changed in terms of the hostile environment in court premises for some witnesses like Ayyubbhai Sindhi, a witness in the Kidiad case, for whom court appearances included facing sloganeeging by supporters of the accused,[15] when it was freshly instituted, the SIT had in 2008 also generated optimism in the minds of some victims for justice.[16]

In the same year as the instituting of the SIT, the Nanavati-Shah Commission, that had been appointed by the Modi administration as early as 6 March 2002, released its report on what is considered to be the immediate cause of the violence in 2002 namely, the burning of the coach of Sabarmati Express in a Muslim locality. The conclusions of the Nanavati-Shah Commission, however, were contrary to the findings of an earlier commission appointed by the central government namely, the UC Banerjee Commission. The UC Banerjee Commission was appointed by the Railway Minister Lalu Prasad Yadav of the Congress-led UPA government, which had just come to power in 2004. The commission used this opportunity to intervene in the aftermath of the violence. It was headed by a retired judge who had submitted its report in 2005. The commission appointed by the UPA led national government, which submitted its report in 2005 and the one appointed by the BJP led state government, which submitted its report in 2008 on the same incident, came to contrary conclusions. The Banerjee Commission in 2005 held that the fire could not have been started by the throwing of flammable liquid from outside, given that some survivors managed to crawl out of the compartment, which would have not been possible had there been flammable liquid on the floor as was alleged in the theory of petrol being poured into the compartment by the Muslim mob outside.[17] Citing the nature of the burns sustained by the victims the UC Banerjee Commission concluded that the fire was accidental given that *karsevaks* who had camped in Ayodhya were carrying inflammable substances within the compartment, rather than what was believed by most people in Gujarat namely, that the fire started because petrol was poured into the compartment and burning rags were thrown by a mob from the Muslim locality outside where the train had temporarily stopped. While the UC Banerjee Commission held that the fire was accidental and not premeditated, the Nanavati Commission held that the fire was not caused by accident but that the train was set on fire by pouring petrol

15 Ayyubhai Sindhi (resident Al Falaha Relief Colony, Sabarkantha) interview by author, 22 March 2009.

16 Imtiaz Shahid Pathan (survivor of Gulbarg Society violence), 12 July 2008.

17 *Frontline*, 28 (06), 12–25 March 2011.

in it as a 'conspiracy to burn the coach of Sabarmati Express coming from Ayodhya and to cause harm to the *karsevaks* travelling in the coach' (Nanavati Commission Report, 2005, pg 172). While the Banerjee Commission questioned the possibility of miscreants entering a coach full of 150–200 VHP or BD activists to pour 60 litres of petrol in it and have the same ignited, the Nanavati Shah Commission held that it would be reasonable to expect that the same happened.[18] The Nanavati-Shah Report concurred with the explanation offered by the Gujarat police that 140 litres of petrol was poured into the coach to set it on fire.

The SIT, that in 2011 completed its first trial of the burning of the coach of the Sabarmati Express, also arrived at the conclusion that the burning of the train coach in Godhra was a preplanned attack. Of the 31 accused 11 were sentenced to death and 20 to life imprisonment while the remaining 63 accused were released after nine years in prison under the stringent Prevention of Terrorism Act (POTA). In November 2011 a verdict was pronounced on the Sardarpura case where 33 Muslims had been killed in 2002 in a village. The special court convicted 31 of the 73 accused who had been charged with murder, attempt to murder, along with the sections of damage to the house, criminal trespass, attacking with dangerous weapons, and causing grievous hurt to innocent people and rioting. The accused included former *sarpanches* of the village and two members of the ruling BJP. Although no significant role was attributed to any of the accused, as many as 31 were awarded life imprisonment along with a fine of ₹ 21,700 each for being a part of an unlawful assembly, which attacked the house causing the death of 33 people. The court, while awarding punishment to those convicted also asked them to pay ₹ 50,000 each towards compensation to the victims which was a significant advance from previous judgments. Importantly, while, the court rejected the defence of the accused that there was no intent to kill but also rejected the prosecution's contention of a previously planned criminal conspiracy and held that the attack was a reaction to the Godhra train carnage. Therefore, while the accused had been convicted collectively and not on account of individual involvement[19] that the crime was targeted violence against a community was not acknowledged. Doing so would have acknowledged international normative advances in human rights law and humanitarian law in Indian legal practice. Given the political reality of Gujarat however, this judgement was lauded by NGOs such as Teesta Setalvad's CJP for

---

18 'Post Godhra Riots: What Lies Ahead?', *Times of India*, 26 September 2008.
19 'Sardarpura Massacre: Gujarat Court Awards Life Sentence to 31', *Indian Express*, 9 November 2011.

being the first time in a case of communal violence that such a large number of people were convicted[20] and was celebrated in some sections of the media as the first verdict pronounced in a case probed by SIT.

A few months later in July 2012 in another case of Deepda Darwaza in Visnagar regarding the killing of 11 people of a family in 2002, the court awarded life sentences to 21 people where once again they were convicted not for murder and preplanned conspiracy but attempt to murder and rioting. One police officer accused of building a weak case was sentenced to one year imprisonment for dereliction of duty and one BJP MLA accused of instigating the mob was given the benefit of the doubt and acquitted. The SIT filed appeals in Gujarat High Court where it challenged the acquittal of those accused saying that there was a criminal conspiracy and that those convicted should be charged of murder instead of attempt to murder.[21]

In the next month another special court in Ahmedabad pronounced a verdict on the Naroda Patiya case where on 28 February 2002, according to official estimates 95 people and according to unofficial estimates more than a hundred were killed on a single day in a slum on the industrial periphery of Ahmedabad. When the Gujarat Police had first investigated the killings, it failed to take into account crucial evidence such as a CD of call detail records collected and compiled by Rahul Sharma who had been transferred to the CBI but was a police officer in Gujarat at the time of the violence and similar evidence put up by lawyer Mukul Sinha-led NGO Jan Sangharsh Manch, which showed state functionaries such as a BJP MLA and police officials in touch with VHP and Bajrang Dal members during the violence. When the SIT took over investigation of the case, it was compelled to take cognizance of this evidence in addition to the testimony of witnesses who saw functionaries of right wing organizations lead and direct the perpetrators of the violence. In 2009, the SIT arrested Babu Bajrangi a leader of the BD, a militant wing of the Sangh Parivar and Mayaben Kodnani, a practicing doctor who was made Minister of Women and Child Development in the state government in 2007. She was an MLA at the time of the violence and when she visited Naroda Patiya she encouraged the mob armed with weapons to attack Muslims. The special court in August 2012 held that Mayaben Kodnani was the

---

20 Mahesh Langa, 'Sardarpura was a Rare Case of Justice Done', *Hindustan Times*, 13 February 2012.

21 'HC Admits SIT Appeals in Deepda Darwaza Massacre Case', *The Hindu*, Ahmedabad, 6 May 2013.

prime conspirator in the violence, who was charged with murder and awarded 28 years in prison while Babu Bajrangi was awarded life imprisonment. SIT sought to file an appeal in the high court for the sentence to be increased to the maximum available sentence for the charge, namely death penalty. However, the Gujarat government initially agreed but subsequently changed its opinion and refused permission to SIT to file an appeal arguing that there was no direct evidence against her. The appeal for death sentence was allowed to be filed in the case of Babu Bajrangi.[22] Mayaben Kodnani however was subsequently granted bail by the Gujarat High Court on medical grounds.

A pivotal case that SIT was asked to investigate by the Supreme Court was based on the complaint by Zakia Jafri whose husband, former MP Ehsan Jafri was killed by a mob in 2002 in front of his Gulbarg Society residence where 69 others were also killed on that day. In 2006 Zakia Jafri along with Teesta Setalvad's CJP filed a complaint with the Gujarat police and then with the Gujarat High Court where it was dismissed. Her complaint however was admitted by the Supreme Court in 2008 and directed to the SIT for preliminary investigation in 2009. The criminal complaint levelled charges against 63 persons including the then chief minister Narendra Modi, ministers of his cabinet, BJP MLAs, six members of other Sangh Parivar organizations and senior Indian Administrative Services (IAS) and IPS officers. It made 32 specific allegations the most serious of which was that as chief minister Narendra Modi convened a meeting at his bungalow on March 27, 2002 in which he instructed senior officials including the chief Secretary and the director general of police to allow Hindus to freely vent their anger against Muslims at the Sabarmati train carnage. On March 2010 Narendra Modi then the chief minister was called to testify before the SIT. Subsequently the SIT submitted three interim reports to the Supreme Court. The functioning of the SIT on certain aspects however raised questions about its impartiality for instance, its acceptance of the version of the local police in the Godhra train case despite its inconsistencies (Jaffrelot, 2012, p. 85; Mitta, 2014, pp. 1–24). Another discrepancy was the little use of incriminating evidence put out in the public domain (Jaffrelot, 2012, p. 84) by investigative journalism of *Tehelka* magazine's journalist Ashish Khetan (Khetan, 2007) who posing as a PhD student and RSS sympathizer managed to get on record[23] those who were then accused in the

---

22 Rohit Bhan and Diana George, 15 September 2013, 'Gujarat Government Asks SIT Not to Seek Death Penalty for Maya Kodnani', *NDTV*.

23 Tehelka made available in public domain 60 hours of video footage from its investigative journalism, which was verified as authentic by the CBI.

Naroda Patiya case, who roamed free or were out on bail such as Babu Bajrangi and Suresh Richard discussing the killing of people and the encouragement they received in person from Narendra Modi (Khetan, 2007). Two public prosecutors even resigned to protest the manner of the functioning of the SIT.

In order to independently assess interim reports of the SIT the Supreme Court appointed an *amicus curiae*, Raju Ramachandran, giving him a wide mandate to assess the reports, as well as to talk to witnesses independent of the reports and advice the court. The SIT filed a summary closure report in the Supreme Court on 8 February 2012. In its report, the SIT took cognisance of inflammatory speeches by Narendra Modi, destruction of crucial records, appointment of members of the family of right wing organisations of the Sangh Parivar as public prosecutors, the illegal positioning of ministers in police control rooms during the riots, senior police officers missing from sites where mass carnages occurred such as Gulbarg Society and Naroda Patiya and the neutral officers being transferred out of their posts. On the important issue of the testimony of suspended Indian Police Service officer Sanjiv Bhatt, who claimed to be present at the meeting on 27 February where chief minister Narendra Modi purportedly asked state functionaries to allow Hindus to vent their anger, that corroborated Zakia Jafri's claim, the SIT held that Sanjiv Bhatt was an unreliable witness. The SIT came to the conclusion that there was no prosecutable evidence against Narendra Modi. The report of the *amicus curiae* of the Supreme Court, on the other hand, held that it was not advisable for the testimony of Sanjiv Bhatt to be discredited at this stage as his position entailed him not unlikely to attend the meeting convened by the then chief minister and that the SIT had not provided evidence to disprove his claims of his whereabouts if he were not at the meeting held by the then chief minister. The *amicus curiae* report also held that while evidence provided by the SIT may not be sufficient to file charges of criminal conspiracy with rioters against Narendra Modi, the many references in the SIT report to communally provocative statements by Modi, which are hate speeches, point to *prima facie* commission of offences under sections 153A, 153B, 166 and 505 of the Indian Penal Code, which are offences punishable with a maximum sentence of imprisonment for up to three years. However, given that the advice of the *amicus curiae* or friend of the court is not binding by law on the investigating agency, the SIT was free to disregard it while the decision on the reports at the first stage fell on the Ahmedabad Metropolitan Magistrate.[24]

---

24 Venkatesan, V., 2012, 'A Tale of Two Reports', *Frontline* 29(4), http://www.frontline.in/static.

Since the time of the SIT's submission of an interim report in 2010, however, several reports in the media carried stories about a 'clean chit' for Narendra Modi who was subsequently made the prime ministerial candidate for the BJP. While the SIT's closure report and Narendra Modi's elevation and meteoric rise to the post of prime minister came as a shock to many who had been involved in campaigns in various capacities for the rights of victims of the violence, the outcome of the journey of these rights claims, that has also led to unprecedented intervention of the Supreme Court and a number of landmark judgments, should not have surprised those familiar with the working of the electoral and legal system of India.

That the verdict in the Bilkis Bano Rape Case was upheld by lawyers and human rights activists as the first conviction in a communal violence rape case since the formation of the modern Indian state since 1947, despite the many riots that have occurred since, is indicative of a lacuna in the system for the delivery of justice in cases related to communal violence. This is because in a situation of communal violence when masses are mobilized and they take to the streets, instances of destruction of property, killings, rapes and even mass crimes (as in 1984 anti-Sikh riots and 2002 violence in Gujarat) can occur. The established practice in law however, is to treat all such cases as criminal offences under the Indian Penal Code. In the logic of criminal law, a criminal act is seen as a crime against the whole of society, which is why the state's prosecution agency, and not the victim, goes to court against alleged criminals and higher penalties such as incarceration are available. The higher penalties available also mean that the burden of proof is higher than in for instance civil tort law, which is extremely difficult to produce given the anonymity afforded by mobs in situations of communal violence, not to mention possible bias against victims by state authorities. Moreover, criminal law takes punitive action like incarceration and a fine if imposed is to be paid to the state and not to the victim. After recent developments in victimology compensation to victims has been introduced through some judgments. More importantly crimes are seen as offences against the society and the state, which in a continuation of the colonial logic cannot commit crimes. While there is a codification of crimes committed against the state, there is no codification of crimes committed by the state (Grover, 2010, pp. 120–53). In fact while defending its report and demanding a rejection of Zakia Jafri's review petition, the SIT's counsel R. K. Jamuar held that the SIT was never asked to probe the conspiracy angle of the post-Godhra riots and asking it to do so would have been unconstitutional.[25]

---

25 'Order on Zakia's Protest Plea Likely Today', *Times of India*, 2 December 2013.

From his study of Aligarh across decades Paul Brass points out that riots are organized productions (Brass, 2003). Persons of experience from the Indian administrative services as well the Indian Police Services have also pointed out that a riot cannot go on for more than 24 hours without political support from somewhere.[26] From his experience in the Indian Administrative Services Harsh Mander has pointed out that a District Magistrate (DM) does not lack the power to summon additional armed forces to quell a riot but most often people in the administration take their cue from political bosses.[27] Moreover, the government and its functionaries that are responsible for safeguarding the lives of citizens are not brought to book for their failure to maintain law and order. Vibhuti Narayan Rai, a senior retired police officer, with experience in riot prone areas of Uttar Pradesh has pointed out,

> in practice senior officers are rarely held responsible for their lapses. At the most junior level officers are placed under suspension after the outbreak of a riot. This in most cases is an eyewash since officers under suspension are reinstated soon after the fury of public criticism subsides. Since suspension cannot be termed as punishment, in most cases practically no punishment was awarded to any guilty official' (Rai 1999, pp. 127–28).

In major instances of communal violence of genocidal proportions such as the anti–Sikh riots in 1984, the Mumbai riots in 1992–93 and the 2002 violence in Gujarat members of a single religious community have been victims of violence. However, the Indian Penal Law and Criminal Procedures Code continue to operate on colonial notions where a riot is defined as 'assembly of five or more persons' engaged in unlawful activities directed against government institutions, the laws, persons or property for the purpose of committing 'mischief or criminal tresspass, or other offense.'[28] The law thus only provides for individual culpability

---

26 Vibhuti Narain Rai, 1999, *Combating Communal Conflicts: Perception of Police Neutrality during Hindu-Muslim Riots in India*, Allahabad: Anamika Prakashan, 50. Harsh Mander has also attested to this from his experience as District Magistrate. In the case of Gujarat RB Sreekumar and Sanjiv Bhatt has testified to the complicity of state authorities in the violence of 2002.

27 Harsh Mander quoted in *The Hindu*, www.hindu.com/2010/07/14 (accessed on 24 March 2011).

28 Ashutosh Varshney and Steven Wilkinson, 1996, *Hindu-Muslim Riots 1960-1993: New Findings Possible Remedies*, New Delhi: Rajiv Gandhi Institute for Contemporary Studies, 19.

where even targeted violence against a group involving mass crimes etc. are all treated as isolated criminal cases. The Indian justice system is yet to appreciate and incorporate international normative developments against violence against groups such as the United Nations (UN) Convention Against Torture, UN Guiding Principles on Internally Displaced Persons and UN Principles on Remedy and Reparation (Grover 2010).

An attempt was made to address this systemic lacuna through legislation on what was commonly referred to as the Communal Violence Bill. In the light of the outrage over the violence in Gujarat in 2002, the UPA government had, following its stated intent in its national election manifesto in 2004, highlighted the need for a comprehensive law to deal with communal violence. The bill was first introduced in the upper house of the Parliament, the Rajya Sabha by the then Home Minister, Shivraj Patil on 5 December 2005 and referred to the Parliamentary Standing Committee on Home Affairs for examination and report on the same. The bill, first introduced as the Communal Violence (Prevention, Control and Rehabilitation of Victims) Bill, 2005 and later rechristened the Communal Violence (Suppression) Act, 2005 and again the Communal and Sectarian Violence Bill, 2010 to its latest and possibly last seen avatar as the 'Prevention of Communal and Targeted Violence (Access to Justice and Reparations) Bill, 2011' is an indication of the gradual weighing up of some of the larger issues that dealing with communal violence entails that has been viewed primarily as a law and order problem to the negligence of the effects of communal violence that result in displacement and gross human rights violations.

In its first version the bill, which had been with a parliamentary standing committee headed by the BJP's Sushma Swaraj since 2006 had for the prevention and control of communal violence, mooted the provision of the declaration of certain areas as communally disturbed areas and also for extraordinary powers for law enforcers to maintain public order. This was in keeping with existing state practices of viewing communal violence primarily as a law and order problem. This version of the bill actually strengthened the power of the state but did not address the main problem, namely the establishment of accountability of state actors who play a crucial role in the effects of communal violence. Since 2010 after the Bill went to the National Advisory Council (NAC) an innovation by the United Progressive Alliance (UPA) government that included the Congress Party leader as well as invited experts and leaders of the civil society to advice the government on policy making its nomenclature was changed to 'Communal and Sectarian Violence Bill, 2010' to widen the scope of the legislation. Although earlier sections of the bill were rejected it retained the structure and created new crimes and offences and accountability for public officials. Also, due to the intervention of civil society groups and activists there was a shift in the bill from empowerment of officials to accountability of officials and an attempt to develop the rights of victims of communal violence such as those of IDPs with regard to relief, reparation, rehabilitation and resettlement. It retained provisions for the setting up of special courts to try offences under this law and provided mechanisms to deliver relief and rehabilitation for victims of violence. The bill also set up guidelines for assessment of compensation for losses suffered by individuals including loss of life, home, belongings, loss of livelihood, injuries, impact of sexual assault or abuse on women.

The final version of the Bill called 'Prevention of Communal and Targeted Violence (Access to Justice and Reparations) Bill, 2011' communal violence bill, made a fresh attempt to establish command responsibility whereby responsibility can be fixed to the person occupying the office. The bill also included a provision enabling the central government to take over the powers of the state government in a situation of major communal violence by the insertion of a clause empowering the central government to invoke Article 355 by declaring a particular instance of communal clash as 'internal disturbance'; the creation of a National Authority for Communal Harmony, Justice and Reparation to take charge in the event of major communal violence; the creation of mechanisms to determine and disburse compensation and importantly; the incorporation and use of the category of IDPs to refer to those displaced by communal violence in the bill.

The bill was criticized by the BJP and other opposition parties for being anti-majority, and damaging the federal structure of constitution. The BJP's principle criticism of the bill was that it privileges minorities and does not address situations when the minority community is an aggressor in a communal conflict. The NAC on the other hand argued that the Bills provisions are informed by the understanding that while existing laws already provide for justice in case a person from a majority community is harmed, this bill's intent was to ensure that minority communities get access to justice especially in a case of state sponsored communal activity as had happened in Gujarat. In keeping with its position against the intervention of the centre in Gujarat in 2002 due to concerns of maintaining the federal balance the BJP argued that the central government was not directly empowered to deal with law and order situations, which are a state subject. Its stated position was that the central government's jurisdiction in such situations was limited to issuing advisories, directions and forming an opinion under Article 356 regarding whether the governance of the state can be carried on in accordance with the constitution. When the UPA government, which by then had taken a beating due to several corruption allegations, tried to introduce a much watered down version of the bill in the upper house of the parliament in 2014 it was met with a united opposition and was forced to defer the bill, which is now buried and unlikely to resurface again.

Despite the upsurge of media interest and the loud and persistent campaign of activists and academics, much of the waves of these campaigns that used the language of rights and human rights have – to borrow Upendra Baxi's analogy – broken on the waves of national sovereignty. The invoking of international standards for human rights violations did not go well with not just the BJP-led NDA government at the centre in 2002 that rejected international condemnation on the violence as interference in its internal affairs but also with the Supreme Court that on one occasion rapped Teesta Setalvad for presenting a report to the UN's Economic and Social Council (ECOSOC) about the violations of social and economic rights of internally displaced Muslims. More importantly however even attempts to imply a moral accountability or popular perception against human rights violations by a government failed to find resonance in the larger political universe both for allies and electoral purposes despite continued academic and media interest.

Good governance as *sushasan*

Since 2003 chief minister Narendra Modi has responded to allegations of human rights violations in the state by pointing out to economic growth. Following the intervention of a statutory body like the NHRC in the state that sought the intervention of the Supreme Court in the Best Bakery case with the reasoning that a free and fair trial would not be possible inside Gujarat, Narendra Modi, argued that 'vested interests are trying to obstruct the path of progress. They are identifying stray incidents and exaggerating them with the sole objective of slowing the pace of development'.[29] The Supreme Court however went on to make unprecedented interventions which in effect kept the verdict on Gujarat 2002 alive in the theatre of the courts. While this faciliated the media, human

---

29   Quoted in Manoj Mitta, 2014, *The Fiction of Fact Finding: Modi and Godhra*, India: Harper Collins, 59.

rights activists and academics to criticize the state in Gujarat using the standards of secularism and human rights, chief minister Narendra Modi, thereafter refusing to engage with what he dismissed as 'vested interests' threw himself headlong into highlighting the alternative standard of economic growth to measure his state with. The Jyotigram Scheme introduced in September 2003 enabled villages in Gujarat to get 24 hour three phase power supply for domestic use in schools, hospitals, village industries and tubewell owners to get eight hours a day power of full voltage on a pre-announced schedule. While this mainly benefitted medium and large farmers and affected marginal farmers and the landless, it enabled a significant improvement in the rural power supply (Shah and Verma, 2008, p. 59). To counter national and international criticism of its governance during the violence in 2002, the Modi government made consistent efforts to counter the perception of a majoritarian right wing state with that of an economically vibrant Gujarat. Since 2003, Vibrant Gujarat Global Investor Summits, that showcase Gujarat's leadership and its attractiveness as a business destination, have been held every two years that according to the state government cumulatively generated investment pledges of 920 billion dollars. Land acquisition processes were liberalized to attract foreign and national investment into Gujarat including the much publicized Tata Nano car project that the chief minister, using executive order rather than the legislative route, successfully invited into Gujarat after it ran into trouble in West Bengal over land acquisition (Sud, 2012, pp. 92–93). The Narendra Modi administration also made important reforms through e-governance, which increased transparency. Soon he acquired the reputation of an efficient administrator who acted with a firm hand against inefficiency and corruption.

Narendra Modi's reputation for being incorruptible also came from the fact that in a country where most political parties follow dynastic politics, he had led the life of extreme austerity, self discipline and self sufficiency without family commitments, making allegations of a conflict of interest difficult to sustain. Although married at a young age of 17, he had he walked walked out of his marriage and found a family in RSS or the Association of National Volunteers, a far right paramilitary organization in whose ranks he grew as a full time worker and pracharak (propogandist). Throughout his political career he has continued to maintain close ties with the organization that attempts to create a corps of dedicated paramilitary zealots who, it is hoped, will form the basis of a revival of a golden age of national strength and racial purity.[30] Under Narendra Modi,

---

30 William Dalrymple, 2014, 'Modi the Man of the Masses', *New Statesman*, 12 May 2014, http://www. newstatesman.com.

Gujarat's rate of state gross domestic product (SGDP) for 2000 to 2008 grew at 10.76 per cent as against India's at 7.68 for the same period. For the year 2007–08 Gujarat had the highest fixed capital investment among all the states in India. Agriculture in the state also showed an annual growth rate of more than 12 per cent during 2000–08 while the national figures for the same period were around 3 per cent. In 2007–08, Gujarat was also ranked first among 20 major Indian states in terms of fixed capital investment, second in terms of total invested capital and fourth in terms of total number of factories (Hirway, 2011a). Gujarat's per capita income at 27027, while not the highest among Indian states, is well above the Indian average at 22580.[31] It also accounted for more than 20 per cent of India's exports that originate from the country (Kohli, 2012). More importantly under Modi, the state government, that had the backing of major industrial and corporate houses, started to promote itself as a model state worthy of emulation by other states in India.

Good governance, described by the World Bank as governance that 'promotes participatory, accountable and transparent government in which streamlined bureaucratic institutions work with actors in the market and civil society to ensure liberal growth' (Kaufmann, *et.al*, 1999), was typically recast for popular parlance as follows,

> Good governance is the ability to differentiate between right & wrong, just & unjust, fair & foul and moral and immoral. Kautilya in his Arthashastra says that in order to ensure this the person who governs should understand that his happiness lies in the happiness of his subjects, his welfare in their welfare. But this in itself does not make it democratic governance. But in the context of democratic good governance, people are no longer subjects but are participants.[32]

Good governance emerged in popular discourse as *sushasan* as, a new form of doing government that was set apart from politicking of the past and was only concerned with getting things done. The BJP promoted Narendra Modi as *'nirnayak neta'* (decisive leader) and *vikas purush* (development man) who delivers on good governance.[33] Gujarat's SGDP under Narendra Modi's tenure as chief

---

31 Per capita net state domestic product for the year 2006–07 was calculated in thousand rupees from indiastat.com.

32 Narendra Modi, retrieved from https://www.bjpgujarat.org/english/listing/ourinitiatives.

33 Bharatiya Janata Party, Gujarat, 2012, Good Governance. Retrieved from www.bjpguj.

minister for 13 years from 2001 to 2014, showed a compounded average growth of 13.4 per cent as compared to the national rate of 7.8 per cent for that period (Bahree, 2014). Narendra Modi ran an economically successful administration with noteworthy achievements. However this was achieved not by affecting a turnaround but rather by carrying forward policies existing in the state for at least a decade before his term. Gujarat's growth for the first decade of this century is comparable with other states that have not had a history of industrial and economic growth and were even regarded as most backward such as Bihar. Its annual rate of growth from 8.01 from 1995–2000 to 8.68 per cent for 2001–10 is comparable with other states such as Uttarakhand at 11.81 per cent and Haryana at 8.95 per cent for the period 2001–10.[34]

Gujarat has been growing at a faster rate than the Indian economy from the 1960s. The state's peculiar economy has had high per capita income that has been 35 per cent higher than the all India average from 1981 to date. Gujarat has also been the fastest growing state under the changing globalized reality with structural changes in the economy in the late 1980s and 1990s. The state had shown the highest rate of growth of per capita income among the major 16 states in the post-liberalization period as well (Hirway, 2000, 3106). While the decade of the 1980s saw a lagging behind of the primary sector, particularly agriculture, due to the enterprising ethic of the Gujaratis, the favourable policies of successive governments in the state set up institutional structures to facilitate industrial development such as the Gujarat Industrial Development Corporation (GIDC) and Gujarat Infrastructure Development Board (set up in 1995) and infrastructural facilities such as continuous availability of power, water and accessibility through road and rail transport to industries. Since the 1980s, Gujarat has maintained its position at the forefront of industrial development. As early as the 1990s the state made special provisions to provide incentives, aggressively pursued industrial investments and introduced of Indextb, which ensured a radical cutting down of red-tapism through a single window processing of applications for proposals for business and industry by the bureaucracy the state. The 1980s and 1990s marked a period of committed industrial investments and the vision to make Gujarat compete not just with other states but other countries in Asia.

---

org/good_ governance.html.

34 Mungekar, B., 'Gujarat Myth and Reality', *Times of India*, 12 June 2012, retrieved from http://articles.timesofindia.indiatimes.com

These developments were not incompatible with developments in other parts of the world where processes of liberalisation were taking root in an increasingly globalised world. Neoliberal theories emerged among new forms of governance in the last few decades of the twentieth century that saw a complex of modernizing theories of doing government in an increasingly globalized world as a result of growing disillusionment in many countries with representative democracies that sought to implement grand theories of justice and citizenship with large unwieldy bureaucracies (Bevir, 2010). In neoliberal narratives, markets that are driven by competition and hold profit as the yardstick of performance are seen as more efficient than the state, that is bound by the yardstick of public interest. In new forms of governance, the state apparatus of bureaucracy, that has formal accountability structures, is sought to be better replaced by what is considered to be a more efficient form of entrepreneurial government with performance accountability where the citizen is redefined as customer and public officials as managers. A wave of reforms in the 1980s saw governments across a number of countries especially in the West 'roll back the state' from functions and sectors, while private actors and the voluntary sector stepped in. While the increasing influence of non-state actors entering roles that were traditionally held by the state led to the perception of the hollowing out of the state on the one hand and the transformation of the vertical bureaucratic accountability of state structure, on the other hand, the expansion of more horizontal patterns of service delivery based on a complex set of organizations drawn from public, private and voluntary sectors in the 1990s was also perceived as the expansion of the state through networks (Bevir, 2010, p. 31). This also resulted in benchmarks of responsiveness, performance and efficiency gaining currency over more traditional concepts of citizenship and representative democracy as criterion for assessing the state.

The language of governance that implies a change in the meaning of government, referring to a new process of governing, a changed condition of ordered rule, or the new method by which society is governed (Rhodes, 1996, pp. 652–53) that is often projected as an improvement to previous ones however raises fundamental tensions between governance and democracy that have larger import for the very formulation of the state where for instance non-state actors are not democratically accountable. More importantly, in the new governance that is largely due to changes in capitalism (Jessop, 1997), the Keynesian state's commitment to demand side growth and labour market maximization has been abandoned in the emerging post-Fordist conception of the state where labour and social policies have been discredited in that they inhibit the flexibility that is said to be vital to competitiveness within the new global economy (Bevir, 2010, p. 57). In this new governance, despite innovations such as participatory democracy by institutionalists in the second wave of reforms, there is also the reasoning that crucial policy areas such as banking and budgeting should be insulated from the vagaries of democracy.[35] Such a reasoning however has lent itself to the argument that less democracy in the interests of efficiency and flexibility are essential to manage the affairs of the state in the new global economy.[36] According to Mark Bevir the rationale offered by neoliberalists, who argue for an insulation of certain policy areas from the stresses of democracy using positive, scientific and empirical argumentation purely from the technical analysis of political transaction costs, is distinct from normative arguments to restrict democracy.[37]

In Gujarat, however, after the violence of 2002 one finds in the avoidance of a government from engaging with allegations of human rights violations citing efficiency and decisiveness to produce economic growth, a manifestation of this distinction between technical and normative arguments with serious implications. While up until 1980s, the governance of communal violence was framed as part of the larger narrative of the development of Gujarat,[38] discussion of communal violence of 2002 was opposed by the BJP as an obstruction to development. BJP MLAs expressed consternation at the mindset of the opposition that wanted to continue to discuss the communal violence when the government wanted to proceed with the important business of introducing a new scheme.[39] This marked a departure from the past where despite the state being exposed then in prolonged instances of communal violence as biased and fragmented there was however an effort to maintain the myth of the state as is evident in the legislative assembly

---

35 Rational choice theorist Giandomenico Majone for instance argues that the political transaction costs of reaching an agreement and then enforcing it and the politicians lack of credibility as their long-term commitments are checked by winning the next elections. (Bevir 2010)

36 China and Singapore have been successful models of the single minded pursuit of development with little regard for democracy.

37 He clarifies that that distinction can blur and acknowledges well known normative arguments for the defence of human rights from majoritarianism.

38 Gujarat Vidhan Sabha Debates, Part I, Book 85, March 1984, 433. Amarsinhbhai Chaudhari the then chief minister argued in the legislative assembly that peace and communal harmony is in the interests of Gujarat's development.

39 Gujarat Vidhan Sabha Debates, 10th Session, 15 March 2002.

debates of that period where chief ministers were at pains to convince the house of their best efforts to maintain communal harmony and its importance to the development of Gujarat.[40] In major instances of violence such as the 1984 anti Sikh violence and post-Babri masjid demolition riots in Mumbai in 1992, the Indian state in the past has sought to reassert its authority and legitimacy that have been undermined and exposed during instances of communal violence through mechanisms such as judicial inquiry commissions, *mohalla* committees and efforts to ensure renewed cohabitation among communities (Tripathi, 1997) in the post-conflict scenario (Hansen 2012, p. 36).

However, in Gujarat while the state's neutrality was severely challenged through scores of reports by civil society groups, the media and statutory institutions that had developed in the decade of the 1990s such as NHRC and NCM, the state administration of Gujarat did not seek to reconfigure governance mechanisms and reverse the perception in order to intervene and remedy polarization of population, the displacement of Muslims and the discrediting of its institutions as biased. In a paradigmatic shift through the leadership of Narendra Modi the state in Gujarat continued to be projected through a majoritarian and exclusivist cultural nationalist vision that sought and received legitimacy by recasting itself as the state that delivers *sushasan* using the language of good governance. Among the majority of the middle classes, rich and poor in Gujarat Narendra Modi has been admired for having stood his ground, and achieving majoritarian justice in the face of what Hindu nationalists decried as the Indian state's appeasement of the minorities. Since the violence in 2002 the BJP led by Narendra Modi, who was projected as the architect of Gujarat's success, not only consolidated its position in repeated elections in the state but also found admirers particularly among the middle class in post liberalisation India.

In an interview to Reuters, that proved to be a defining moment, when Narendra Modi was asked if he was a Hindu nationalist he replied in the affirmative that he was a Hindu and a nationalist and therefore a Hindu nationalist. The interview sparked uproar among the press, particularly sections of English media for his oblique reference to the death of Muslims in the 2002 violence to a puppy coming under the car when someone else is driving it. The reference to himself as a Hindu and a nationalist however allowed him to connect, in addition to

---

40 Komi eklas Gujaratna vikasna hitma cche (communal harmony is in the interest of development in Gujarat) Gujarat Vidhan Sabha Debates, Part I, Book 85, March 1984, 433. (Amarsinhbhai Chaudhari).

those who subscribed to the BJP's majoritarian ideology of cultural nationalism, to many others who didn't necessarily subscribe to the ideology of Hindutva but who identified with the broad categories of 'Hindu' and 'nationalist'. Sections of the media severely criticised the comment particularly against the benchmark of secularism, an ideal which is enshrined in the Indian constitution (both in spirit during the framing of the constitution and in letter through a subsequent ammendment). In practice however, since the early days of the modern Indian state there has been a disconnect between the stated ideal of secularism and evident biases of the state. It has been argued that this is because secularism is a western construct (Madan in Bhargava 1998, Nandy 1988, Chatterjee, 2010) and that its namesake in India is vastly different in the West, where the state is not separate from but maintans a principled distance from religion (Bhargava 1998). It has also been argued that a blind imitation of western secularism by Indian elite has led to the disconnect between secularists and the majority of people for whom religion and matters of faith are an essential reality of life and where religion appears to be ubiquitous not just in private but also in the public sphere.

Citizenship deficit

In run up to the 2014 elections the BJP in a massive campaign successfully projected Narendra Modi as the man who gets the job done. He promised better days through good governance, combating corruption and bold reforms. On the other hand the party that engineered India's economic liberalization[41], the Indian National Congress, from 2004 to 2014, despite a policy environment of ascendant neoliberalism, sought to give an impetus to social citizenship through a spurt of legislation on social and economic rights. The Congress-led UPA government a coalition made up of a loose alliance of centrist, left and regional parties, introduced a number of important legislations as rights such as the right to food, right to education, right to information, minimum wage and work through the Mahatma Gandhi National Rural Employment Guarantee Act or MGNREGA and even the right to compensation for land acquisition under the landmark Land Acquisition, Rehabilitation and Resettlement Bill, 2011 derided

---

41 Policies of economic liberalization were introduced in a calibrated manner and definite manner in the early 1990s when Manmohan Singh was the Finance Minister of the national government led by the Congress although antecedents to economic liberalization have been traced to almost a decade before that.

as unaffordable populist measures that led to vociferous criticism from powerful pro-reform lobbies on the extent of public spending on such legislation even though the projected overall spending on NREGA was less than 1 per cent of gross domestic product (GDP) (Jayal, 2013, p. 193).

In their second term i.e., the Fifteenth Lok Sabha frequent disruptions by opposition parties led to the worst performance in the lower house of the Parliament in 50 years with the lower house working for 61 per cent and the upper house for only 66 per cent of its scheduled time.[42] In a political landscape of neoliberalism allegations of corruption in the allotment of 2G spectrum, coal blocks and the Commonwealth Games exposed by a vigilant media and the Right to Information Act, where even bureaucrats were reluctant to move files and take decisions there was a policy paralysis and a 'governance deficit' where legislation for social citizenship seemed anachronistic and paled into insignificance. What emerged instead as a burning issue was that of corruption fuelled by massive media coverage to the anti–corruption movement led by Anna Hazare that saw the emergence of the erstwhile apathetic and expanding middle class into political significance at the national level and the subsequent rise of Arvind Kejriwal and the Aam Aadmi Party (AAP). Corruption emerged popularly as an all embracing narrative to channel social resentment, explain inequality and even hold together competing values and interests. Despite points of divergence this is not unrelated to the global movement against corruption that spans a variety of unlikely values and interests that construes corruption as a quantifiable and technocratic problem in need of remedies such as a larger role for civil society, a smaller or redefined role of the state, institutional reform, deregulation and liberalisation (Ivanov 2009, 146–153). AAP went on to snatch victory at the assembly elections in New Delhi but had a short lived and tumultuous stint at the Delhi government before Kejriwal resigned as chief minister to try and replicate the same at the national level by joining the race for the 2014 national elections for the lower house of the Indian parliament. In a toughly contested and vitriolic campaign to the national elections in 2014 the BJP emerged as the party with the single largest majority with a vote share of 31 per cent while the Congress could not even immediately lay claim leadership to the opposition in the lower house of parliament. Narendra Modi proved to be popular with the rich and the middle classes across religious communities with his campaign that emphasized change

---

42 Malik Kusum and Mandira Kala, 21 February 2014, 'Vital Stats: Performance of Parliament during the 15[th]Lok Sabha', PRS Legislative Research, Institute for Policy Research Studies.

through good governance. That he was in power at the time of the violence in 2002 where a large number of human rights violations occurred, was lost on a large part of the electorate for whom he had gone on to achieve success as an able administrator.

In the discourse of good governance as *sushasan* that has emerged in the backdrop of the violence in 2002, economic growth has emerged as the ultimate criterion of assessing the state. In the copious literature on the long standing issue of communal violence that includes sectarian violence as well as targeted violence against a group while there is the understanding that communal violence is endemic to India (Brass 2003), there is also a reasoning in recent times that with increase in economic growth the frequency of communal violence will diminish (Bohlken and Sergenti, 2010, p. 589).[43] There is the perception, the sharply polarized living spaces, underlying fear, minor instances of communal violence and major terrorist attacks based on revenge for violence in 2002 notwithstanding, that communal violence has actually declined after 2002 given that there has not been a major riot in Gujarat and that this will follow in other parts of India. Within the first year of its institution at the national level the Narendra Modi led government passed an ordinance to remove obstacles to land acquisition, cut spending on healthcare by nearly 20 per cent, said little on the mobilisation of right wing groups to reconvert minority Muslims and Christians into Hinduism, but was very vocal on economic reforms and its intention to make India the easiest place to do business in the world.

Thomas Hobbes had famously argued that suppression of memories of past wrongs was essential because if society is treated as a building made of stones then some stones "that have an irregularity of figure take more room from others and must be discarded." Following the horrors of the world wars however where the danger inherent in the very structure of the nation state was brought to sharp relief where people could very democratically agree to act to even eliminate a minority(Arendt, 1962, pp. 275, 299), normative instruments at the international level to protect minorities from targeted violence have been accorded the importance of *jus cogens* and there have also been instances of apologies by imperial powers, albeit a few centuries late for violence against members of a community to acknowledge the wrongs that had happened and to initiate a process of reconciliation between the two communities. While among

---

43 Ashutosh Varshney, 'A Strange Fire: Why the Muzzafarnagar Riots were a Departure from Past Trends', *Indian Express*, 20 September 2013.

the watchwords in new governance is transparency that seeks accountability by mobilizing the 'power of shame'[44], the language of transparency, efficiency and accountability however have thus far been used in the context of technical rather than normative standards.

The events of Gujarat in 2002 that brought to sharp contrast the systemic problems with regard to communal violence offered a window of opportunity to address a longstanding question. The question however is not limited to the issue of communal violence but also the entity of the state and what can be reasonably expected from it in neo liberal times.

---

44 Fox J., 'The Uncertain Relationship between Transparency and Accountability', quoted in Rosie McGee and John Gaventa, 2011, 'Shifting Power? Assessing the Impact of Transparency and Accountability, November 2011', IDS Working Paper, 383, *Development in Practice* 17(4): 663–71.

Bibliography

Primary Sources

African Union. 2009. African Union Convention for the protection and assistance of internally displaced persons in Africa (Kampala Convention). Kampala Uganda.

African Union. 2014. List of countries that have signed, ratified/acceded to the African Union Convention for the protection and assistance of internally displaced persons in Africa (Kampala Convention). Available at: http://www.au.int/en/sites/default/files/Convention. Accessed on 11 April 2014.

Deng, Francis M. Representative of the Secretary–General. 1998. *Internally Displaced Persons: Compilations and Analysis of Legal Norms*, by New York and Geneva: United Nations.

Deng, Francis M. 1993. Comprehensive Study prepared by Dr Francis M. Deng, Representative of the Secretary General on the human rights issues related to internally displaced persons, pursuant to commission on Human Rights, Resolution 1992/73, UN document E/CN.4/1993/35. Geneva: United Nations Commission on Human Rights.

_____. 2001. *Census of India*. New Delhi: Ministry of Rural Development, GoI.

Government of Gujarat. 1962. *Gujarat State Gazeteer*, Ahmedabad Ahmedabad District, 1984 Broach District, 1961, Junagadh District, 1975, Kheda District, 1977, Surat District (revised edition). Gujarat.

_____. 29 October 1986. 'The Gujarat Prohibition of Transfer of Immovable Property and Provisions for Protection of Tenants from Eviction from Premises in Disturbed Areas Act, 1986', *The Gujarat Government Gazette* XXVII.

Government of India. 1998. *Draft National Policy, Packages and Guidelines for Resettlement and Rehabilitation, 1998*. New Delhi: Ministry of Rural Development, GoI.

Gujarat Vidhan Sabha. 1947–2002. . *Gujarat Vidhan Sabha Charchao*. Gujarat, Gandhinagar: Gujarat Vidhan Sabha Secretariat.

National Human Rights Commission. 2002a. Proceedings of 1 and 6 March 2002, *Suo motu* Case No. 1150/6/2001-2002. New Delhi: National Human Rights Commission, Law Division.

_____. 2002b. Proceedings of 1 April: Transmittal of Preliminary Comments and Recommendations, together with Confidential Report, to the Government of Gujarat, Ministry of Home Affairs, Government of India and Prime Minister, *Suo motu* Case No. 1150/6/2001-2002. New Delhi: National Human Rights Commission, Law Division.

_____. 2002c. Proceedings of 1 May 2002: Response of the Government of Gujarat, dated 12 April 2002 to Preliminary Comments and Recommendations of 1 April 2002. New Delhi: National Human Rights Commission, Law Division.

_____. 2002d. Proceedings of 31 May 2002: in respect of the situation in Gujarat in continuation of those recorded by the Commission on 1 and 6 March 2002 and 1 April and 1 May 2002, *Suo motu* Case No. 1150/6/2001-2002. New Delhi: National Human Rights Commission, Law Division.

Singh, K. S. (ed). 2002. *Anthropological Survey of India, People of India, Gujarat, Volume XXII, Part One.* Mumbai: Popular Prakashan Pvt. Ltd.

United Nations. 1998. *UN Guiding Principles on Internal Displacement,* UN Document E/CN.4/ 1998/ 53/ Add.2. New York and Geneva: UN.

Government Reports

Government of Gujarat. August 2008. *Status Report of the Displaced Families in Gujarat with Reference to NCM Delegation visit on 15/10/2006,* No. RTI-102008-Information-18-A1. Gandhinagar: Social Justice and Empowerment Division, Sachivalaya.

_____. August 2008. *Second Report on the Status of the Identified Resettlement Colonies of the 2002 Riots Affected in Gujarat.* Presented to the National Commission for Minorities, New Delhi, 9 August 2002, No. RTI-102008-Information-18-A1. Gandhinagar: Social Justice and Empowerment Division, Sachivalaya.

Government of India. November 2006. *Social, Economic and Educational Status of Muslim Community of India: A Report,* Justice Rajindar Sachar, Prime Minister's High Level Committee, Cabinet Secretariat. New Delhi..

_____. 2008. *Dalits in the Muslim and Christian Communities: A Status Report on Current Social Scientific Knowledge.* Satish Deshpande. National Commission for Minorities.

United States Commission on International Religious Freedom. May 2004. *Annual Report of the United States Commission on International Religious Freedom.* Available at: http://www.uscirf.gov/images/stories/PDFs/. Accessed on 12 May 2010.

Commissions of Enquiry

Justice G. T. Nanavati and Justice Akshay H. Mehta. 2008. *Report by the Commission of Inquiry(COI) Into the Facts, Circumstances and All the Course of Events of the Incidents*

That Led to Setting on Fire Some Coaches of the Sabarmati Express Train On 27.2.2002 near Godhra Railway Station and the Subsequent Incidents of Violence in the State in the Aftermath of the Godhra Incident. Ahmedabad: Government of Gujarat.

Justice J Reddy. 1970. *Report of the Commission of Inquiry: Ahmedabad Communal Disturbances 1969.* Ahmedabad: Government of Gujarat.

Justice V. S. Dave. April 1990. *Report of the Commission of Inquiry: Into the Incidents of Violence and Disturbances which Took Place at Various Places in the State of Gujarat since February 1985 to 18ᵗʰ July 1985.* Ahmedabad: Government of Gujarat.

Non-official Reports

Aman Biradari. 2002. *Campaign for Peace and Harmony: Goals and Strategies.* New Delhi.

Amnesty International. 2002. *Justice, the Victim: Gujarat State Fails to Protect Women from Violence.* Available at: http://www.amnesty.org/en/library/info/ASA20 /001/2005. Accessed on 12 May 2010.

_____. 28 February 2002. *A Memorandum to the Government of Gujarat on its duties in the Aftermath of the Violence.* Available at: www.amnesty.org/en/library/info/ ASA20/005/2002. Accessed on 4 December 2009.

Anhad. 2005. *Gujarat 3 Years Later: Living with Injustice and Fear.* New Delhi.

Centre for Social Justice and Anhad. February 2007. *The Uprooted Caught Between Existence and Denial: A Document on the State of the Internally Displaced in Gujarat.* Ahmedabad.

Centre for Social Justice. November 2004. *A Status Report on Rehabilitation of Victims of Communal Violence in Gujarat in Year 2002: A Study based on the UN Guiding Principles of Internally Displaced.* Ahmedabad.

Citizens Initiative. April 2002. *How has the Gujarat Massacre Affected Minority Women? The Survivors Speak, Fact Finding by a Women's Panel.* Ahmedabad.

Concerned Citizens Tribunal Report. 2002. *Crimes against Humanity: An Inquiry into the Carnage in Gujarat* (Vols 1–3). Mumbai: Citizens for Justice and Peace.

Dabhi, Jimmy. 2007. *The Flip Side of the Vibrant Gujarat.* New Delhi: Indian Social Institute.

Fernandes, Walter ed. 2005. *The Land Acquisition Bill: For Liberalisation or for the Poor.* New Delhi: Indian Social Institute.

Forum against Oppression of Women and Awaaz-e-Niswaan. May 2002. *Genocide in Rural Gujarat: Experience of Dahod District.*

Ganguly, Varsha, ZakiaJowher and Jimmy Dabhi. 2006. *Changing Contours of Gujarati Society-Identity Formation and Communal Violence.* New Delhi: Indian Social Institute.

Human Rights Watch. April 2002. *"We have No Orders to Save You": State Participation and Complicity in Communal Violence in Gujarat* (Vol. 14 No. 3(C)). Available at: http://www.hrw.org/legacy/reports/2002/india. Accessed 12 May 2010.

International Initiative for Justice in Gujarat. December 2003. *Threatened Existence: A Feminist Analysis of Genocide in Gujarat.*

Islami Relief Committee. 2004. *Horror of Earthquake and Genocide: A Journey of Relief and Pain, Report Upto 2004, Gujarat.* Ahmedabad.

Kumar, Ajay (ed). 2004. *Modi-fied Justice and Rule of Law: The Case of Best Bakery.* Delhi: Udhbavana.

Mander, Harsh and Kiran Nanavati. 2006. *Surviving State Hostility and Denial: A Survey of Relief Colonies for People Affected by Mass Violence in Gujarat 2002- A Report.* Ahmedabad: Nyayagrah and Oxfam.

Mitra Chenoy, Kamal., S. P. Shukla, K. S. Subraamaniam and Achin Vinaik. 2002. *Gujarat Carnage 2002: A Report to the Nation, An Independent Fact Finding Mission.* Available at: http://www.sacw.net/Gujararat2002/GujCarnage.html. Accessed on 7 April 2009.

Oza, Digant. 2009. *Vibrant Lapodshankhni Global Varta: Political Commentary.* Mumbai: Nisbat.

Patel Aakar,, Deleep Padgaonkar and B. G. Verghese May 2002. 'Rights and Wrongs: Ordeal by Fire in the Killing Fields of Gujarat', *Editors Guild Fact Finding Mission Report.* New Delhi, Editors Guild.

Patnam, Manasa and Sahir Raza 2005. *In Search of Faith Unconquered: A Journey in Three Acts.* New Delhi: Anhad.

People's Union for Civil Liberties (PUCL). June 2002. *Violence in Vadodara.* Available at: http://www.onlinevolunteers.org/gujarat/reports/pucl/index.htm. Accessed 5 July2010.

People's Union of Civil Liberties and Vadodara Shanti Abhiyan. May 2002. *At the Receiving End: Women's Experience of Violence in Vadodara.* Vadodara.

_____. May 2002. *Violence in Vadodara: A Report.* Vadodara.

Peoples Union for Democratic Rights (PUDR).. 2002. *Gujarat Genocide 'Act Two': Six Months Later, September.* New Delhi.

_____. 2002. *Maaro! Kaapo! Baalo!: State, Society and Communalism in Gujarat.* New Delhi: Secretary, Peoples Union for Democratic Rights.

Punjabi, Kavita and K Bandopadhyay. May 2002. *The Next Generation: In the Wake of the Genocide.* Available at: http://www.onlinevolunteers.org/gujarat/reports/children/. Accessed in December 2009.

Raza, Gauhar, and Surjit Singh. 2008. *The Wretched: A Profile: A Report on the Socio-Economic Condition of the Internally Displaced in Gujarat*. New Delhi: Anhad and AVHRS.

Report of the Investigation by Medico Health Circle. 13 May 2002. *Carnage in Gujarat: A Public Health Crisis*. Pune.

SAHMAT. March 10–11, 2002. . *Ethnic Cleansing in Ahmedabad: Preliminary Report*. Fact Finding Team to Ahmedabad. .

Sen, Amartya. 2004. *Social Exclusion: Concept Application and Scrutiny*. New Delhi – Critical Quest

Newspapers and Magazines

Combat Law

Communalism Combat

Frontline

Hindustan Times

Tehelka

The Hindu

The Indian Express

The Times of India

Secondary Sources

African Union and Norwegian Refugee Council. 2013. *The Kampala Convention One Year On: Progress and Prospects*. Switzerland: Internal Displacement Monitoring Centre and Norwegian Refugee Council.

Ahmed, Ishtiaq. 1996. *State, Ethnicity and Nation in Contemporary South Asia*. London and New York: Pinter.

Amnesty International. 2000. *Persecuted for Challenging Injustice: Human Rights Defenders in India*. London: Amnesty International.

Arendt, Hannah. 1962. *Origins of Totalitarianism*. Cleveland and New York: Meridian Books, The World Publishing Company.

_____. 1969. *On Violence*. London: Allen Lane and the Penguin Press.

_____. 2006. *Eichmann in Jerusalem: A Report on the Banality of Evil*. New York: Penguin Classics.

Attwood D. W. and B. S. Baviskar. 1988. *Who Shares? Co-operatives and Rural Development*. Delhi: Oxford University Press.

Banerjee, Paula, Sabyasachi Basu Ray Chaudhuri and Samir Kumar Das (eds). 2005. *Internal Displacement in South Asia*. New Delhi: Sage Publications.

Baratuscki, M. 2000. *Addressing Legal Constraints and Improving Outcomes in Development Induced Resettlement Projects*. Oxford: RSC and DfID.

Barbalet, J. M. 1997. *Citizenship*. Delhi: World View.

Baruah, Sanjib. 1999. *India against Itself: Assam and the Politics of Nationality*. New Delhi: Oxford University Press.

_____. 2005. *Durable Disorder: Understanding the Politics of Northeast India*. New Delhi: Oxford University Press.

Bastian, Sunil and Robin Luckham (eds). 2003. *Can Democracy be Designed?: The Politics of Institutional Choice in Conflict Torn Societies*. London: Zed Books.

Basu, Amrita and Atul Kohli (eds). 1998. *Community Conflicts and State in India*. New Delhi: Oxford University Press.

Basu, Amrita and Srirupa Roy. 2004. 'Prose After Gujarat: Violence, Secularism and Democracy in India', in *Will Secular India Survive?*, edited by Mushirul Hasan, 320–55. Gurgaon: Imprint One.

Baviskar, B. S. and Donald W. Attwood. 1995. *Finding the Middle Path: The Political Economy of Cooperation in Rural India*. New Delhi: Vistaar Publications.

Baviskar, Amita. 1995. *In the Belly of the River: Tribal Conflicts over Development in the Narmada Valley*. Delhi: Oxford University Press.

Baxi, Upendra (ed). 1988. *Law and Poverty: Critical Essays*. Mumbai: N. M. Tripathi.

_____. 2002. *The Future of Human Rights*. New Delhi: Oxford University Press.

Benhabib, Seyla. 2004. *The Rights of Others: Aliens, Residents and Citizens*. Cambridge: Cambridge University Press.

Bevir, Mark. 2010. *Democratic Governance*. New Jersey: Princeton University Press.

Bevir, Mark and R. A.W. Rhodes. 2010. *The State as Cultural Practice*. Oxford: Oxford University Press.

Bhavnani, Nandita. 2014. *The Making of Exile: Sindhi Hindus and the Partition of India*. Delhi: Tranquebar Press.

Bhargava, Rajeev and Helmut Reifeld (eds). 2005. *Civil Society, Public Sphere and Citizenship: Dialogues and Perceptions*. New Delhi: Sage Publications.

Bhargava, Rajeev. 1998. *Secularism and its Critics*. New Delhi: Oxford University Press.

Biswal, D. N. 2000. *Forced Displacement: Illusion and Reality*. New Delhi: Manas Publications.

Bond, E., James. 1974. *The Rules of Riot: Internal Conflict and the Law of War*. New Jersey: Princeton University Press.

Bookman, Milicia Z. 2002. *Ethnic Groups in Motion: Economic Competition and Migration in Multiethnic States*. Oregon, US: Frank Cass Publishers.

Bose, Tapan K. and Rita Manchanda (eds). 1995. *States, Citizens and Outsiders: The Uprooted Peoples of South Asia*. Kathmandu: South Asia Forum for Human Rights.

Brass, Paul R. 1991. *Ethnicity and Nationalism: Theory and Comparison*. New Delhi: Sage Publications.

_____ (ed). 1996. *Riots and Pogroms*. London: Macmillan.

_____. 2003. *The Production of Hindu-Muslim Violence in Contemporary India*. New Delhi: Oxford University Press.

Breman, Jan. 2004. *The Making and Unmaking of an Industrial Working Class: Sliding down the Labour Hierarchy in Ahmedabad, India*. New Delhi: Oxford University Press.

Bunsha, Dionne. 2006. *Scarred: Experiments with Violence in Gujarat*. New Delhi: Penguin Books.

Buzan, Barry. 1991. *People, States and Fear: An Agenda for Internal Security in Post-Cold War Era*. Second edition. London: Harvest Wheatsheaf.

Carens, Joseph H. 2000. *Culture, Citizenship, Community: A Contextual Exploration of Justice as Evenhandedness*. New York: Oxford University Press.

Cernea, Michael and Christopher Mc.Dowell (eds). 2000. *Risks and Reconstruction-Experience of Resettlers and Refugees*. Washington DC: The World Bank.

Chadha, G. K., Sucharita Sen and H. R. Sharma (eds). 2004. *State of the Indian Farmer*. New Delhi: Academic Foundation and Ministry of Agriculture.

Chandra, Bipan. 1994. *Communalism in Modern India*. New Delhi: Vikas.

Chatterjee, Joya. 2007. *The Spoils of Partition: Bengal and India, 1947-1967*. New York: Cambridge University Press.

Chimni, B. S. ed. 2000. *International Refugee Law: A Reader*. New Delhi: Sage Publications.

Cohen, Roberta and Francis Deng. 1998. *Masses in Flight*. Washington DC: Brookings Institution.

Cohen, Roberta and Francis M. Deng (eds). 1998. *The Forsaken People: Case Studies of the Internally Displaced*. Washington DC: Brookings Institution.

Collier, Paul, V. L. Elliott, Havard Hegre, Anke Hoeffler, Marta Reynal-Queral and Nicholas Sambanis. 2003. *Breaking the Conflict Trap: Civil War and Development Policy*. Washington DC and New York: The World Bank and Oxford University Press.

Crawford, James. 1988. *The Rights of Peoples*. Oxford: Clarendon Press.

Dahl, Robert A. 1971. *Polyarchy: Participation and Opposition*. New Haven, Connecticut: Yale University Press.

Daniel, E. Valentine, and John Chr. Knudsen (eds). 1995. *Mistrusting Refugees*. Berkeley and Los Angeles: University of California Press.

Das, Veena, Arthur Kleinman, Mamphela Ramphele and Pamela Reynolds (eds). 2001. *Violence and Subjectivity*. New Delhi: Oxford University Press.

Das, Veena (ed). 1992. *Mirrors of Violence: Communities, Riots and Survivors in South Asia*. New Delhi: Oxford India Paperbacks.

_____. 2007. *Life and Words*. London, England: University of California Press.

Dayal, John. 2003. *Gujarat 2002: Untold and Retold Stories of the Hindutva Lab*. Delhi: Justice and Peace Commission.

Deshpande, Satish. 2005. 'Hegemonic Spatial Strategies: The Nation-Space and Hindu Communalism in Twentieth Century India', in *Community, Gender and Violence, Subaltern Studies XI*, edited by Partha Chatterjee and Pradeep Jeganathan, pp. 167–211. Delhi: Permanent Black. First Published in 2000.

Dhattiwala, Raheel. 2014. *The Puzzle of the BJP's Muslim Supporters in Gujarat*. Policy Report No. 5. Chennai: The Hindu Centre for Politics and Public Policy.

Dreze, Jean, Meera Samson and Satyajit Singh (eds). 1997. *The Dam and the Nation: Displacement and Resettlement in the Narmada Valley*. New Delhi: Oxford University Press.

Dye, Thomas R. 2002. *Understanding Public Policy*, 10th Edition. New Jersey: Princeton Hall.

Engineer, Ashgar Ali. 1989. *Muslim Communities of Gujarat: An Exploratory Study of Bohras, Khojas and Memons*. Delhi: Ajanta Publications.

_____. 1991. *Communal Riots in Post Independence India*. Hyderabad: Sangam Books.

_____. 2004. *Communal Riots After Independence: A Comprehensive Account*. Mumbai: Shipra Publications.

Evans, P. 1995. *Embedded Autonomy: States and Industrial Reformation*. Princeton, New Jersey: Princeton University Press.

Fernandes, Walter and Vijay Pranjapai (eds). 1997. *Rehabilitation Policy and Law in India: A Right to Livelihood*. New Delhi: Indian Social Institute and Pune: Econet.

Fernandes, Walter. 2009. 'India's Forced Displacement Policy: Is Compensation up to its functions?' in *Can Compensation Prevent Impoverishment? Reforming Compensation through Investments and Benefit Sharing*, edited by M. Cernea and H. Mathur, 180–207. New Delhi: Oxford University Press.

Fernandez, Walter and Enakshi Ganguly Thukral (eds). 1989. *Development, Displacement and Rehabilitation*. New Delhi: Indian Social Institute.

Frankel, Francine R. 1978. *India's Political Economy, 1947-1977: The Gradual Revolution.* Delhi: Oxford University Press.

Freeden, Michael. 1991. *Rights.* Buckingham: Open University Press.

Fukuyama, Francis. 2004. *State Building: Governance and the World Order in the Twenty First Century.* Ithaca, New York: Cornell University Press.

Ganguly, Varsha. 2004. *Conservation, Displacement and Deprivation: Maldhari of Gir Forest of Gujarat.* New Delhi: Indian Social Institute.

Garre, Marianne. 1999. *Human Rights in Translation: Legal Concepts in Different Languages.* Denmark: Copenhagen Business School Press.

Ghosh, Partha S. 2004. *Unwanted and Uprooted: A Political Study of Migrants, Refugees, Stateless and Displaced of South Asia.* New Delhi: Samskriti.

Giddens, A. 1985. *The Nation-State and Violence.* Cambridge: Polity Press.

Glibney, Matthew J. and Randall Hansen (eds). 2005. *Immigration and Asylum: From 1900 to the Present,* Vol. 1. California: ABC-CLIO.

Global IDP Project and Norwegian Refugee Council. 2003. *Internally Displaced People: A Global Survey.* Second Edition. London: Earthscan.

Grover, Vrinda (ed). 2010. *Kandhamal: The Law Must Change its Course.* Research and Writing by Saumya Uma. New Delhi: Multiple Action Research Group (MARG).

Gupta, Dipankar. 2011. *Justice before Reconciliation: Negotiating a 'New Normal' in Post-riot Mumbai and Ahmedabad.* New Delhi: Routledge.

Hampton, Jamie. (ed). 1998. 'Internally Displaced Persons: A Global Survey', *Norwegian Refugee Council, Global IDP Survey.* London: Earthscan.

Hansen, Thomas Blom. 2012 . 'Governance and Myths of State in Mumbai', in *The Everyday State and Society in Modern India,* edited by C. J. Fuller and Veronique Benei, 31–67. New Delhi: Social Science Press. First published in 2000.

Hardiman, David. 1981. *Peasant Nationalists of Gujarat: Kheda District, 1917-1934.* New Delhi: Oxford University Press.

Hasan, Mushirul. (ed). 2004. *Will Secular India Survive?* New Delhi: Imprint One.

Hasan, Zoya. 2005. 'Shah Bano Affair (Overview)', in *Encyclopedia of Women and Islamic Cultures: Family, Law and Politics,* Vol. 2: 741–44. Netherlands: Brill Publishers.

Henckaerts, Jean-Marie. 1995. *Mass Expulsion in Modern International law and Practise.* The Hague: Martinus Nijhoff Publishers.

Hinton, Laban Alexander (ed). 2002. *Annihilating Differences: The Anthropology of Genocide.* Berkeley: University of California Press.

Holtzman, Steven B. and Taies Nezam. 2004. *Living in Limbo: Conflict Induced Displacement in Europe and Central Asia.* Washington DC: The World Bank.

Horowitz, Donald L. 2001. *The Deadly Ethnic Riot*. New Delhi: Oxford University Press. Available at: http://plato. stanford. edu /archives/spr2009/entries/ citizenship. Accessed on 11 April 2013.

Iyengar, Sudarshan. 2002. 'Resettlement and Rehabilitation in the Sardar Sarovar Project: A Review of Policy Reforms and Implementation', in *The Other Gujarat: Social Transformations Among Weaker Sections*, edited by Takashi Shinoda, 119–58. Mumbai: Popular Prakashan.

Ivanov, Kalin. 2009. 'Fighting Corruption Globally and Locally', in *Ethics and Integrity in Public Administration: Concepts and Cases*, edited by Raymond W. Cox III, 146–154. New York: M. E. Sharpe, Inc.

Jaffrelot, Christoffe. 2001. 'The Vishnu Hindu Parishad: A Nationalist but Mimetic Attempt at Federating the Hindu Sects', in *Charisma and Canon: Essays on the Religious History of the Indian Subcontinent*, edited by Vasudha Dalmia, Angelika Malinar and Martin Christof, 388–411. New Delhi: Oxford University Press.

Jasani, Rubina. 2010. 'A Potted History of Neighbours and Neighbourliness in Urban Ahmedabad', in *The Idea of Gujarat: History, Ethnography and Text*, edited by Edward Simpson and Aparna Kapadia, 153–67. Hyderabad: Orient Blackswan.

Jayal, Niraja Gopal. 2013. *Citizenship and its Discontents*. Ranikhet: Permanent Black.

Jayawickrama, Nihal. 2002. *The Judicial Application of Human Rights Law*. Cambridge: Cambridge University Press.

Jefferey, Patricia and Roger Jeffery. 2006. *Confronting Saffron Demography: Religion, Fertility and Women's Status in India*. Haryana: Three Essays Collective.

Kakar, Sudhir. 1990. 'Some Unconscious Aspects of Ethnic Violence in India', in *Mirrors of Violence: Communities, Riots and Survivors in South Asia*, edited by Veena Das, 134–45. Delhi: Oxford University Press.

_____. 1995. *The Colors of Violence*. Delhi: Viking Penguin India.

Kalin, Walter. 2000. *Guiding Principles on Internal Displacement Annotations*. Washington DC: The American Society of International Law and The Brookings Institution.

Kaur, Ravinder (ed). 2005. *Religion, Violence and Political Mobilisation in South Asia*. New Delhi: Sage.

Khan, Ayesha. 2002. *Scattered Voices: An Anthology of Poetry*. New Delhi: Books for Change.

Kleinman, Arthur, Veena Das and Margaret Lock (eds). 1997. *Social Suffering*. New Delhi: Oxford University Press.

Kohli, Atul. 2012. *Poverty Amid Plenty in the New India*. New Delhi: Cambridge University Press.

_____. 1990. *Democracy and Discontent*. Cambridge: Cambridge University Press.

Korn, A. David. 1999. *Exodus Within Borders: An Introduction to the Crisis of Internal Displacement*. Washington DC: Brookings Institution Press.

Kriemer, Alcira, John Eriksson, Robert Muscat, Margaret Arnold and Colin Scott. 1998. *Experience with Post-Conflict Reconstruction*. Washington DC: The World Bank.

Kumar, Amrita and Prashun Bhaumik, eds. 2002. *Lest We Forget Gujarat 2002*. New Delhi: World Report and Rupa and Co.

Laydete, Dominique. 2006. 'Citizenship', in *Stanford Encyclopedia of Philosophy*, edited by Edward N. Zalta. First published on 13 October 2006. Accessed on 12 December 2010.

Lazreq, M. 1979. 'Human Rights, State and Ideology: An Historical Perspective', in *Human Rights: Cultural and Ideological Perspectives*, edited by A. Pollis and Swab. New York: Praeger.

Lijphart, Arendt. 1990. *Conflict and Peacemaking in Multiethnic Societies*. Lexington Books.

Lobo, Lancy and Biswaroop Das (eds). 2006. *Communal Violence and Minorities: Gujarat Society in Ferment*. Jaipur: Rawat Publications.

Lobo, Lancy and Shashikant Kumar. *Land Acquisition, Displacement and Resettlement in Gujarat 1947-2004*. New Delhi: Sage Publications India.

Louis, Prakash. 2006. *Policy Documents of the Government of India, Compendium II*. New Delhi: Indian Social Institute.

Mahadevia, Darshini. 2003. *Development Dichotomy in Gujarat*. New Delhi: Research Foundation for Science, Technology and Ecology.

_____. 2007. 'A City with Many Borders: Beyond Ghettoisation in Ahmedabad', in *Indian Cities in Transition*, edited by Annapurna Shaw, 341–89. Hyderabad: Orient Longman.

Mahajan, Gurpreet. 1998. *Identities and Rights*. New Delhi: Oxford University Press.

Mander, Harsh. 2004. *Cry My Beloved Country: Reflections on the Gujarat Carnage 2002 and its Aftermath*. Noida, UP: Rainbow Publishers.

Marshall, T. H. and Tom Bottomore (eds). 1992. *Citizenship and Social Class*. London: Pluto Press.

Mehta, Swaranjit. 1990. *Migration: A Spatial Perspective*. Jaipur: Rawat Publications.

Metcalf, Barbara D. and Thomas R. Metcalf. 2006. *A Concise History of India*. Cambridge, UK: Cambridge University Press.

Migdal, Joel, Atul Kohli and Vivienne Shue (eds). 2001. *State in Society: Studying how State and Societies Transform and Constitute One Another*. New York: Cambridge University Press.

Migdal, Joel. 1988. *Strong Societies and Weak States: State Society Relations and State Capabilities in the Third World*. New Jersey: Princeton University Press.

Migdal, Joel. 2001. *State in Society: Studying how States and Societies Transform and Constitute one Another*. Cambridge, UK: Cambridge University Press.

Mishra, Omprakash (ed). 2004. *Forced Migration in the South Asian Region: Displacement, Human Rights and Conflict Resolution*. Jadavpur: Centre for Refugee Studies, Jadavpur University.

Mishra, Satish C. 1964. *Muslim Communities in Gujarat*. London: Asia Publishing House.

_____. 1985. *Muslim Communities in Gujarat: A Preliminary Study in their History and Social Organisation*. Bombay: Asia Publishing House.

Morse, Bradford and Thomas R. Berger. 1992. *Sardar Sarovar - Report of the Independent Review*. Ottawa: Resource Futures International.

Nandy, Ashis, ShikhaTrivedy, ShailMayaram and Achyut Yagnik. 1998. *Creating a Nationality: The Ramjanmabhumi Movement and Fear of the Self*. New Delhi: Oxford University Press.

Newman, Edward and Joanne Van Selm (eds). 2003. *Refugees and Forced Displacement: International Security, Human Vulnerability and the State*. New York: United Nations University Press.

Norwegian Refugee Council. 2001. *Profile of Internal Displacement: India* [Compilation of Information Available in the Global IDP Database of the Norwegian Refugee Council]. Geneva: Norwegian Refugee Council.

Nussbaum, Martha, C. 2007. *The Clash Within: Democracy, Religious Violence and India's Future*. Ranikhet: Permanent Black.

Oza, Rupal (ed). 2007. *The Geography of Hindu Right-Wing Violence in India*. New York: Routledge.

Pandey, Gyanendra. 1990. *The Construction of Communalism in Colonial North India*. New Delhi: Oxford University Press.

_____. 2006. *Routine Violence*. Delhi: Permanent Black.

Parsuraman, S. and P. V. Unnikrishnan (eds). 2000. *Disaster Report: Towards a Policy Inititative*. New Delhi: Oxford University Press.

Patel, Alka. 2004. *Building Communities in Gujarāt: Architecture and Society during the Twelfth through Fourteenth Centuries*. The Netherlands: University of California Press.

Patkar, Medha. 1988. *Sardar Sarovar: Vikas ki Vansh*. Dhule: Parisar.

Peteet, Julie M. 1995. 'Transforming Trust: Dispossession and Empowerment Among Palestinian Refugees', In *Mistrusting Refugees*, edited by Daniel, E. Valentine and John Chr. Knudsen, 168–186. Berkeley and Los Angeles: University of California Press.

Penz, P. 2002. 'Development, Displacement, Coercion and Harm: A Theoretical treatment', paper for the 8th Conference of the IASFM, 5–9 January 2003 in Chiang Mai, Thailand.

Pocock, David F. 1972. *Kanbi and Patidar: The Study of the Patidar Community of Gujarat*. Oxford: Oxford University Press.

Puri, Balraj. 1993. *Kashmir Towards Insurgency*. Hyderabad: Orient Longman.

Rai, Vibhuti Narain. 1999. *Combating Communal Conflicts: Perception of Police Neutrality during Hindu-Muslim Riots in India*. Allahabad: Anamika Prakashan.

Raju, G. C. Thomas (ed). 1992. *Perspectives on Kashmir: The Roots of Conflict in South Asia*. Oxford: Westview Press.

Ricoeur, P. 1986. 'Introduction', in *Philosophical Foundations of Human Rights*. Paris: UNESCO.

Robinson, Rowena. 2005. *Tremors of Violence: Muslim Survivors of Ethnic Strife in Western India*. New Delhi: Sage Publications.

Roy, Anupama. 2005. *Gendered Citizenship: Historical and Conceptual Explorations*. New Delhi: Orient Longman.

Rutten, Mario. 2002. 'Elite Attitudes Towards the Poor: Patidar Enterpreneurs in Rural Central Gujarat', in *The Other Gujarat: Social Transformations Among Weaker Sections*, edited by Takashi Shinoda, 260–83. Mumbai: Popular Prakashan.

Samaddar, Ranabir. (ed). 2004. *Peace Studies: An Introduction to the Concept, Scope and Themes*. New Delhi: Sage Publications.

Satyanarayana, G. 1999. *Development, Displacement and Rehabilitation*. Jaipur and New Delhi: Rawat Publications.

Scudder, Thayer. 2005. *The Future of Large Dams: Dealing with Social, Environmental, Institutional and Political Costs*. London: Earthscan.

Sen, Amartya. 2006. *Identity and Violence: The Illusion of Destiny*. New Delhi: Allen Lane and Penguin Books.

Shah, A. M. 2002. *Exploring India's Rural Past: A Gujarat Village in the Early Nineteenth Century*. New Delhi: Oxford University Press.

Shah, Ghanshyam. 1975. *Caste Association and Political Process in Gujarat: A Study of Gujarat Kshatriya Sabha*. Bombay: Popular Prakashan.

Shani, Ornit. 2007. *Communalism, Caste and Hindu Nationalism*. New Delhi: Cambridge University Press.

Sheth, Achyut Yagnik and Suchitra Sheth. 2005. *The Shaping of Modern Gujarat: Plurality, Hindutva and Beyond*. New Delhi: Penguin Books India.

Sheth, Pravin and Ramesh Menon. 1989. *Caste a Communal Timebomb*. Ahmedabad: Het Varsha Prakashan.

Shinoda, Takashi (ed). 2002. *The Other Gujarat: Social Transformations Among Weaker Sections*. Mumbai: Popular Prakashan.

Simpson, Edward and Aparna Kapadia (eds). 2010. *The Idea of Gujarat: History, Ethnography and Text*. Hyderabad: Orient Blackswan.

Simpson, Edward. 2004. 'Hindutva as a Rural Planning Paradigm in Post-Earthquake Gujarat', in *The Politics of Cultural Mobilization in India*, edited by John Vavos, Andrew Wyatt and Vernon Hewitt, 136–65. New Delhi: Oxford University Press.

Singh, Tavleen. 1995. *Kashmir : A Tragedy of Errors*. New Delhi: Viking Penguin Books.

Sondhi, M. L. and Apratim Mukarji. 2002. *The Black Book of Gujarat*. New Delhi: Manak Publications Ltd.

Srinivas, M. N. 1955. 'The Social System of a Mysore Village', in *Village India*, edited by McKim Marriott, 25–36. Chicago: University of Chicago Press.

Stephen, Ryan. 1995. *Ethnic Conflict and International Relations*. Second edition. Aldershot, UK: Dartmouth.

Stewart, Pamela J. and Andrew Strathern. 2002. *Violence: Theory and Ethnography*. London: Continuum.

Stremlau, John J. 1998. *People in Peril: Human Rights, Humanitarian Action and Preventing Deadly Conflict*. A Report to the Carnegie Commission on Preventing Deadly Conflict. Washington DC: Carnegie Commission on Preventing Deadly Conflict.

Sud, Nikita. 2012. *Liberalization, Hindu Nationalism and the State: A Biography of Gujarat*. New Delhi: Oxford University Press.

Summary Report, Regional Conference on Internal Displacement in Asia, at Brookings Institution website. Available at: http://www.brook.edu/fp/projects/idp/idp.htm, accessed on 12/10/2008.

Taseer, Bilqees C. 2005. *The Kashmir of Sheikh Muhammad Abdullah*. Srinagar: Gulshan Books.

Tata Institute of Social Sciences. 1997. 'Experiences with Resettlement and Rehabilitation in Maharashta', in *The Dam and the Nation: Displacement and Resettlement in the Narmada Valley*, edited by Jean Dreze, Meera Samson and Satyajit Singh, 184–214. Delhi: Oxford University Press.

Thapar, Romila. 2004. *Somnatha: The Many Voices of a History*. New Delhi: Penguin, Viking.

Thomas, C. J. (ed). 2002. *Dimensions of Displaced People in North East India*. New Delhi: Regency Publications.

Tonkiss, Fran. 2005. *Space, the City and Social Theory: Social Relations and Urban Forms*. Cambridge: Polity Press.

Tripathi, Satish. 1997. *Relief and Rehabilitation Measures for Persons Affected by the Bombay Riots of 1992-1993*. Mumbai: Tata Institute of Social Sciences.

UNHCR. 2001. *State of the World's Refugees: 50 Years of Protection*. Oxford: OUP.

United Nations University Press. 2004. *International Security, Human Vulnerability and the State*. New Delhi: Manas Publications.

United States Committee for Refugees. 2000. *Worldwide Refugee Information, Country Report: India*.

Vanaik, Achin. 1998. *The Furies of Indian Communalism*. London: Verso.

Vardarajan, Siddharth (ed). 2002. *Gujarat: The Making of a Tragedy*. New Delhi: Penguin Books.

Varshney, Ashutosh and Steven Wilkinson. 1996. *Hindu-Muslim Riots 1960-1993: New Findings, Possible Remedies*. New Delhi: Rajiv Gandhi Institute for Contemporary Studies.

Varshney, Ashutosh. 2002. *Ethnic Conflict and Civic Life: Hindus and Muslims in India*. New Haven and London: Yale University Press.

_____. (ed). 2004. *India and the Politics of Developing Countries: Essays in Memory of Myron Weiner*. New Delhi: Sage Publications.

Vincent, Mark and Birgette Refslund Sorensen. 2001. *Caught between Borders: Response Strategies of Internally Displaced Persons*. London: Pluto Press.

Walzer, Michael. 1989. 'Citizenship', in *Political Innovation and Conceptual Change*, edited by Terence Ball, James Farr and Russell Hanson, 211–19. Cambridge: Cambridge University Press.

Weiner, Myron. 1978. *Sons of the Soil: Migration and Ethnic Conflict in India*. Princeton: Princeton University Press.

Widmalm, Sten. 1998. 'The Rise and Fall of Democracy in Jammu and Kashmir, 1975-1989', in *Community Conflicts and State in India*, edited by Amrita Basu and Atul Kohli, 149–82. New Delhi: Oxford University Press.

Wilkinson, Steven I. (ed). 2005. *Religious Politics and Communal Violence*. New Delhi: Oxford University Press.

Wollstonecraft, Mary. 1996. *A Vindication of the Rights of Men*. New York: Prometheus Books.

Yagnik, Achyut and Suchitra Sheth. 2005. *Shaping of Modern Gujarat : Plurality, Hindutva and Beyond.* New Delhi: Penguin.

Yuval-Davis, Nira and PninaWerbner (eds). 1999. *Women, Citizenship and Difference.* London: Zed.

Zamindar, Vazira Fazila and Yacoobali Zamindar. 2008. *The Long Partition and the Making of Modern South Asia: Refugees, Boundaries, Histories.* New Delhi: Penguin Viking.

Zolberg, A. R., A. Suhrke and S. Aguayo. 1989. *Escape from Violence: Conflict and Refugee Crisis in the Developing World.* Oxford: Oxford University Press.

Articles

Ahmad, Aijaz. March–April 1993. 'Fascism and National Culture: Reading Gramsci in the Days of Hindutva', *Social Scientist* 21(3–4): 32–68.

Agamben, Gorgio. Summer 1995. 'We Refugees', *Symposium* 49(2): 114–19. Translated by Michael Rocke.

Anand, S. 2 February 2008. 'Bilkis Bano's Brave Fight', *Tehelka*, 5(4). Available at: http://archive.tehelka.com. Accessed on 23 February 2010.

Appadurai, Arjun. Spring 1990. 'Disjuncture and Difference in the Global Cultural Economy', *Public Culture* 2(2): 1–11, 15–24.

Badigar, Sanjeevini. 28 September 2013, 'Gujarat and its Protean State', Economic and Political Weekly 48(39): 35–37.

Bahree, Megha. 12 March 2014. 'Doing Big Business in Modi's Gujarat', *Forbes Asia*. Available at: http://www.forbes.com. Accessed on 12 April 2014.

Bohlken, Anjali Thomas and Ernest John Sergenti. 2010. 'Economic Growth and Ethnic Violence: An Empirical Investigation of Hindu Muslim Riots in India', *Journal of Peace Research* 47(5): 589–600.

Brass, Paul. 'The Gujarat Pogrom of 2002', *Contemporary Conflicts.* Available online at the website of the Social Science Research Council, http://conflicts.ssrc.org/gujarat/brass. Accessed on 22 March 2006.

Breman, Jan. 20 April 2002. 'Communal Upheaval as Resurgence of Social Darwinism', *Economic and Political Weekly* 37(16). :

Bunsha, Dionne. 06–19 July 2002. 'Refugees Without Refuge', *Frontline* 19(14).

Cernea, Michael. 1997. 'The Risks and Reconstruction Model for Resettling Displaced Populations' Elsevier 25(10): 1569-1587.

_____. 2000. 'Some Thoughts on Research Priorities', *The Eastern Anthropologist,* Sp. Resettlement 53(1–2): 3–12.

Chakrabarty, Dipesh. 1992. 'Postcoloniality and the Artifice of History: Who Speaks for the Indian Past', *Representations* 37 (Special Issue: Imperial Fantasies and Postcolonial Histories, winter: 1–26.

Chandoke, Neera, Praveen Priyadarshi, Silky Tyagi and Neha Khanna. 2007. 'The Displaced of Ahmedabad', *Economic and Political Weekly* 42(43): 10–14.

Chandoke, Neera. 8 October 1994. 'Why People Should have Rights', *Economic and Political Weekly* XXIX(41): 2697–98.

Chatterjee, Joya. 2007. '"Dispersal" and the Failure of Rehabilitation: Refugee Camp-Dwellers and Squatters in West Bengal', *Modern Asian Studies* 41(5): 995–1032.

Chatterjee, Partha. 9 July 1994. 'Secularism and Toleration', *Economic and Political Weekly* XXIX(28): . 1768–77.

_____. 1998. 'Beyond the Nation? Or Within', *Social Text* 56/16(3): 57–69.

Chinkin, C. M. 1989. 'The Challenge of Soft Law: Development and Change in International Law', *International and Comparative Law Quarterly* 38(4): 850–66.
Crisp, J. Spring 2001. 'Mind the Gap! UNHCR Humanitarian Assistance and the Development Process', *International Migration Review* 35(1): 168–91..

Dacyl, Janina W. 1996. 'Sovereignty Versus Human Rights: From Past Discourses to Contemporary Dilemmas', *Journal of Refugee Studies* 9(2): 131–65. Available at: doi: 10.1093/jrs/9.2.136.

Das, Veena. 15 June 1996. 'Dislocation and Rehabilitation: Defining a Field', *Economic and Political Weekly* XXXI(24): 1509–14.

Engineer, Ashgar Ali.6 July 6. 'Communal Fire Engulfs Ahmedabad Once Again', *Economic and Political Weekly* XX(27): 116–20.

Fernandes, Walter and Samyadip Chatterjee. March-April 1995. 'A Critique of the Draft National Policy', *Lokayan Bulletin* (Special Issue on Displacement and Rehabilitation) 11(5): 29–40.

Ferraro, K. F. 1982. 'The Health Consequences of Relocation Among the Aged in the Community', *Journal of Gerontology* 38(1): 90–96.Gardner, Katy and Filippo Osella (ed). 2003. 'Migration, Modernity and Social Transformation in South Asia: An Overview', *Contributions to Indian Sociology* (n.s) 37(1 and 2). New Delhi: Sage Publications.

Gold, Joseph. 1983. 'Strengthening the Soft International Law of Exchange Arrangements', *American Journal of International Law* 77(3): 443.

Gopal Jayal, Niraja. 31 January 1998. 'Displaced Persons and Discourse on Rights', *Economic and Political Weekly* XXXIII(5).

Gruchalla-Weisieski, Tadeusz. 1984. 'A Framework for Understanding Soft Law', *McGill Law Journal* 30: 37–88.

Gupta, A. 1995. 'Blurred Boundaries: The Discourse of Corruption, The Culture of Politics and the Imagined State', *American Ethnologist* 22(2): 375–402.

Handl, Gunther F. 1988. 'A Hard Look at Soft Law', *ASIL Proceeding of 82nd Annual Meeting* 20–23 April 20-23: 371–73.

Hardiman, David. 20–26 June 1998. 'Well Irrigation in Gujarat: Systems of Use, Hierarchies of Control', *Economic and Political Weekly* 33(25): 1533–44. Available at: http://www.jstor.org/stable/4406907. Accessed on 14 May 2012.

Harriss, John. 2012. 'For an Anthropology of the Modern Indian State', in *The Everyday State and Society in Modern India*, edited by C. J. Fuller and Veronique Benei, 1–30. New Delhi: Social Science Press.

Hathaway, Oona A. June 2002. 'Do Human Rights Treaties Make a Difference?', *The Yale Law Journal* 111(8): 1935–2042.

Hein, Jeremy. 1993. 'Refugees, Immigrants and the State', *Annual Review of Sociology* 19: 43–59.

Hirway, Indira and Neha Shah. 5 November 2011. 'Labour and Employment in Gujarat', *Economic and Political Weekly* XLVI(44 and 45): 62–64.

_____. 28 May 2011. 'Labour and Employment under Globalisation: The Case of Gujarat', *Economic and Political Weekly* XLVI(22) 57–65.

Hirway, Indira. 26 August–2 September 2000. 'Dynamics of Development in Gujarat: Some Issues', *Economic and Political Weekly* XXXV(35-36): 3106–120.

Jaffrelot, Christophe. 25 February 2012. 'Gujarat 2002: What Justice for the Victims?', *Economic and Political Weekly* XLVII(8): 77–89.

Jessop, Bob. Autumn 1997. 'Capitalism and its Future: Remarks on Regulation, Government and Governance', *Review of International Political Economy* 4(3): 561–81.

Kaplan, Robert. 1 April 2009. 'India's New Face', *The Atlantic*. Available at: http://www.theatlantic.com. Accessed on 2 July 2013.

Kaviraj, Sudipta. 1994. 'Crisis of the Nation State in India', *Political Studies* 42: 115–29. Oxford: Blackwell Publishers.

Khan, Ayesha. 3 October 2012. 'How to Profit from a Disturbed Area', *Fountain Ink*. Available at: http://fountainink.in/?p=2784. Accessed on 12 December 2013.

Kirmani, Nida. 8–14 March 2008. 'History, Memory and Localised Constructions of Insecurity', *Economic and Political Weekly* 43(10): 57–64. Available at: http://www.jstor.org/stable/40277231. Accessed on 14 May 2011.

Kothari, Rajni. 30 November 2002. 'Culture of Communalism in Gujarat', *Economic and Political Weekly* 37(48): 4823–25.

Kothari, Smitu. 1996. 'Whose Nation? Displaced as Victims of Development', *Economic and Political Weekly* 31(24): 1476–79.

Lobo, Lancy. 30 November 2002. 'Adivasis, Hindutva and Post-Godhra Riots in Gujarat', *Economic and Political Weekly* 37(48) : 4844–49.

Madan, T. N. 1993. 'Whither Indian Secularism?', *Modern Asian Studies* 27(3): 680–82.

Mahadevia, D., R. Joshi and A. Datey 15–31 May 2013( ). 'Travellers on an Eco-friendly Route', *Down to Earth* 21(21): 60–62.

Mahajan, Gurpreet. December 1999. 'Rethinking Multiculturalism', *Seminar* 484. Available at: http://www.india-seminar.com/1999/484/484%20mahajan.htm. Accessed on 28 June 2011.

Malkki, Liisa. February 1992. 'National Geographic: The Rooting of Peoples and the Territorialisation of National Identity among Scholars and Refugees', *Cultural Anthropology* 7(1): 24–44. Space, Identity and the Politics of Difference.

_____. 1995. 'Refugees and Exile: From Refugee Studies to the National Order of Things', *Annual Review of Anthropology* 24(1): 495–523.

_____. August 1996. 'Speechless Emissaries: Refugees, Humanitarianism and Dehistoricization', *Cultural Anthropology* 11(3): 377–404.

March, Andrew F. 2006. 'Liberal Citizenship and the Search for an Overlapping Consensus: The Case of Muslim Minorities', *Philosophy and Public Affairs* 34(4): 373–421.

Mendelsohn, Oliver. October 1993. 'The Transformation of Authority in Rural India', *Modern Asian Studies* 27(4): 805–42. Available at: http://www.jstor.org/stable/312832. Accessed on June 2012.

Mohan, Dinesh, GautamNavlakha, Sumanta Banerjee and Tapan Bose. March 1990. 'India's "Kashmir War"', *Economic and Political Weekly* XXV(13)31: 650–52.

Muggah, Robert. 2000. 'Capacities in Conflict: Resettlement of Conflict-Induced Internally Displaced in Colombia', *The Eastern Anthropologist* 53(1–2): 259–92.

_____. Summer 2003. 'A Pressing Humanitarian and Development Issue: Reflections on Internal Displacement and Resettlement', *Global Security and Cooperation Quarterly* 9.

_____. 2003. 'A Tale of Two Solitudes: Comparing Conflict and Development-Induced Internal Displacement and Involuntary Resettlement',*International Migration* 41(5): 5–31.

Mungekar, B. 12 June 2012. 'Gujarat Myth and Reality', *Times of India*. Retrieved from http://articles.timesofindia.indiatimes.com.

Nandy, Ashish. 2002. 'Obituary of a Culture', *Seminar* May.

Narayanan, Dinesh. 1 May 2014. 'RSS 3.0: Mahesh Bhagwat Brings a Resurgent RSS to the Cusp of Political Power', *Caravan*. Available at: http://www.caravanmagazine. in/reportage/rss-30.

Parekh, Bhikhu. May 2002. 'Making Sense of Gujarat', *Seminar* 513.

Patel, Girish. 30 November 2002. 'Narendra Modi's One Day Cricket: What and Why?', *Economic and Political Weekly* 48: 4826–37.

Ramanathan, Usha. 1996. 'Displacement and the Law', *Economic and Political Weekly* 31: 1486.

Ratner, Steven R. Spring 1998. 'International Law: The Trials of Global Norms', *Foreign Policy* 110(Special Edition Frontiers of Knowledge)..

Roy, Anupama. 15 April 2006. 'Overseas Indian Citizen: A New Setubandhan?', *Economic and Political Weekly*.

_____. January-April 2007. 'Towards a Practice of Democratic Citizenship', *Indian Journal of Gender Studies* 14(1): 1–15.

Sarkar, Sumit. February 2003. 'The Limits of Nationalism', *Seminar*.

Sarkar, Tanika. 13 July 2002. 'Semiotics of Terror: Muslim Women and Children in Hindu Rashtra', *Economic and Political Weekly* 37(28): 2872–76.

Shah, Ghanshyam. January 1970. 'Communal Riots in Gujarat: Report of a Preliminary Investigation', *Economic and Political Weekly* (Annual Number): 187–200.

_____. 10 August 1974. 'The Upsurge in Gujarat', *Economic and Political Weekly* 9(32–34): 1429–54.

_____. May 1987. 'Middle Class Politics: A Case of Anti Reservation Agitation in Gujarat', *Economic and Political Weekly* 22(Annual Number): 155–72.

_____. 1994. 'BJP and Backward Castes in Gujarat', *South Asia Bulletin* 14(1): 57–65.

_____. 7 May 1994. 'Identity, Communal Consciousness and Politics', *Economic and Political Weekly* 29(19): 1133–40. Available at: http://www.jstor.org/ stable/4401169. Accessed on 1 February 2014.

_____. 30 November 2002. 'Contestations and Negotiations: Hindutva Sentiments and Temporal Interests in Gujarat Elections', *Economic and Political Weekly* 37(48): 4838–43.

Shah, Tushar and Shilp Verma. 16–22 February 2008 . 'Co-management of Electricity and Groundwater: An Assessment of Gujarat's Jyotirgram Scheme', *Economic and Political Weekly* 43(7): 59–66.

Sikand, Yoginder. 2000. 'The Tablighi Jamaat in Post-1947 Mewat', *Eastern Anthropologist* 53(3–4): 341–50.

Simpson, Edward and Malathi de Alwis. 2008. 'Remembering Natural Disaster: Politics and the Culture of Memorials in Gujarat and Sri Lanka', *Anthropology Today* 24(4): 6–12.

Simpson, Edward and Stuart Corbridge. September 2006. 'The Geography of Things That May Become Memories: The 2001 Earthquake in Kachchh Gujarat and the Politics of Rehabilitation in the Prememorial Era', *Annals of the Association of American Geographers* 96(3): 566–85. Available at: http://www.jstor.org/stable/4124433. Accessed on 14 May 2012.

Sood, Jyotika. 1–15 February 2014. 'The New Milky Way', *Down to Earth* 22(18): 26–35.

Spencer, Jonathan. 1997. 'Postcolonialism and the Political Imagination', *Journal of the Royal Anthropological Institute* 3: 1–19.

Spodek, Howard. 1989. 'From Gandhi to Violence: Ahmedabad's 1985 Riots in Historical Perspective', *Modern Asian Studies* 23(4): 765–95.

Srinivasan, Bina, Rohit Prajapati and Wilfred D' Costa. 18 February 1989. 'Dam Workers on Strike', *Economic and Political Weekly* 24 (7) : 339–41. Available at: http://www.jstor.org/stable/4394395. Accessed on 5 June 2012.

Teltumbde, Anand. 2 April 2011. 'From the Underbelly of Swarnim Gujarat', *Economic and Political Weekly* XLVI(14): 10–11.

Trimble, Phillip R. 1990. 'International Law, World Order, and Critical Legal Studies', *Stanford Law Review* 42(3): 811–45.

Upadhya, Carol and Mario Rutten. 12 May 2012. 'Migration, Transnational Flows and Development in India: A Regional Perspective', *Economic and Political Weekly* XLVII (19): 54–62.

Varshney, Ashutosh. 20 September 2013. 'A Strange Fire: Why the Muzzafarnagar Riots were a Departure from Past Trends', *Indian Express*.

_____. 26 March 2004. 'Understanding Gujarat Violence', Contemporary Conflicts. Available at: http://conconflicts. ssrc.org/archives/gujarat/varshney/. Accessed on 26 March 2004.

Wilkinson, Steven. 27 April 2002. 'Putting Gujarat in Perspective', *Economic and Political Weekly* XXXVII(17): 1579–83.

Yagnik, Achyut. 'The Pathology of Gujarat', *Seminar* 513. Accessed on 17 June 2010.

Yagnik, Achyut and Anil Bhatt. Spring 1984. 'The Anti-Dalit Agitation in Gujarat', *South Asia Bulletin* IV: 45–60.

Young, Iris Marion. 1989. 'Polity and Group Difference: A Critique of the Ideal of Universal Citizenship', *Ethics* 99: 257.

Index